IN DEFENSE
OF WYAM

NATIVE-WHITE ALLIANCES & THE
STRUGGLE FOR CELILO VILLAGE

KATRINE BARBER

A HELEN MARIE RYAN WYMAN BOOK

CENTER FOR THE STUDY OF THE PACIFIC NORTHWEST
in association with
UNIVERSITY OF WASHINGTON PRESS
Seattle

Helen Marie Ryan Wyman was intelligent, curious, and gregarious; she took great stock in books and reading, and books abounded in her life. The Wyman family is proud to sponsor this book fund in Native American and Indigenous studies in her name.

Copyright © 2018 by the University of Washington Press
Printed and bound in the United States of America
Composed in Minion, typeface designed by Robert Slimbach

22 21 20 19 18   5 4 3 2 1

CENTER FOR THE STUDY OF   UNIVERSITY OF WASHINGTON PRESS
THE PACIFIC NORTHWEST   www.washington.edu/uwpress
http://cspn.uw.edu

LIBRARY OF CONGRESS CATALOGING-IN-PUBLICATION DATA
Names: Barber, Katrine, author.
Title: In defense of Wyam : native-white alliances and the struggle for Celilo Village / Katrine Barber.
Description: Seattle : Center for the Study of the Pacific Northwest in association with University of Washington Press, [2018] | Series: Emil and Kathleen Sick series in Western history and biography | Includes bibliographical references and index. | Identifiers: LCCN 2017059144 (print) | LCCN 2018002203 (ebook) | ISBN 9780295743592 (ebook) | ISBN 9780295743578 (hardcover : alk. paper) | ISBN 9780295743585 (pbk. : alk. paper)
Subjects: LCSH: Indians of North America—Land tenure—Oregon—Celilo. | McKeown, Martha Ferguson, 1903–1974. | Thompson, Flora Cushinway, 1893–1978. | Indians of North America—Government relations—Oregon—Celilo. | Celilo Falls Indian Relocation Project—Political aspects. | Indians of North America—Relocation—Oregon—Celilo. | Women—Oregon—Celilo—Biography. | Wyam Indians—Biography. | Whites—Columbia River Valley—Relations with Indians. | Celilo (Or.)—History.
Classification: LCC E78.O6 (ebook) | LCC E78.O6 B375 2018 (print) | DDC 323.11970795/62—dc23
LC record available at https://lccn.loc.gov/2017059144

MAPMAKER: Erik Memmott COVER PHOTOGRAPH: The tribal tents at Celilo, 1901. Photograph by Lee Moorhouse. Courtesy of Special Collections and University Archives, University of Oregon Libraries, PH036_2305. FRONTISPIECE: *Left:* Martha Ferguson McKeown in a photograph taken when she was the Dean of Women at Multnomah College, 1938–1941. She would have been in her mid-thirties. Oregon Historical Society, #bb00633. *Right:* Flora Thompson in 1966 in a photograph taken by newspaper editor, author, and artist Click Relander. Courtesy of the Yakima Valley Regional Library.

CONTENTS

A Note on Terminology and Sources   *vii*
Acknowledgments   *ix*

ONE
Homelands in Transition   3

TWO
Maintaining/Making Home   25

THREE
Growing Up   49

FOUR
Converging Paths of Leadership   89

FIVE
Protecting Home   125

SIX
New Narratives in an Ancient Land   161

SEVEN
Aftermath   193

Notes   *229*
Bibliography   *275*
Index   *287*

A NOTE ON TERMINOLOGY
AND SOURCES

In the service of readability, I use the first names of Martha Ferguson McKeown and Flora Cushinway Thompson frequently, especially when writing about them as children and during periods when their last names changed due to marriage and remarriage. In a single chapter, Flora is Cushinway, Boise, George, and Thompson. Moreover, Flora's mother was named Martha. Martha Ferguson was named after her grandmother, Martha Hawthorne, and changed her name to McKeown and then to Dana as she married. While their last names changed over time, Martha and Flora's first names remained constant.

I traced the lives of both women through government documents, including census records, Indian census rolls, and marriage records. Periods of Flora's life were captured in BIA records such as field matron notes and boarding school records. I drew also from newspaper coverage, especially after she married Tommy Thompson in the early 1940s. Martha Ferguson was, during her childhood, a frequent subject of the *Hood River Glacier*, a small local newspaper that chronicled the activities of Hood River Valley residents in great detail. McKeown's own writings about her family history, in four books published between 1948 and 1951, were also helpful.

McKeown wrote about two families more than anything else—hers and the Thompsons'. I relied heavily on McKeown's writings about the Thompsons and Celilo Village as a source that documented both and as a source that helped construct them in the imaginations of other Oregonians.

In the 1970s, several years after the death of her husband, Tommy Thompson, and a few years before her own, Flora conducted two oral history interviews that I've relied on here. One is available at the Oregon Historical Society. Linda George Meanus, Flora's granddaughter, gave me the second when she learned of my research.

Finally, this book is supported and shaped by the correspondence that James (Jimmie) James collected between 1950 and 1967. His correspondence with both women as well as with mutual friends provided insight into their personalities and details about their lives not available anywhere else. Sources about Martha Ferguson McKeown and Flora Thompson dating after James's death are scarcer and less detailed. James sometimes wrote dozens of letters a day and rarely took the time to revise his hurried correspondence or strike through mistakes. I have corrected the misspellings and punctuation in James's letters when necessary for clarity and readability.

ACKNOWLEDGMENTS

When I was ten or eleven, my parents took me to a bookstore in the Columbia River Gorge to pick something out for the ride home to Portland. I chose a picture book with an infant laced in her cradleboard on its cover, *Linda's Indian Home* by Martha Ferguson McKeown. As she rang the book up, the elderly cashier leaned over the counter to ask me if I'd ever heard of Flora Thompson, who was featured in the book and a legend in the area. McKeown made my introduction.

I owned the book for a long time but eventually gave it away and forgot about it until I started researching Celilo Village as a graduate student. I came across McKeown's book again, and memories of buying and reading it flooded back. As a child, I'd pored over the black-and-white photographs that Archie, Martha's husband, took of the George and Thompson families. Things that I'd missed then—McKeown's loving characterization of Celilo Village families and the importance of the book as a *history* of the place—became more apparent to me as an adult. *Linda's Indian Home* and McKeown's follow-up, *Come to Our Salmon Feast,* occupied prominent places on my bookshelf as I wrote my own history of Celilo Village and its inundation by The Dalles Dam in 1957, which was published as *Death of Celilo Falls* in 2005.

The book that you now hold in your hands is a result of that first discovery and the later rediscovery of Martha McKeown and Flora Thompson. I have them to thank for the resulting project, as well as many others who have supported my work in myriad ways over the last several years.

I am especially grateful to Linda George Meanus, Flora Thompson's granddaughter, and Davinne McKeown-Ellis, Martha McKeown's granddaughter, for their occasional input and for never asking me *not* to write this book. I imagine that reading a historian's interpretation of your own family history can be unsettling, and I truly appreciate the conversations they were willing to have with me and the materials and information they shared.

I am fortunate to share my professional and personal life with a group of energetic, smart, and charming historians. Eliza Canty-Jones, Janice Dilg, Johanna Ogden, and Donna Sinclair—my history sisters—have provided constant support and inspiration. Thank you for the dinners, telephone conversations, walks, and work sessions. Thank you for reading my work and allowing me to read yours. We have shared much, including a fateful November night in 2016. We persist.

Donna and I have chewed through historical methods, research conundrums, and teaching victories and disappointments on a weekly walk for more than a decade. She read multiple drafts, sharing my excitement when things were going well and refusing to let my spirits flag when they weren't. This book is better for all those steps.

My father, Steve Barber, was an excellent sounding board who, among other things, reminded me not to downplay the role Martha McKeown took in turning her uncle's reminiscences into vivid, powerful prose. He caught my own artless phrases and typos and helped me correct them. A writer himself, he has taught me much about what it means to be one.

Over the course of this project, I met weekly with other Portland State University faculty in small writing groups. Peter Collier and Maude Hines sustained this project for two years, and Megann McGill and Lindsay Skog saw it through to completion. I am especially grateful to Dannelle Stevens, professor emeritus in PSU's School of Education and faculty-in-residence for academic writing. Dannelle has been an amazing writing coach and all-around mentor for me and for dozens of other faculty members. We are all so lucky to have her in our lives.

William Robbins and Susan Armitage have played vital roles in my continuing development as a historian. Thank you to Melinda Jetté for her enthusiasm and to Johanna Ogden and Donna Sinclair for ensuring that writing was not a solitary business even when I was on sabbatical. I also extend my gratitude to the many PSU History graduate students who have participated in regular writing sessions, especially Melissa Lang, Alecia Giombolini, Greta Smith, Nicole Kindle, Carolee Harrison, and Taylor Bailey.

Dave Hedberg was another superb writing buddy. His outstanding 2017 MA thesis, "'As Long as the Mighty Columbia River Flows': The Leadership and Legacy of Wilson Charley, a Yakama Indian Fisherman," documents Yakama tribal leader Wilson Charley's efforts to protect salmon runs and treaty fishing rights in the 1950s and '60s, using Charley's correspondence with Jimmie James. It was a joy to work beside and advise the thesis of someone who was as excited about that trove of letters as I was. Joshua Ross generously read an early draft and provided insightful comments. Kirsten Straus cheerfully organized all of the images and made sure the press had permission to use them.

Portland State University provided a sabbatical and research funds, the time and money necessary for a project such as this. I am very grateful to all of my colleagues in the history department, especially our chair, Tim Garrison, who is steadfast in his support of faculty research and our public history program. My talented students in the public history seminar "Indigenous Histories in Public Places" refined the practices of research return, communication with tribal culture committees, and other decolonizing research methodologies with me.

The staffs at the Oregon Historical Society Research Library, the National Archives and Records Administration—Pacific Alaska Region, Reed College, the University of Washington Library's Special Collections, the History Museum of Hood River County, and the University of Oregon Library's Special Collections helped me identify and track down materials. Thomas Robinson of Historic Photo Archives helped me locate photographs of Martha McKeown and members of the Thompson family and generously granted permission to publish them.

I am grateful to the University of Washington Press staff who have shepherded the project from an idea to a manuscript to a published book, especially Ranjit Arab (now at the University of Iowa Press) for helping me narrow my scope at a critical early stage and Larin McLaughlin for help in the later stages. Anonymous readers provided insightful feedback that strengthened the manuscript.

Finally, I want to thank my Portland, Damascus, Silverton, and Minot families for their support and love. I dedicate this book to Donna Marie Croker—librarian, reader, and the world's best mother-in-law. Thank you for raising my favorite person.

Proceeds from the sale of this book will go to the PSU Honor Day ceremony, a celebration of the scholastic achievements of the university's Native American, Alaskan Native, and Pacific Islander students, in honor of educator Martha McKeown, and to Linda George Meanus, Flora Thompson's granddaughter and protagonist of *Linda's Indian Home*.

IN DEFENSE OF WYAM

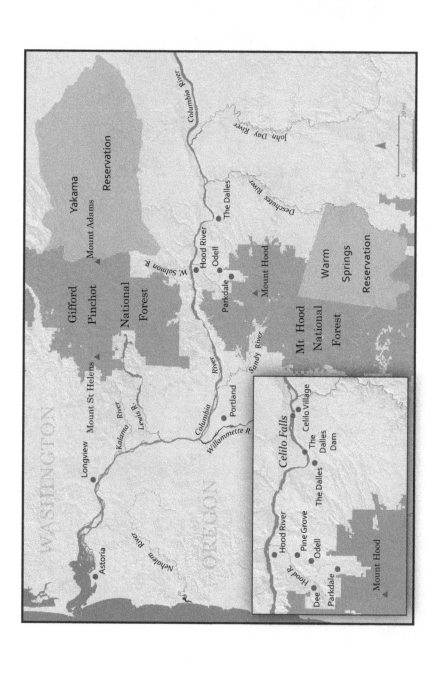

ONE

Homelands in Transition

When historians write about the making of modern
Indians, they are writing about the making of other
Americans, too. Or at least they should be.

DANIEL HERMAN, *Rim Country Exodus*

*As the sun rose to illuminate the roaring Columbia River on
April 19, 1953, Flora Thompson emerged from her home to
join other women in the longhouse kitchen as they prepared
the feast for the salmon ceremony hosted annually at Celilo
Village in Oregon. People from up and down the river had
already gathered at the village, but more—nearly four hundred
in all—would drive in from neighboring reservations or from
The Dalles, Gresham, or Portland over the course of the day.
By the time they were ready to eat that afternoon, Flora would
be in regalia, attending to guests. Her elderly husband and
hereditary salmon chief of the Wyam, Tommy Thompson, was
not well. Although he would attend, she planned to take over
some of his ceremonial tasks that day. Flora was grateful for*

the help of her older sister, Effie Cushinway, and the other women of the village. Martha McKeown, a white woman and longtime friend, had spent all of Saturday at the village and would remain for Sunday.

Archie McKeown, Martha's husband, snapped photographs of the people beautiful in their regalia—the men in headdresses, the women in scarves and wing dresses—and the children and dogs who ran about in equal measure, darting between the legs of adults and playing on the hillside that bounded the village to the south. The first salmon ceremony tied contemporary Native residents to their ancestors and renewed the relationship between salmon and the people they sustained. Indigenous people throughout the Pacific Northwest commemorated the first salmon caught in the spring with first foods feasts that varied among them in detail but not importance. The ceremony had been held at Celilo Village for as long as anyone could remember and marked the onset of fresh foods with the start of the fishery and the special reciprocal relationship that River People had with Salmon Nation.[1]

The ceremony brought far-flung people together for a few days, renewing the relationships between kin and friends as those who lived on reservations or in cities and towns traveled to the village to join the festivities. By the 1950s, the ceremony was also a chance for the region's Indigenous people to teach non-Native people about the centrality of the river and its resources to their culture. By opening it to non-Natives, participants made the ceremony, at least in part, into public relations, a way "to explain and interpret their lives" through prayer, dance, song, and oratory.[2] It was a risk. Some guests, especially journalists, distorted ceremony into

Undated photograph of women dancing at the First Salmon Ceremony, Celilo Village, by Archie McKeown. Special Collections and Archives, Eric V. Hauser Memorial Library, Reed College

spectacle, turning what was sacred tradition into stereotype. But others prayed and ate with their Indigenous neighbors with humility, receptive to the lessons village residents imparted.

Chief Thompson briefly acknowledged the people within the longhouse, men and women sitting separately as was the custom, before giving the floor over to his wife. Flora ignored her fatigue as she addressed the crowd: "Chief Thompson welcomes all of you as his brothers and sisters. The dear old chief has suffered for a long time, and now he greets you with a deep heart. He told his children he wanted this gathering continued, even though he might be on his deathbed."[3] Chief Thompson was too thin, noticeably smaller than this same time last year, when dynamite blasts from construction on the dam

punctuated the ceremonial drumming, the juxtaposition of
ancient ceremony and transformative explosion readying
tribal leaders for a year of struggle. But that was last year.

This year, Thompson's call, voiced by Flora, to continue the
annual ceremony echoed his concern about the alterations on
the mid-Columbia River, under way for more than a year.
How would the river support the salmon celebrated that day
once the dam went online? No one knew. What they did know
was that The Dalles Dam would irrevocably alter the river-
scape and inundate fishing stations owned and operated by
Indigenous families for hundreds of generations. But "to lose a
ceremony is to lose the past; to create a ceremony is to create
the future."4 On April 19, 1953, the future at Celilo Village was
being created; it was also in crisis.

DOCUMENTING NATIVE-WHITE ALLIANCES

This book juxtaposes the lives of two women on the mid-Columbia
River in the twentieth century to examine a central animating
force in the Pacific Northwest, the effects of settler colonialism and
Native resistance to it. Martha Ferguson McKeown was a prominent author from a Hood River Valley farming family, and Flora
Thompson was a Celilo Village resident and leader, enrolled at the
Confederated Tribes of the Warm Springs Reservation. Martha
and Flora would indelibly shape how Oregonians and others
understood Celilo Village and the mid-Columbia River. The
women were contemporaries, neighbors, and eventually friends
through a connection with Flora's third husband, Wyam chief
Tommy Thompson. Flora Thompson's life reveals the continuity
as well as the flexibility of Columbia Plateau gender constructions, including the gendered employment of influence within

Dip-netting salmon at Celilo Falls. National Oceanic and Atmospheric Administration Historic Fisheries Collection

Native communities of the Northwest. As a regional author and clubwoman, Martha aimed to interrupt the legacies of settler colonialism.

By illustrating the ongoing patterns of settler colonialism, the intersecting lives of Flora and Martha disrupt often-repeated narratives of the Pacific Northwest that cast the region as peripheral to the nation's history. It is true that for much of its history, the American Pacific Northwest was an isolated outpost, far from the economic or political levers of the nation, lightly populated, and insular in its culture. These characteristics and the exploitation of the region's natural resources by capitalists in faraway places led historian Carlos Schwantes to coin the term *colonial hinterland* to describe the states in the Columbia River watershed.[5] The term captures an economic relationship between region and nation, in which the nation relies on raw materials exports to manufacturing and trade centers beyond the region's borders. But it elides the equally important relationship between region and nation that was founded on American territorial expansion and the violent colonization of the region's original inhabitants. From that perspective, the Northwest was not a hinterland but rather a hub of colonial activity. For Indigenous and settler populations, the twined tensions inherent in the region's economic and political relationship to the nation-state and their own unequal relationships to one another characterized what it meant to be northwestern even into the twentieth century.[6]

This book developed out of an earlier one, *The Death of Celilo Falls*, in which I examined the negotiations between the US Army Corps of Engineers and the four Columbia River treaty tribes—the Confederated Tribes of the Warm Springs Reservation, the Yakama Nation, the Confederated Tribes of the Umatilla Indian Reservation, and the Nez Perce—who were compensated for fishing sites lost to the construction of The Dalles Dam in the 1950s.[7] While I documented opposition to the dam in my earlier book, a discovery of hundreds of letters between Portlander Jimmie James and numerous Indian and non-Indian opponents of the dam in the University of Oregon Special Collections allowed me to document that opposition with more precision and in greater detail here. Jimmie James's correspondence with Flora Thompson and Martha McKeown, who both appear in my first book, similarly allowed for a greater examination of their lives.

Flora Cushinway (*La moosh Cush-nee-yi*)[8] was born in 1893 to Jim and Martha (*Hu leh*) Cushinway on the Warm Springs Reservation. Flora was temporally close to a period of full and uncompromised Native sovereignty as well as to the most direct violence aimed at sequestering Indians onto reservations. Her parents were born just a few years before the treaty council that delineated the Warm Springs Reservation, and her father was an Indian Scout in a war to the south that forcibly placed Indians on the Klamath Reservation.[9] After their father died in 1906, Flora and her older brother lived with their mother, who did not remarry, on the family's allotment land on the Warm Springs Reservation. She attended reservation school through the sixth grade, where she learned to read and write in English.

Flora married three times over the course of her life. In 1919, she married Young Boise, an enrolled member of the Warms Springs Reservation nearly two decades her elder. It was Boise's second marriage, and he had children who were near adulthood. Flora brought a son into the marriage as well.[10] After nearly two decades of marriage, Boise died of a stroke. Flora then married Timothy George in 1939, a religious leader thirty-five years older than she. They lived adjacent to Flora's now adult son and his young wife on the Yakama Reservation in Washington State, where George was enrolled. Flora left George after a few years and married Tommy Thompson in 1943. Flora remained with Thompson until he died in 1959.

Traditionally on the Plateau, parents arranged first marriages while subsequent marriages were the purview of the individuals. Divorces were easy to secure, and most adults would marry several times over the course of their lives.[11] Flora Thompson may have married out of love or responsibility, but her unions were also strategic. She married older men who were ensconced leaders in the communities in which she traveled. The households she shared with them were multigenerational and filled with relatives, both close and distant. Her husbands brought political influence to the relationships while Flora brought skills in reading and writing, her own leadership ability, and a personality that garnered the respect of the non-Indian community.

When Flora Cushinway married Tommy Thompson in 1943, the relationship placed her in the public eye and into an important leadership role at Celilo Village. Tommy Thompson was the hereditary salmon chief at the village, tracing his lineage back to Chief Stocket-ly, a signatory of the Middle Oregon treaty, which created the Warm Springs Reservation. Thompson managed the fishery and officiated at religious ceremonies held at the village. Flora Thompson assisted her husband, attending to his correspondence, stepping in to speak for him when his health faltered, aiding in village public relations, and advising him. Although for the most part women were not traditionally chiefs in Plateau societies, they held status and responsibilities through their marriages. It was a position to which Flora had long aspired. As she said in an oral history interview, "I had a chance to get a chief husband this time."[12]

Flora Thompson was not unique in her time. Native women took on important leadership roles in Indigenous communities across the Columbia Plateau, reflecting the gender equality that anthropologist Lillian Ackerman has documented in economic, domestic, religious, and to a lesser degree political spheres.[13] Flora Thompson held influence because she was the wife of a chief, a role traditionally associated with tasks that extended the abilities and influence of the chief. To marry a chief required that a woman be able and willing to take on those tasks within the community and with outsiders. Native women leaders in the twentieth century altered their strategies, rooted in past practices, to meet contemporary concerns and issues. They were called on to intervene in the mainstream that surrounded and often sought to assimilate them, they used their Western-style educations to interrupt the ongoing legacies of colonization, and they maintained cultural and political practices within their own communities that connected them to their ancestors and provided sustenance for their acts of resistance. Contemporary First Nations theorist Taiaiake Alfred names such acts of resistance to assimilation "dangerous dignity."[14]

Martha Ferguson McKeown was born in 1903 in Astoria to James Ernest Ferguson and Almira E. Hawthorne, both from prominent settler families.[15] Her paternal grandfather, Albert, traveled along the Oregon Trail in the mid-1800s while her paternal grandmother reached Oregon after crossing the Isthmus of Panama, losing the couple's two children on the trip to fever. In Oregon, the family would grow by six more children. Albert Ferguson designed and built Salem's first courthouse (completed in 1854), spent two terms as the Wasco County sheriff (1866–1870), and in 1876 moved to Astoria, where he built several of the city's Victorian homes and served as justice of the peace and director of schools. McKeown would eventually record the history of her maternal grandparents in her 1950 book, *Them Was the Days*, which traced the Hawthorne family's migration in 1870 from a farm in northwestern Pennsylvania to a plantation in Richmond, Virginia, and finally to Astoria, Oregon, by 1883.

McKeown earned her undergraduate degree from Willamette University in 1923 and a master's degree in English fifteen years later, and she dedicated herself to a career in teaching. She also developed an important, if largely forgotten, reputation as a regional writer. Her first publication was a five-page history of the Umatilla House, a mid-nineteenth century hotel that had recently been torn down. The article was published in 1930 in the *Oregon Historical Quarterly,* the journal of the state's historical society, and is her only publication to follow the conventions of an academic historical narrative.[16] She began collecting the stories of her maternal uncle, Mont Hawthorne, about joining the Klondike gold rush, which she published as *The Trail Led North* in 1948. She followed that with *Them Was the Days* (1950) and *Alaska Silver* (1951), both also based on her uncle's recollections. She turned her attention to Celilo Village with two children's books, *Linda's Indian Home* (1956), which focused on Flora Thompson's granddaughter, Linda George Meanus, and *Come to Our Salmon Feast* (1959). Both were illustrated with photographs that McKeown's husband, Archie, took at the community and were written with the Thompsons' input. Her final book was a historical novel about the Oregon Trail, *Mountains Ahead*, published in 1961. McKeown's writing defies placement into a single genre—she wrote local history articles for the *Oregonian* newspaper, as-told-to memoirs in collaboration with her uncle, nonacademic ethnographies about Celilo Village at midcentury, and a somewhat clunky novel about the Oregon Trail. Even when they were critical of her books, reviewers often praised her extensive research and attention to accurate historical and ethnographic detail. Regionalism is the thread that runs through her body of work, placing her in the company of many other nonprofessional women regionalists of the early and mid-twentieth century.[17]

McKeown enjoyed a genuine friendship with the Thompsons, which Chief Thompson publicly recognized by adopting her. She cared for him as he aged and grew infirm, and she also looked after others at Celilo Village. She wrote about the lively and resilient community she found at the village and used her connections in women's voluntary associations to advocate for Indian rights. Her children's stories are populated with relatives and friends of the Thompsons. She took care to review her work with Thompson and other consultants. She welcomed River Indians into her home, made sure they had the supplies they needed for their traditional arts, brokered the sale of the jewelry and dolls they made, and organized the delivery of apples and winter coats to the village at Christmas. She rallied the organizations of which she was a member to attend to the policy and cultural issues that arose at Celilo Village. Perhaps most importantly, she provided venues for the Thompsons and other Indigenous spokespeople to address dominant audiences in Hood River, Portland, and beyond.

NATIVE REFORM AND WOMEN'S VOLUNTARY ORGANIZATIONS

In addition to her publications, Martha McKeown used her club memberships to disseminate information about Celilo and its imminent inundation. In doing so, she joined a movement that preceded her birth by nearly half a century. After the Civil War through the mid-twentieth century, women's clubs were important venues for the articulation and demonstration of the power and influence of women with economic and racial privilege at a time when other forms of professional work and political life were closed to them. Women's voluntary organizations also were key sites in promoting Native assimilation and a domesticity founded in white supremacy. The first voluntary association—either male or female—to focus its entire energies on Native issues was the Women's National Indian Association (WNIA), founded in 1879, during a period of tremendous military violence directed at Indians. The WNIA hoped to turn federal policy away from annihilation and toward what historian Lori Jacobson calls *de-Indianization*.

Reformers claimed a special role for themselves in the push to assimilate Native people, especially women and children. WNIA cofounder Amelia Stone Quinton contended that there was "a sacred responsibility laid upon the white women of the land" to attend to the welfare of Native people.[18] Although its members were unable to vote or hold elected office, the WNIA greatly influenced federal Indian policy for five decades, including successfully lobbying for passage of the Dawes General Allotment Act in 1887. What reformers did not recognize was that their "sacred responsibility" to modernize Indian people "was the culmination of a cycle of cultural annihilation that had been taking place for more than two centuries."[19] Members of the WNIA, according to historian Lori Jacobson, "remained largely untouched by a sense of responsibility for their role in the violent cultural genocide enforced by an assimilationist agenda."[20]

The overwhelming focus on assimilation among women's organizations fractured by the 1920s when, as Margaret Jacobs has shown, white feminists critical of industrialization and modernization looked to Indigenous gender roles to inform their own. Anthropology's turn toward cultural pluralism, which posited that the nation's diversity of cultures was its strength, influenced this new generation of reformers. Women's networks continued to shape federal Indian policy, now reversing some assimilationist policies of the Bureau of Indian Affairs in concert with the Collier administration. Yet while Indian women's social and political roles, especially among Native societies of the Southwest, inspired white reformers to rethink their own, they persisted in setting the parameters of proper Indigenous female conduct, demanding authenticity rather than assimilation.[21]

Oregon's organized women largely followed these national trends, pivoting from full support of assimilation during Martha's grandmother's career to at least some support of Native cultural and religious practices by the time Martha McKeown was an adult. Following the lead of the General Federation of Women's Clubs, which created a national committee on Indian welfare in

1921, the Oregon Federation of Women's Clubs turned toward Indian issues as its primary cause in 1933.[22] Through the 1930s, Oregon's women's organization leadership was composed of white women who, like previous generations, understood themselves to have an important role in statewide and national Indian issues, doing *to* rather than doing *with*. That began to change when Elizabeth Bender Cloud, born to a German father and Ojibwe mother, came to the Umatilla Indian Reservation in 1940 when her husband, Henry Roe Cloud (Winnebago), was appointed its superintendent. Henry was a nationally renowned leader in Indian affairs, a founding member of the first national Native political organization, the Society of American Indians (1911), and advisor on the watershed 1922 Meriam Commission study.

A community organizer and reformer in her own right (she met Henry at a meeting of the Society of American Indians), Elizabeth helped organize an all-Indian women's club on the reservation. Under her leadership, the Oregon Trails Women's Club eventually affiliated with the Oregon Federation of Women's Clubs. In 1948, Elizabeth rose to state leadership as the Indian Welfare chair of the Oregon Federation of Women's Clubs, one of only four Indian women nationwide to hold such a position. In that same year, members of the Oregon Trails Women's Club played a prominent role in the OFWC's annual conference in Portland.[23] Elizabeth Bender Cloud helped push women's organizations in Oregon toward acceptance of Native self-determination and autonomy. Whether Martha McKeown knew Cloud is unclear, but it's nearly certain she knew of her.

As a girl and young woman on the Warm Springs Reservation, Flora Cushinway felt the effects of the Women's National Indian Association's influence on federal policies like property ownership in severalty—focused on individuals rather than on tribes. Her parents and siblings accepted allotments, land whose sale in the early 1960s secured Flora an income in the final years of her life. Also as a result of lobbying by the WNIA, the Bureau of Indian Affairs instituted a system of field matrons who visited reservation homes and taught Native women "proper" housekeeping. Minnie Holcomb, the Warm Springs field matron, reported on Flora's housekeeping and parenting, as well as on those of her sisters and mother. But like the Pueblo women in the 1920s that Margaret Jacobs studied, Flora harnessed the energy of white clubwomen in the Pacific Northwest to *resist* assimilationist policies by forming alliances with them.

These alliances took on various forms that ranged from the maternal assistance white women often offered to Indigenous people to more equitable relationships that could even be described as friendships. By their nature, these alliances were caught in the web of settler colonialism and the history of Indian reform. They were unstable, quick to change from equitable associations to ones that exploited the "exoticism" of "traditional" Indigenous people.[24] But they were also valuable connections both for Native people and for the clubwomen themselves.

Flora and Tommy Thompson leveraged non-Native alliances to broadcast their resistance to threats to the Celilo community. Alliances provided space, sometimes within Native control and sometimes manipulated by the needs of clubwomen, to rearticulate their identities vis-à-vis the state of Oregon and the nation. The Thompsons demonstrated difference, cultural pluralism, and sovereignty through these relationships. Furthermore, they asked clubwomen to write and speak publicly on their behalf, galvanizing women who were often of means and connected to powerful men in the state to their ends. Nearly two decades later, McKeown brought attention to the planned inundation of the mid–Columbia

River by instigating the passage of a resolution in support of financial compensation for those living at Celilo Village at the forty-first annual conference of the Oregon Daughters of the American Revolution (DAR) in 1955.

FACING THE LEGACIES OF SETTLEMENT

Despite important similarities—Martha and Flora were both very religious, were strong female leaders in their communities, and worked to shaped the historical memory of the region's residents—in many ways their lives were inversions of one another because American expansionism shaped their experiences so very differently. McKeown's history as a descendant of settlers represents the colonial systems that upended Indigenous land histories. But Thompson's lived experiences reveal the limits of resettlement. Because the women's stories start with settler and Indigenous relationships to the land, the next chapter sketches out the federal land policies that legitimated Martha's family's ownership and segregated Flora's family to a small reserve, and how those policies affected the women's grandparents and parents.

Chapter 3 explores Flora and Martha's childhoods. Although Martha was born in Astoria, by the time she was seven she lived in the Hood River Valley about seventy miles from Flora's home on the Warm Springs Reservation. The valley was scene to a new wave of twentieth-century frontier settlement characterized by scientific agriculture. In contrast, after just five decades, many reformers considered reservations backward, limiting, and economically untenable. They were also laboratories for forced assimilation through boarding and day schools, Christian missions, and Bureau of Indian Affairs supervision. In that way, optimism shaped Martha's early years while the overwhelming pressure to assimilate and resistance to it shaped Flora's. This section also examines one of the foundational texts of white supremacy in Oregon, the state's first novel, Frederic Homer Balch's *Bridge of the Gods: A Romance of Indian Oregon*. Like other popular fiction of the period, the novel romanticized an Indigenous past in the state that simultaneously erased the lived experiences of actual Indian people like Flora and her family. White Oregonians embraced Balch's book. Martha's mother and grandmother were members of women's voluntary associations that refashioned the novel into theatrical performances and readings. Martha's mother performed a forty-five-minute recitation of the novel. However, Martha's own writings about Celilo Village and Flora decades later can be read as a corrective to earlier writers like Balch.

By the 1940s, the period covered in the fourth chapter, Flora and Martha's lives began to converge at Celilo Village. They likely met in 1942, when Flora married Chief Thompson. McKeown and Tommy Thompson shared a close relationship, which she considered a piece with the work of her grandfather and grandmother in the Indian communities on the mid–Columbia River. Following in the footsteps of her mother and aunt, McKeown was an active member of the DAR, which gave her access to networks of potential Celilo allies and a platform for her activism, despite the organization's problematic racial history and hyperpatriotism.[25] As a published author, McKeown had an active speaking schedule, and she often invited the Thompsons and other Celilo Indians to share those engagements. When highway widening threatened village homes, Flora turned to Martha's network of women's voluntary organizations for assistance. The lobbying that the Thompsons and Martha embarked on to mitigate changes to Celilo Village illustrate the strategies they would use time and time again to publicize problems at the fishing community—presentations to local and state clubs and writing by Martha to familiarize Oregonians with the community. These efforts stand in contrast to those that would come later to halt the construction of The Dalles Dam.

Subsequent chapters examine opposition to The Dalles Dam, which threatened to obliterate age-old Indigenous fisheries as it reconfigured a salmon-bearing Columbia River into a series of lakes rationalized for hydroelectric output and transportation. Unlike any other river project, the building of The Dalles Dam drew the attention of non-Native advocates of Indian rights who opposed the dam. Flora and Martha worked on river issues for years before construction of The Dalles Dam spurred other Indian rights advocates to help resist the construction. Their proximity to the project and history of activism on issues important at Celilo Village put them in the middle of this new interest. While neither woman was central to Jimmie James's dam opposition efforts, his activism helps contextualize theirs. Moreover, their shared correspondence after completion of the dam illustrates the ongoing complexities of settler-Indigenous relationships in the mid-twentieth century.

The Dalles Dam was one of eight large federal dams that would eventually be built in the Columbia River Basin. Collectively, the dams would transform the riverscape and the fishing practices of Native people. Bonneville and Grand Coulee Dams, completed in 1938 and 1941 respectively, had already inundated Native fisheries at Kettle Falls and the Cascade Rapids, washing away burial grounds and other sacred places and forcing the relocation of Native town sites. Well before the American entrance into World War II, Indian fishers tracked reductions in annual salmon runs as massive concrete barriers interrupted fish migration and denied access to ancestral reaches of the basin.

Although it was only one of many, The Dalles Dam in particular symbolized the heavy cost Indigenous people bore in river development. Army Corps of Engineers contractors drilled test holes into the basalt outcroppings at the ancient sites of Celilo and the Long Narrows to locate footings for a dam that would permanently transform the river. Photojournalists and tourists rushed to the midriver to document the final fishing seasons of a wild river before its taming. Indians on the Warm Springs, Yakama, Umatilla, and Nez Perce reservations braced to preserve a sacred landscape and treaty fishing rights while families at Celilo Village also rallied to save their homes and livelihoods.

Complicating negotiations to mitigate the dams' effects on Indian communities was the invidious federal policy of "termination" under Public Law 280, which was on the brink of implementation in the Northwest. The policy sought to terminate federal responsibility to the nation's recognized tribes, shift tribal services to individual states, and liquidate the remnant land base reserved over the previous century through the treaty process and reservation system. The idea originally emerged among a coalition of western governors, including Oregon's Douglas McKay, who had been governor from 1949 to 1952 and whom President Eisenhower appointed to head the Department of the Interior.[26] Promising to release Indigenous communities from the Bureau of Indian Affair's paternalistic oversight, on the surface the policy appeared to be a dramatic shift in federal approaches to the colonization of Indian people. But the results of termination followed a familiar pattern—"rapid assimilation with little concern for Indian culture, property, or treaty rights."[27]

Recommendations to terminate the BIA's guardian relationship over Indian tribes energized debates in Indian communities about sovereignty and how to maintain rights codified in treaties as well as access to ancestral lands.[28] The critical tribal deliberations regarding termination were backdrop to the negotiations with federal agencies about Columbia River fishing rights. Termination threatened to divert attention and resources from river issues such as those immediately concerning the Thompsons. But if lost, the battle to resist termination would make efforts to protect the Columbia River's Native fisheries moot; termination would nullify treaty-protected rights to fish.

Indian leaders on the reservations and at Celilo and other off-reservation villages bore the brunt of these battles, but white allies joined them. Allies organized letter-writing campaigns in support of relocating The Dalles Dam to preserve the falls and requesting just compensation for the losses to the Native fishery. They publicized the effects of development on Native communities. Supporters created the "Save the Celilo Falls Committee" and surveyed the state's population to determine opposition to the dam. Conservationist Gertrude Jensen introduced river chiefs to potential allies in New York City. Martha McKeown rallied the members of the women's clubs she attended and wrote two children's books that documented the history of Celilo Village. Click Relander, newspaper editor and author of *Drummers and Dreamers: The Story of Smowhala the Prophet and His Nephew Puck Hyah Toot, the Last Prophet of the Nearly Extinct River People, the Last Wanapums* in 1956, advocated strategies of resistance. Jimmie James, a retired Port of Portland employee, kept copious correspondence with tribal leaders and non-Native allies throughout the region between 1950 and 1967, building a network of opposition.

The letters James circulated prompted and helped organize opposition to the dam. The correspondence also reveals the actions that many people, whites in particular, believed *should* have happened but didn't—that Indians across the region would register and then vote as a bloc, that Native people would borrow a page from the region's labor organizers and picket the dam site, and that the diverse bands and nations of the region would unify in opposition to federal policies. Actions taken and those advocated for but not taken expose competing ideas about citizenship, community, region, and even time. National citizenship conscribed the imagination of white advocates, who envisioned regional Native people acting as a unified interest group rather than as individual sovereign nations. For many whites, voting, passing resolutions, and appealing to national leaders were ceremonial, part of democracy's civic religion. The battle to halt construction of the dam was a fight to be won or lost in a matter of months; strategies would unfold rapidly, and changing policy would be evident quickly if those strategies were effective. Ceremony at Celilo Village and the region's reservations, involving an equally complex and much older set of relationships, brought a world embroiled in conflict back into spiritual balance. The First Salmon Ceremony, which the Thompsons hosted and the regional press persistently proclaimed in danger of dying out in the early years of the 1950s, suggests an Indigenous "long game." The preservation of fishing rights, entrenched in the transformations resettlement brought, was a marathon of generations, not a sprint over a few years' time.

James and his letters also aid in tracing the lives of Martha and Flora in the aftermath of the dam's closing, the events of which constitute the final chapter. Both women became widows as the dam quieted the river. Within a few years, Martha married a family friend and moved to Portland, but she remained connected to Flora, who continued to monitor treaty fishing rights struggles on the mid-Columbia. Their interests overlapped one last time when Jimmie James tried to permanently place Flora's granddaughter and the subject of Martha's book *Linda's Indian Home*, Linda George Meanus, in an adoptive home.

Read against one another, the personal histories of Flora Thompson and Martha McKeown reveal cross sections of Indigenous and settler regions and the intersections where they meet. The midcentury crisis on the Columbia River was rooted in several generations of conflict about the relationships between the region's landscapes and its people, with Indigenous people losing ground, literally, to settlers and the policies they engendered. Native people constructed a rational worldview based on relationships, sacredness, and longevity that settler perceptions of and incursions into the same region dangerously destabilized. Indigenous people within the Northwest never relinquished their relationships with their homescapes, despite the cession of lands, forced assimilation, and a colonial legal system that assumed limited aboriginal title and imposed guardianship. Losses to settlers weren't total. Remnant homelands on reservations and at village sites like Celilo remained. These sites became spaces of entrenched indigeneity, creating a regional landscape that was both non-Native and Native.

TWO

Maintaining/Making Home

One needs to reflect upon U.S. history and its troubling legacy of "placemaking" manifested in acts of displacement, removal, and containment.

ROBERTO BEDOYA, "Placemaking and the Politics of Belonging and Dis-belonging"

Young Boise stumbled over human remains near Mud Creek on Mount Hood's south side while out with a group of huckleberry harvesters in the early autumn of 1929. The next year, another Warm Springs huckleberry picking party spotted the body again and rumors about it spread, eventually alerting officials.[1] The Clackamas County sheriff's office suspected that the bones belonged to Leslie Brownlee, a twenty-year-old mountaineer who had attempted the first official summit of Mount Hood in 1927 with a climbing partner who was filming the event. Exhausted, Brownlee separated from his partner to return to Government Camp but was caught in a blizzard and never made it to safety.

County officials immediately launched a massive search,
which they periodically renewed for several months even as
hopes of finding Brownlee alive waned.[2]

The rumor reinvigorated the search, and the sheriff hoped
Boise would lead them to the body. But Boise needed to hunt.
The commercial harvest season had been one of the worst in
years, with "at least three would-be workers for every job that
is available," as the unemployed competed with Indians for
work in the fields.[3] *Subsistence hunting and fishing would*
have to make up the year's loss in wages. Boise's wife, Flora,
offered to lead the search party in his stead. Flora was
familiar with Mud Creek, where her family picked berries, but
she hadn't actually seen the skeleton. The sheriff's office
pressed on, despite the unfavorable circumstances. They didn't
locate any remains that day. That evening the sheriff's office
promised a $25 award, which impelled a second search led by
Young Boise the following day. When they were still unable
to locate the body, "the Indians stayed on the ground and
announced their intention of remaining until the skeleton was
found."[4] *They were unsuccessful, leading the* Oregonian *to*
announce that Brownlee's remains were "unfound." Brown-
lee's body has yet to be recovered.[5]

In the summer of 1924, her twentieth year, Martha Ferguson
pulled on a "draped gown of cream white crepe" "caught with
rose point lace" that her grandmother had made and married
Archie McKeown on her parents' expansive lawn, enclosed
by the fruit trees of their orchard.[6] *The elaborate wedding*
included live musical accompaniment and a reception and
buffet lunch for two hundred guests. The Oregonian *covered*
the festivities in three columns in its society section,

concluding with a list of those who had traveled from out of town to observe the rite. Although the guest list must have included many men, women populated the newspaper's coverage. Female friends, who were each fully named, "presided at the coffee urn" or were put "in charge of the arrangements of the gift room."[7] They presided over lunch, sliced and served cake, and, of course, were bridesmaids. Because her father had recently died, Martha's mother even walked her down the aisle.[8]

These two accounts call out the ways in which American resettlement of Oregon's Indigenous lands transformed definitions of place, belonging, and home. They tell two divergent stories about women's lives that fractured along lines of race and class, and along the relationship between the Pacific Northwest's white dominant settler culture and its Indigenous cultures. Land policies set into motion generations before Flora and Martha were born bounded their relationships with the region and ultimately to each other. The legal system that legitimated settler farms and designated reservation boundaries reverberated as each woman moved through the valleys and plateaus of the Columbia River Basin.

When twenty-year-old Martha Ferguson became Martha McKeown, she enacted a marriage ritual that fastened her to a narrative of American expansion and nationalism. A personal decision—whom to marry and when—resonated with the historic role of marriage and family in a settler dynamic in which new families secured new lands to the nation. Marriage and family, essential to the structure of settlement, had historically opened the possibility of claiming vast acreage in what seemed like "new" land, leading to the orchard the Fergusons venerated in the McKeowns' ceremony. "Settler women's lives," historian Albert Hurtado states, "were a *routine* part of the day-to-day transformation of the American West from Indian country to public domain and to private property."[9] Settlement mandated families, and in the American mythos, families necessitated expansion.

In contrast, Flora Boise's experience on the trails of Mount Hood in 1930 was ambiguous, at least as narrated by local reporters. Young Boise's decision to hunt instead of search is understandable; October was a busy month of fishing, gathering, and hunting for most people at Warm Springs. It's less clear why Flora guided the first search when she hadn't seen the body. Maybe she hoped for a reward. In the news coverage, Flora Boise and other Native helpers journeyed on the periphery of the main event—the failed summit of Mount Hood; Indians were within the narrative frame but only in ineffectual supporting roles. However, their presence on Mount Hood speaks to resilience, to successfully maintaining traditions of food gathering in spite of the profound transformations of their homeland, and to the unfinished, even unstable nature of settler colonization.

The straightforwardness of Martha's wedding sits in contrast to the ambiguity of Flora's aid to the Clackamas County sheriff. Telescoped beyond single events in the lives of two women, they reveal much about the settlement of Oregon in the early twentieth century. At root are competing notions of place and belonging—what Mishuana Goeman calls the "spatial tendencies"—held by settlers and Native peoples.[10] Martha's wedding tied her to the centrality of the nuclear family in settlement, to a kind of colonial belonging manifested in nineteenth-century land policies like the Oregon Donation Act. Flora's story caught her beyond the artificial confines of the reservation imposed by settlement's logic, signaling the critical issue for members of the Warm Springs Reservation: maintaining connections to resources and sacred sites on lands ceded in 1855 in the face of a system designed to alienate them from those very resources and sites.[11] Martha's wedding, a celebration of the nuclear family within the bounds of private property, reflects the supposed order of white settlement. Flora's perseverance in cultivating the broader homeland is a rip in the fabric of settlement, which relied on the segregation and othering of Oregon's Indigenous people. Warm Springs huckleberry gathering parties indicated the potential for disorder and chaos in the newly Americanized place. Land is at the heart of these stories.

The productive land Martha's father bought in 1911, when she was eight, surrounded the newly wed McKeowns. The orchard was her birthright; after a brief honeymoon, she and Archie lived in her mother's home while he managed the family business. When Martha's mother died in 1943, the two officially took over the farm and continued to live in the family home. The land was also a metaphorical birthright, reflecting a pioneering mythology that celebrated families like McKeowns as tamers of the wilderness frontier. The Fergusons founded Oregon, literally building some of the state's most important homes and buildings, developing its industries, and acting as government officials in its counties.

In Oregon's "settler terrains," federal reservation policy and the practice of allotment shaped Flora Cushinway's access to her ancestors' land by turning the region into a false colonial binary: reservation space / off-reservation space.[12] Unlike Martha, Flora experienced two contradictory traditions of land use: a foreign system of private landownership embodied in allotment policy, and the migratory seasonal rounds delineated by kin connections that predated the reservation system. Off-reservation sites such as those on federally owned land bound Flora to her ancestors. She harvested the same foods sometimes into the very cedar-root baskets they had used. But getting to those sites was increasingly difficult as Indians were forced onto reserves where they were expected to farm, and as families like the McKeowns and their neighbors locked land into private, non-Native ownership, turning fields of camas and wild celery into acres of strawberries and pear trees.

Kinship created a web of Indigenous connections across space and time that was often illegible to colonial outsiders. As the federal government sought to control Indigenous placemaking, it also attempted to streamline the complexity of Indigenous relationships to the land and to one another. Federal agencies emphasized the biological nuclear family over the numerous biological and nonbiological aunts, uncles, grandparents, and cousins that characterized Native kinship patterns. Marriages, births, and deaths became the jurisdiction of the state, which documented each and in turn required such documentation to legitimate relationships between Indigenous individuals. Even naming practices were simplified into permanent customary American designations to aid in tracking an individual over time and space. Likewise, private landownership—the compulsory allotment—with clearly marked boundaries and clear transmission to the next generation was to replace Indian usufructuary rights. But one system did not replace the other. Oregon's Native peoples moved between and among them; claims to allotments coexisted with claims to ancestral root fields. Kinship connected families to one another as well as to place, the resource sites throughout the region that made Indigenous life possible.

Kinship was also important for Martha because it tied her to the conceptual space of the nation as well as to a historic narrative of the American Pacific Northwest. Martha, her mother, and her maternal grandmother were all members of the Daughters of the American Revolution through ancestor John Lupher, a private in the Pennsylvania Cumberland Company militia.[13] Martha's fraternal grandfather came to Oregon in 1850 and served as Wasco County's sheriff (1866–1870) before moving to Astoria, where Martha was born. Albert Ferguson designed the buildings of Oregon's statecraft, policed the emerging American society along the Columbia River, and founded Free Mason chapters in many of the state's developing cities.[14] Martha's family had deep roots in Oregon, at least compared to other white families. Moreover, they shared in the migration to the region, which eventually Americanized it.

Events before Flora Cushinway and Martha Ferguson were born set the trajectory of their personal histories within a changing history of place and kinship. Their very lives were the legacies of the past and embodied the continual refreshing of settler colonial takings into the twentieth century. Pull on the threads of two foundational pieces of legislation—the Oregon Donation Land Act (1850) and the Dawes General Allotment Act (1887)—and expropriation becomes visible. Congress passed both measures "during the heyday of Americans' celebration of the home as the keystone of their political, economic, and social order";[15] and as such, they represent the ways in which land policy delineated and limited definitions of "home" and "region." Together, they explain why Martha's marriage was a legible component of American expansion and the conquest of Oregon and why Flora's off-reservation ventures onto Mount Hood, activities that mirrored those of her ancestors, had become transgressive by the time Flora was a young woman.

Resettlement of Oregon required land and the reproduction of settler families in equal measure. From its inception, public land policy in Oregon secured both. Expansionists in Congress, hoping the promise of generous land grants would tempt citizens to trek to isolated and lightly populated territories, passed land-grant acts in the mid-nineteenth century to "create a landowning agricultural class in the western territories."[16] As winter turned to spring in 1850, Oregon's territorial delegate, Samuel R. Thurston, lobbied in Washington, DC, for passage of the Oregon Donation Land Act, which was modeled on liberal land claim laws passed by Oregon's provisional government before it was a US territory. The new federal law, passed in late September of that year, secured 320 acres for men at least twenty-one years old who arrived in Oregon Territory prior to December 1, 1850. (Those who arrived after 1850 but prior to 1853 could also claim land under the act, but the acreage was halved. Congress eventually extended the act to include settlers arriving as late as 1855.) Married couples could claim 640 acres—a full square mile. The law reflected and shaped the expectations of settlers in regards to landownership opportunities in Oregon.

The act was one piece of a global project—a "settler revolution" of "explosive settlement" in the United States, Canada, New Zealand, Australia, Argentina, and South Africa that remade significant regions of the world during the nineteenth century.[17] Throughout distant locales, settlers and their lawmaking champions established legal processes that legitimated their claims to Indigenous land in what historian John Weaver calls "the great land rush."[18] Oregon's contribution to that legal apparatus was notable in two ways: first, Congress passed the act before securing title to the land from its Indigenous owners; and second, the act provided Oregon's white women with a path toward landownership. Concerned about maintaining family integrity in cases where the patriarch died, Congress passed provisions that allowed wives to hold property in their own names.

The Indian Appropriations Act of 1851 was intended to provide an orderly schematic whereby Indian people willingly gave up large tracts of land to the federal government and reserved select portions of their traditional homelands, as well as rights to resources on and off those reserves, in exchange for annuities and other forms of payment. The Oregon Donation Land Act inverted that process by securing private property for settlers before the region's Native people ceded their lands. That reversal reflected deeply embedded settler assumptions about settlement, namely that the land would ultimately be theirs, with treaty negotiation outcomes predetermined. Although federal officials later negotiated cessions from the region's Indigenous peoples, the Oregon Donation Land Act symbolically and literally erased Native landownership and tenure in legislation that reimagined the region as one of pastoral, American-owned family farms.

In 1850, the year Congress passed the Oregon Donation Land Act, twenty-nine-year-old Albert W. Ferguson, Martha's grandfather, arrived in Oregon, like many young men who traveled west: ambitious and ready to make his mark.[19]

Albert Ferguson's family was originally from southern Virginia, where he apprenticed as a carpenter. Ferguson moved to Lewisburg, married Margaret Jane Wetzel in 1844, and started a family. Soon, the Fergusons moved again, this time more than eight hundred miles west, to the county seat of Lexington, Missouri. Lexington, on the banks of the Missouri River, had an economy based on agriculture sustained both by slave labor and by its geographical position as a jumping-off point for westward emigration. After a short period spent preparing for the six-month overland journey, Albert left his young wife and two young sons for the goldfields of California. Ferguson must not have found the fortune he was seeking; he quickly left the Sacramento River on a steamer, chartered by several would-be miners, that landed in Astoria, Oregon, after battling a storm at the notorious Columbia River bar. Once he settled in his new state, Ferguson's wife and two children traveled around the Isthmus of Panama to join him; only his wife survived the trip and the fevers that killed the couple's children.[20]

Albert W. Ferguson was a builder as well as a settler. In Oregon he was appointed to a three-person committee tasked with locating and erecting public buildings in the state's new capital, Salem.[21] Ferguson designed and built Marion County's first courthouse as well as other Salem buildings. When he moved his family to The Dalles in 1862 to improve his health in the dry air east of the Cascade Mountains, Ferguson established his wealth and secured political standing. He cofounded a planing mill (a plant that turns boards into dimensional lumber), and he was twice elected sheriff for the enormous Wasco County.[22] The family returned to Astoria in 1876, where Ferguson worked as an architect and founded a sash and door company.[23] Albert and his youngest son, James (Martha's father), built homes for Astoria's most prominent residents, including the home that Martha lived in during her first seven years, and other late Queen Anne structures that still characterize the city today.[24]

Martha's family history connected her to two of the most important events of the nineteenth century: the crisis of the Civil War and the promise of westward expansion. By moving west, Ferguson missed Civil War battles. Two older brothers, however, remained in Virginia and joined the Confederate Army. One was badly wounded and the other sustained fatal injuries in the war. More than one thousand miles separated Albert from his brothers and the bloody battles in the South. But settlers like Albert came west with the devastation of sectional crisis and slavery's brutality as much a part of their baggage as the clothes and tools they packed. Political debates regarding the Oregon Donation Land Act centered on its exclusion of nonwhite claimants ("American half-breed Indians" could claim grants under the bill, which excluded Hawaiians, Indians, and African Americans), and Albert made his home in a state whose constitution excluded slavery *and* black settlement. Moreover, as his older brothers were embroiled in the Civil War's destruction, Albert built the infrastructure that Americanized Flora Cushinway's homeland and systematically reordered Indigenous lifeways in the far corner of the Pacific Northwest.

CREATING THE WARM SPRINGS INDIAN RESERVATION

In 1855, five years after the passage of the Oregon Donation Land Act, federal officials commenced treaty negotiations with the tribes and bands that would populate the Yakama, Umatilla, and Nez Perce reservations. Later that same year, the bands and tribes that would live on the Warm Springs Reservation—Tygh, Wyam, Tenino, John Day, Wasco, Dog River, and Dalles—negotiated the Treaty with the Tribes of Middle Oregon with Oregon Superintendent of Indian Affairs Joel Palmer. One of the treaty's signatories was Tommy Thompson's uncle, Chief Stocket-ly, the salmon chief who named Thompson his successor.

The council met near Dalles City (renamed The Dalles in 1860), at the time one of the Pacific Northwest's largest population centers, with more than eight hundred residents.[25] Situated near the region's most important Native trade sites at Celilo Falls, the burgeoning American city got its start as the end of the overland portion of the Oregon Trail. By 1850 it boasted a new military fort (Fort Dalles), and in the next decade it would become an important stop for stagecoaches and steamers.[26] The town burst with travelers and merchants eager to connect the resource-rich valleys of the West with the rest of the nation. The treaty simply codified a sweeping upheaval already in progress and visible in the generations of Flora's family. Her grandparents lived in a territory governed by Native bands and marked by the influence of the global fur trade. The birth of Flora's father and mother (1842 and 1852, respectively) coincided with a demographic revolution and the forced relocation of Indigenous people to reservations throughout the region.

The Treaty with the Tribes of Middle Oregon created a reserve of more than half a million acres seventy miles south of the Columbia River.[27] In return, bands ceded 10 million acres to the United States, including the many village sites that dotted the banks of the Columbia. Treaty negotiators spoke about the new reservation with little specific knowledge of the land on which it would be placed. As a result, the boundaries were initially vague. Indian agent R. R. Thompson and several band leaders surveyed the reservation boundaries a few years after the treaty council, and R. R. Thompson blazed trees while the Indians piled rocks to mark the borders. Nonetheless, the borders would remain contested for decades.

The remote reserve was a journey of "four days' travel over steep rocky trails" from the river.[28] Warm Springs superintendent A. O. Wright described the reservation in his 1900 annual report:

It is bounded west by the summit of the Cascade Range, south by the Metolins [Metolius] River, east by the Des Chutes [Deschutes] River, and north by the range of hills near Wapinitia. The surface slopes from the mountains eastward. In the mountains and their foothills there is a growth of pine timber of considerable value, but far from being equal to that in the moister climate on the other side of the mountains. . . . In the mountains there is still pretty good hunting, and there are berries in profusion, which the women pick at this season. Farther east there are openings with good pasturage, and which probably are humid enough to raise good crops, at least of small grain. Indian ponies in large numbers range here half wild. There are also many cattle and one flock of sheep which finds amply [*sic*] pasturing here. The cattle belong partly to the Indians and partly to encroaching whites. . . . Still farther east the plateau is broken more and more by the streams, which have cut down many hundred feet in canyons. This leaves the plateau a desert with a growth of sagebrush, while the canyons have more or less fertile land which is occupied as farms. These could all be irrigated if the soil were not a volcanic sand, which does not hold the water in the ditches.[29]

When hundred-year-old Albert Kuckup testified before the US Court of Claims in 1931, he described the contested northern boundaries of the reservation.

The beginning of the selection they started for the boundary is on the northern side, toward west. There is a butte there known as Taihan is the name of the butte. Another butte still remains is called Pato-Pato. . . . That is where the line runs. That is the boundary line. Then from that Pato-Pato it went on to Soo-lee, now known as Jefferson's Mountain, Mount Jefferson. Then from Soo-lee or Mount Jefferson it went on to known by Indians as Ktha-tee-wapt-kee.

Q: What is the white name?

A: Three Fingered Jack is the name now at the present time; and from that Three Fingered Jack or Ktha-tee-wapt-kee it went on over Three Sisters. From Three Sisters it went, it went from Three Sisters right to Sumiee, and then from Sumiee, passing Sumiee, into another big lake, which is the head of the Deschutes River.[30]

Eighty years after he attended the treaty council and accompanied the Thompson survey team to care for their horses, Kuckup relied on both Indigenous and American place-names as if to underscore the lack of common language in the complicated negotiations over land claimed in two separate traditions.

Native leaders chafed at moving so far from the Columbia River. The reservation isolated them from the Indigenous trading center at Celilo and the economic hub that emerged with white settlement. Tribal historian George Aguilar called the reservation "the Warm Springs wastelands" and described removal as "a funeral death march" to a "desolate" land.[31] Distance limited opportunities for wage labor and curtailed access to the marketplace established on the river over centuries. Moreover, the reservation required removal from fishing stations, hunting spots, and the high mountain meadows where berries were harvested. Sacred sites marked by pictographs and cairns would have to be maintained remotely amid the settler invasion, and the myths and place-names that animated the gorge landscape remembered and taught to subsequent generations from afar. The land held everything—sustenance, history, religion, and law.

As a result, the treaty provisions to fish, gather roots and berries, hunt, and process foods—activities that required tribal members to be absent from the reservation for months at a time—were crucial to Native treaty negotiators. Jeff Van Pelt, an enrolled member of the Confederated Tribes of the Umatilla Indian Reservation, described the off-reservation rights reserved by his ancestors in a 1999 interview:

> If you're going to put us on that little bitty Indian reservation you need to understand that our economic base is very broad. We have many horses. We need to take care of the horses; we need pasturing for them horses. We need to have access to our usual and accustomed fishing areas where we always go to gather our fish. We need areas to go hunt. We need areas to go gather different kinds of foods and roots and berries. Those are things that specifically they take out in the articles of the treaty.

By reserving rights to pasture their horses, and fishing, hunting, and gathering sites, Jackson's ancestors were "in reality . . . saying . . . we want to continue our way of life as we always have."[32]

For the very reasons off-reservation rights were so critical to Indian people, they did not square with the assimilationist goals of federal Indian policy. Within a decade of signing the treaty, J. W. Perit Huntington, Oregon's Superintendent of Indian Affairs from 1863 to 1869, sought to eliminate those rights. Huntington fraudulently secured the approval of a new treaty from reservation leaders. The agreement, which became known as the Huntington Treaty, purchased Warm Springs enrollees' off-reservation rights. Tribal leaders thought they had agreed to a pass system that would monitor but not prohibit their off-reservation movements. Congress ratified the treaty in 1867, though it was quickly determined to be wrongfully negotiated and was seldom enforced.[33]

Despite the Huntington Treaty, Indians from the Warm Springs Reservation continued to periodically travel to the Columbia River and the region's mountains to fish, hunt, and gather traditional foods. As historian Andrew Fisher points out in his examination of "River Indians," reservations were "porous," lacking the definitive boundaries to segregate Indians that many envisioned.[34] Those who peopled Fisher's important book—like Tommy Thompson—stayed in communities along the river, eventually developing identities that distinguished them from the Indians who lived at least part-time on the region's reservations. When Indians left reservations to travel, work, and live, they challenged the ability of federal agents to carry out their work, namely supervising Indian enrollees and maximizing efforts to assimilate them into mainstream American values and lifeways.

Progressive superintendents of Indian Affairs, like Huntington's replacement, Alfred B. Meacham, recognized the necessity of seasonally returning to the fishing and hunting sites beyond the bounds of the reservation. But most officials became exasperated at the frequent trips made by Warm Springs enrollees and sought to limit off-reservation excursions, believing they slowed assimilation. Movement off the reservation and between reservations characterized Flora's life as she collected traditional foods, sought out religious gatherings, moved temporarily to the Yakama Reservation in Washington State, and eventually settled permanently at Celilo Village. The descendants of settlers who venerated migration in their own families defined the movements of Indian people as transgressive.

Flora's father, Jim Cushny or Cushinway, took advantage of an officially sanctioned leave of the reservation when he joined the Warm Springs Indian Scouts, led by Donald McKay, in 1873.[35] The scouts—seventy in total—fought on behalf of the United States in the Modoc War on the Oregon-California state line.[36] The details of the Modoc War were widely reported in newspapers across the country, with the Warm Spring scouts heralded as "Indian allies" to the United States. The dispatches of fanciful reporters intent on demonstrating the success of Indian policies introduced the Warm Springs people to a national audience. The *San Francisco Bulletin* described the Warm Springs as "really a nation of farmers" whose small family plots of eight to ten acres, school, church, and emerging industries were transforming Indians so thoroughly it was evident in their facial features:

> Each year's work upon the Indian mind improves the face, as the clever brush of the artist softens the outlines of the portrait, and develops harmonious beauty.[37]

Implausible accounts of assimilation's triumph matched the realities of Native lives no better than newspaper accounts of ten-acre farms producing the crops needed to sustain Indian families.

At the conclusion of hostilities in June 1873, Cushinway mustered out. McKay and Superintendent of Indian Affairs Alfred Meacham capitalized on the national interest in the conflict by creating separate touring groups that reenacted fictionalized accounts of the war. McKay's troupe included more than a dozen scouts, but contemporary advertisements and newspaper accounts do not identify the participants, making it difficult to know whether Flora's father traveled with them. When he returned to the reservation, Cushinway lived with his wife, Martha, and mother-in-law and started a family. After he died in 1906 (when Flora was eight or nine), Martha petitioned the federal government for his pension, which she was finally awarded in the early 1920s, a quarter century after his service.[38] Otherwise, according to the field matron's records, Martha was "very poor."[39]

"Mama used to tell me these stories," Flora recalled decades later. When the hostilities stopped, the Warm Springs women who lost husbands "wipe[d] each other[']s tears and they became widows." A parade was held at Pulpit Rock just outside of the city of The Dalles. "Citizen American armies" joined with the scouts and they feasted.

> After the feast, the men were given blankets apiece, brown and black, brown and black. . . . And socks, probably shoes, too. . . . And then the ladies were given blankets, shawls, same kind, black and brown. And then they were given paint. Red, yellow, orange.

Flora's mother "painted herself, just red up here and then orange and then yellow. . . . Like sunrise. Sunrise. . . . And I used to laugh at her, 'Oh, Mother! You must have looked like a clown!' I wasn't born yet. I must have been born just about that time."[40] Like a sunrise that marks the transition from night to day, Flora's recollections suggest a liminal time—when local communities recognized Indian veterans and the federal government denied them benefits, when Indian people satisfied the obligations of citizenship without holding its privileges.

This stereograph image produced for the commercial market is of Warm Springs Scout leader Donald McKay and four unidentified scouts. Photo by Eadweard J. Muybridge, 1873. Courtesy of the George Eastman Museum

DOMESTICITY AND LAND POLICY

Flora's childhood home sat on land allotted to her father and mother under the Allotment Act passed in 1887. The Women's National Indian Association's lobbying was so influential that Senator Henry Dawes remarked that the new Indian policy "was born of and nursed by" this women's association.[41]

The Dawes Allotment Act was the fun-house mirror distortion of federal land policies like the Oregon Donation Land Act and the subsequent Homestead Act, which was modeled on the Oregon legislation.[42] The Land Claim Act originated with the settlers of Oregon, justifying plots they had claimed before the United States had undisputed jurisdiction of the territory, and reverberated with the values of yeoman democracy. Conversely, the Dawes Act was coercive. Congressional leaders and Indian reformers advocated a land policy for reservations similar to the land giveaways that justified long-distance migrations among settlers. But this time the values were imposed from outside as the legislation crafted individually owned parcels from the collective landholdings of the tribe. Private land, nuclear families, and agriculture would provide paths toward assimilation and citizenship, according to advocates of the measure. Moreover, provisions allowed for "surplus" land—any not allotted to living Indians—to be sold to non-Indian buyers. Compulsory allotment assumed *the lack* of reproduction among Indian families, which would lead to a diminishment of reservation populations over time. Patrick Wolfe refers to this and other assimilationist policies as "the logics of elimination" of Indigenous people.

Statistics tell the same story. American homesteaders secured 2.5 million acres during the short life of the Donation Land Act.[43] Indians lost 90 million acres of land nationwide during the period between the Allotment Act's passage in 1887 and its reversal in 1933 under the Indian Reorganization Act. These facts make explicit the common purpose of each law—to transfer the lands of Indigenous people to American landowners. The Land Act provided a net gain of property to mostly white Oregonians, and the Dawes Act further alienated Indians from their traditional homelands.

Both the Oregon Donation Land Act and the Dawes Severalty Act extended property rights to women as they scripted a future of nuclear landowning families for the nation. The "cult of domesticity"—or what Amy Kaplan calls "manifest domesticity" as the cult moved west—drove the vision.[44] Congress did not set out to protect women's property rights, but politicians were certain that the same narrow definition of "home" was both the strength of the white nation and the Native path toward full assimilation into American society.

Assimilationist ideas about domesticity diminished the autonomy of most Native women. "From being she who worked, who controlled lines of descent, who may even have ruled politically," Bethany Ruth Berger writes, "she was to become she who inspired others to work and who depended on others for her support."[45]

Allotment altered traditional familial modes that included extended family networks and polygamy. The small size of allotments limited the number of family members in a single household, and the policy sought to eliminate polygamy by restricting allotments to single men, single women, and married couples. Nonetheless, property rights were extended to women as well as to their husbands to ensure that wives were not vulnerable to changing circumstances.

Congress did not specify protections specifically for Native women when they revised the 1887 Dawes Act in 1891. Pressured by Native activists to alter the law, Congress revised the act to equalize allotments awarded to each enrollee. In the original law, "heads of households" could claim 160 acres, while single people could claim 80 acres and minors could claim 40. Arguing that every tribal member shared land rights equally, tribal leaders successfully urged Congress to allocate 80 acres to each member, which, of course, included women and girls. Alice Fletcher, perhaps the best-known female Indian reformer at the time and an ardent advocate of breaking up tribal lands into individual holdings, urged these revisions, arguing, "by the present allotment the women are losers."[46]

Determining that widows needed protection, Congress specifically named white wives as beneficiaries of the Oregon Donation Land Act. Section five stipulated that male American citizens, twenty-one years and older, who had emigrated to Oregon by December 1, 1853, could be "granted the quantity of one quarter section, or one hundred and sixty acres of land, if a single man; or if married, or if he shall become married within one year after becoming twenty-one years of age as aforesaid, the quantity of one half section, or three hundred and twenty acres, one half to the husband and the other half to the wife *in her own right.*" Women's property rights in this legislation were inextricably linked to their role as wives, but nonetheless they could hold land as individual property owners. Historian Richard Chused credits delegate Samuel Thurston with extending women's property rights. As the likely drafter of the bill and an advocate of women's education, Thurston wanted to "surround wives with sufficient protections so they could act as a moral bastion and source of comfort for their husbands,"[47] declaring in a public letter that women "hold the future destiny of the nation in their gentle grasp."[48]

By 1900, land policies had redistributed lands and resources from Native peoples to the region's new settlers, which numbered well over 400,000 in Oregon alone. Cities like Portland (population 90,426), Astoria (population 8,381), and The Dalles (population 3,542) supplanted Indigenous village sites. They were river cities, located at passable junctures on the Columbia. Portland, which had become the region's largest city, lay at the confluence of the Columbia, which flowed east to west, and the Willamette River, which flowed south to north. Astoria, Oregon's western-most city, welcomed oceangoing vessels at the mouth of the Columbia. Located on the mid–Columbia River, The Dalles tied the hinterlands of Idaho and eastern Oregon and Washington to the port cities of Portland and Astoria.

New settlement demands for transportation connections between resource areas and markets gave rise to good roads campaigns at the turn of the century and within a few decades embraced the systematic damming of the Columbia River. Conversely, the Warm Springs Reservation removed Indian peoples from the Columbia and its fish-filled tributaries, from the berries, deer, and elk on Mounts Adams and Hood, and from the plateau root fields that sustained their ancestors. By design, the reservation was cut off from the regional connections that supported past Native communities, and it also segregated Indians from their white neighbors. But the necessities of survival propelled Indians into the realm of whites. Tommy Thompson and other Indians met orchardists when they ventured onto farms in search of seasonal work, creating spaces for meaningful interactions between peoples.[49]

The legal apparatus of American settlement of Oregon—the Land Act and allotment policy among others—transformed the meaning of land and home as it opened economic opportunities for Martha and her family and limited those of Flora's family. When the women married, traveled away from home, raised their children, worked for wages, or volunteered in community efforts, the past colored every aspect of their lives. It wasn't the fault of either woman, but settlement meant that one people suffered "the logics of elimination" while the other collectively thrived. The wealth of one family was indirectly built on the impoverishment of another. But it also made neighbors of tribal people and settlers and their descendants. Both Flora and Martha made innumerable daily decisions about how they would live with the legacies of settlement and its ongoing manifestations in their own lives, decisions that were shaped by their earliest years.

THREE

Growing Up

The story begins, of course, long before the submergence
of the falls with the seeds of ambition to make an Eden
where Eden was not needed.

ELIZABETH WOODY, "Recalling Celilo"

BY THE TURN OF THE NINETEENTH CENTURY, OREGON'S
settlers had developed a regional identity that inscribed familiar
narratives about settlement and indigeneity from other places
on the specific landscapes of the state. In these narratives, Anglo
Protestant settlers repopulated an Eden made divinely available
to them while remnant Indian people, whose communities had
been decimated by diseases, provided colorful backdrop to the
nation-building actions of pioneers and their children. In stories
at once tragic and celebratory, Oregon's intellectuals knit the Far
West into the national fabric with notions of fading indigeneity and the triumph of benevolent and peaceful pioneering to
bind Oregon to a prosperous continental future. The mythology

overwhelmed alternative understandings of the past and the region, making the domination of Indian people inevitable and their assimilation into American society the best outcome in an otherwise tragic tale of demise. This was the milieu into which both Flora and Martha matured: it shaped federal policy, local and national cultures, and the very identity of western residents.

Martha's mother, Almira, devoured the state's most popular novel, Frederic Balch's *The Bridge of the Gods: A Romance of Indian Oregon*, reading it several times, giving public recitations of it, and visiting "every part of the country mentioned in the book, from New England to Astoria."[1] The turgid story charts the demise of the region's Indian peoples and their replacement by white settlers, embodied in a well-meaning male missionary whose intelligence and morality surpass that of the Indians with whom he makes his temporary home, save for the mixed-heritage "princess" with whom he predictably falls in love. The collapse of the title's natural land bridge signals the collapse of Indian Oregon and the rise of American settler dominance.

The romantic tale, first published in 1890, exploits and distorts Indian oral traditions to establish an origin myth of white supremacy in Oregon. Its central characters are the idealistic missionary, Cecil Gray, and the tragic leader of a tribal confederacy on the mid–Columbia River, Chief Multnomah. Set just as the ocean-based fur trade emerged in Oregon, the novel follows Gray as he treks alone from New England to the wilds of the West, drawn by a vision of a land bridge over a swift-flowing river and the desire to bring Indians to God so that "savage hearts might be touched and softened."[2]

After spending eight years imprisoned by the Cayuse east of the Cascade Mountains, Gray was taken to the Willamette Valley with a war party convened by Multnomah, the leader of their confederacy. On their journey, they passed the Bridge of the Gods, a natural basalt expanse near the Columbia's Cascade Rapids and, according to the novel, the spiritual epicenter of Willamette tribal peoples, who were "the strongest of all the tribes as long as the Bridge of the Gods should stand."[3] When Gray and his captors reached Multnomah's village, the eminent chief immediately recognized Gray as a great spiritual leader and invited the outsider to speak at council, conferring status to the missionary.

Gray quickly discovers the presence of someone he thinks is a young, beautiful white woman. When he greets her, he discovers that Wallulah is mixed-race, the daughter of Multnomah and a woman from the "Orient" who was shipwrecked at the Columbia's mouth. Her mother, Sea Flower, was married to the chief but has since passed away. Though her father has promised her to another high-status chief, Wallulah and Gray fall in love, finding that they share much more in common with one another than either does with the Indians that surround them. Given how central visions of "home" have been to settler identity, Balch's focus on Native homes is no surprise.

When Gray first enters Wallulah's lodge he is immediately taken by an interior that is at once both exotic and familiar, echoing the female space Gray left behind when he embarked on his journey west. Wallulah's home, which she alone inhabits, contrasts sharply with the alien and inferior spaces of the Indians around her. "Rich many-hued products of Oriental looms covered the rough walls," capturing Gray's attention. "The carpet was like a cushion; mirrors sparkling with gems reflected his figure; luxurious divans invited to repose."[4] As with her racial heritage, her furnishings set Wallulah apart, reflecting her elevated level of civilization and making her less connected to the people around her. She reveals to Gray that she has never even entered another lodge in the village; her "mother forbade it, for fear that I might grow like the savage occupants." Gray "knew now how she had preserved her grace and refinement amid her fierce and squalid surroundings."[5]

Balch used the Indigenous Bridge of the Gods mythology as the foundation for a new origin story that distorted Native lifeways and plotted white supremacy. The Indians populating Balch's novel were overwhelmingly male, obtuse and brutal, indulgent, savage, and animal-like in appearance and character. One young man intentionally rode a horse to death while another whipped an elderly woman who inadvertently blocked his path. A trade gathering was "a rude of civilization, the picture of society in its infancy, the rough dramatization of that phase through which every race passes in its evolution from barbarism."[6] Balch leavened his cruel depictions of Indian people with an admission of their potential for civilizing change, much like the federal Indian policy of the period. During one of Gray's sermons "there came to all those swarthy listeners, in dim beauty, a glimpse at a better life . . . a moment's fleeting revelation of something above their own vindictiveness and ferocity."[7] Balch revised the fraught history of Christian missionizing on the Columbia by intimating that Gray's attempts at conversion would bring a "better life" to his Native listeners. In his novel, Balch racialized barbarism, but biology did not entirely dictate one's future. Even recent critics have described Balch's Indian caricatures as "reveal[ing] a genuine interest and respect for native culture" because of the story's prospect for shared humanity.[8] The novel was racist but not anti-Indian.

The popular novel, which was reprinted seven times by 1902 and declared "a realistic picture of the powerful tribes that inhabited Oregon country two centuries ago" by *Publishers Weekly*, became a touchstone for many Oregonians, including Martha's mother.[9] Oregon's boosters and clubwomen kept the story in circulation for decades, with multiple theatrical renditions and dramatic readings of the novel especially in the second and third decade of the twentieth century.[10] When a women's auxiliary arranged for a dramatization as part of Astoria's centennial celebrations in 1911, they helped launch a "splashy extravaganza" with a cast of "more than 500 persons and costing in excess of $35,000 to stage" that included performances in Portland and Oklahoma in addition to Astoria.[11]

Astoria fell in line with a national obsession over historical pageantry in which the aims of hereditary patriotic organizations, civic leaders, and educational elites converged to produce large-scale public celebrations of Anglo American superiority.[12] When the play came to Portland in 1912 as part of the city's annual Rose Festival, performers from the Warm Springs Indian Reservation were added to the cast, their presence meant to lend "an air of realism" to the open-air performance.[13] The *Oregonian* reported on the sold-out performances, highlighting the participation of Jackson Spooms, a former Warm Springs Scout in the Modoc War. The newspaper boasted—certainly incorrectly—that at approximately one hundred years of age Spooms saw his first railroad, automobile, streetcar, and "other delights of civilization" during his visit to Portland.[14] The meaning was clear: even into the twentieth century, Warm Springs Indians were suspended in an early premodern time in contrast to the modernity of settler Oregon. In response, Spooms helped organize another retelling of the Bridge of the Gods myth, this time written by Native people in a

Native language (the newspaper doesn't indicate which) to be performed on the reservation and at intertribal gatherings less than a month after his Portland performances. When A. Du Gas arrived on the reservation to recruit Native performers for the original pageant, he discovered a "strange spectacle": dozens of Indians rehearsing their own play. Spooms gave Du Gas a defiant message for the show's Portland producers: "Tell white men we play a great play here. We [are] greater than white men. We tell [the] story of our own bridge our way. We [will] not come to Portland."[15]

Settler origin myths tethered a recent pioneer past to a more distant Indigenous one and linked the contemporary lives of Martha and Flora into a chain of Oregon identities.[16] The mythological Oregon they created did not leave much space for an Indigenous present, but it did not completely obliterate its possibility. Indeed, Indigenous leaders successfully exploited the romance that whites expected—and sometimes demanded—to pry open space for Indian agency. Like Spooms, they wrote and performed their own stories.

The very mythologies that shaped Martha's Oregon in childhood and early adulthood distorted Flora's Oregon by negating, denying, and destroying Indigenous space, even as they revered a fictionalized Native past. Settler fantasies conjured imaginary first peoples, but Flora and her family, as well as Jackson Spooms and his, stood outside this vision of Oregon. They weren't the fictional Indians of settler invention, yet they also refused assimilation into mainstream American society. They persisted *as* Indian. Daily Native activity in Oregon's Indian Country sustained Indian identities, countering the destructive assimilating and belittling forces of settler colonization that threatened to transform them into caricatures in service to Manifest Destiny.[17] Below, Martha's story precedes Flora Cushinway's although Flora preceded Martha in birth; by the onset of the twentieth century, Flora's was already counternarrative.

MARTHA ALMIRA FERGUSON

September 13, 1903. Astoria was in the final days of summer when Almira went into labor. Her mother Martha, a midwife, was almost certainly in an upstairs bedroom with Almira, an open window letting in the salty air and sounds from town down the hillside. Maybe Martha assisted with the births of all her grandchildren. This little girl, the last of Almira's babies, would bear her grandmother's name. The men in the family may have sat in the parlor, listening for sounds of distress while they pretended to read and waited for good news.

Martha was born into an extended family whose members all had stories of moving to Oregon from other places. Baby Martha and her older brother were the first generation of Oregon-born children on her mother's side, the second generation on her father's.

Martha was born into a family of homebuilders. Her paternal grandfather designed and supervised the building of homes for some of Astoria's most prominent families. Toward the end of his life he oversaw the construction of the family home from his bed, where roughhousing grandchildren and his own coughing spells interrupted his rest. This final home was built to make a statement. After decades of moving from east to west, following the progression of the United States across the continent, the family was settling at its most western edge, where the Columbia River spills its waters into the Pacific Ocean. Astoria was Oregon's largest, most diverse city when Martha was born. A burgeoning salmon industry fueled innovation in canning systems and fishing methods and tools, while new populations of Chinese, Scandinavian, and Greek migrants, mostly men, added their foreign tongues to the chatter of busy wharves that substituted for cement sidewalks in a town wholly oriented toward water. Alfred Ferguson took advantage of timber-mill waste to decorate the homes he built with gingerbread and ornamental moldings. In his own, he added a spiral staircase, the house's centerpiece. Years later, his home was placed on the national historic registry, bearing his name: the Ferguson House.

When Alfred died in 1891, Martha's father, James, took over the family business and designed and constructed Astoria's homes and public buildings in his own right. Perched on the cliffs of Astoria, homes like the Ferguson House overlooked the bustle of the town and were a safe distance from the sea. As much as its salmon carcasses rotting in the salt air, the fancy Queen Anne homes on the hillside characterized nineteenth-century Astoria. While fish canneries, Chinese-owned businesses, and Finnish saunas disappeared as the region's salmon industry diminished, the homes remain, reminding tourists of an earlier period now relegated to nostalgia. Because Alfred and James were builders, the Ferguson name remains a fixture in Astoria, adorning houses identified as historically significant.

James, his wife Almira (Hawthorne), and their four children shared a home with Almira's brother Mont and their widowed mother, Martha Lupher Hawthorne (for whom Martha Ferguson was named).[18] Grandmother Martha and the younger Martha would live in the same household until Mrs. Hawthorne died in 1921. Grandmother Hawthorne was born in Pennsylvania, where she was raised on a 640-acre federal land grant property held by her father.[19] As a middle-aged wife and mother, she moved to Virginia and then to Nebraska, the Black Hills, and finally Astoria with her husband, son Mont, and three daughters.[20] She was a devoted member of the Methodist church for the duration of her life. As a young woman, she participated in war work related to the Civil War. Later, during the Spanish American War, she was a member of the Oregon Emergency Corps, and when World War I erupted, she joined the American Red Cross.[21] She also worked as a midwife and farm wife and ran a cattle operation for a year. Her husband was an unsuccessful breadwinner and struggled with periodic bouts of drunkenness. Mont described his father as "a good man when he was sober,"[22] while his mother was "a proud woman" who worked around her husband's weaknesses by keeping "still," a strategy that belied her usual activity.[23] When his father violently destroyed the family's only water bucket in a burst of drunken anger, Mont "took the pledge" to abstain from alcohol.[24] His mother joined the Women's Christian Temperance Union (WCTU).[25]

As an adult, Martha's daughter Almira would also work toward the prohibition of alcohol. At twenty-five years old, Almira delighted Oregon's WCTU and Knappa's Loyal Temperance Legion members with recitations and song when they gathered for their annual convention at the Oregon coast in 1901.[26] Like others, Almira combined her support of temperance with participation in the vast networks of national Sunday schools.[27] She presided over the Clatsop Sunday School Association as its elected president for seven years, raised money for Astoria's Methodist Episcopal Sunday School, and taught weekly classes for much of her adult life.[28] Given Almira's engagement with the Sunday school and temperance movements, it would be surprising if she was not familiar with the assimilationist agenda of the Women's National Indian Association, even if she was not a member. The evangelism that was at the root of the WTCU also informed the WNIA, and the reform movements frequently overlapped and converged.[29]

Sunday schools, which originated in the first half of the nineteenth century and proliferated in the second, were quickly dominated by female teachers who found in them "a positive image of womanhood, useful and engaging work in a variety of benevolent causes, and opportunities for social interactions beyond the family circle."[30] They were critical outlets for ambitious, skilled women who had few occupational options. National Sunday school associations generated local and state chapters, held annual conventions, and drew from nationally disseminated curricula. Teachers—Almira would eventually become the Hood River Valley's most prominent—received pedagogical and theological training, developed skills in organizations that championed their social influence, and, like Almira, were often elected to leadership positions. Almira, though unpaid, nonetheless developed an impressive career that affected the communities in which she lived. If her husband's inheritance to their children was the literal homes in which they lived, Almira passed on a legacy of women's work centered in community development and education.

Almira followed her mother's participation in civic and religious organizations and eventually passed this interest on to her own daughter. The energy that all three women put into associational activity also mirrored national trends; voluntary organizations flourished between 1870 and 1920.[31] According to historian Anne Firor Scott, for their female members "voluntary associations became a place to exercise the public influence otherwise denied them."[32] Membership in women's voluntary associations diminished after the passage of woman suffrage in 1920 opened other avenues of political influence but rose again at the conclusion of World War II.[33] But in the lives of Martha Hawthorne, her daughter Almira Ferguson, and finally Martha Ferguson McKeown, leadership within women's organizations was a constant.

"APPLE PARADISE"

In 1906, Almira's brother and husband purchased forty acres of land more than 150 miles inland in the Hood River Valley, where new opportunities lured land speculators and prospective farmers to the state's most recent land boom. Mont moved to the valley and began clearing the land that summer, accompanied temporarily by his mother and Martha's older brother, Almont. It was the first of many extended visits various Fergusons would make over the next five years while Mont supervised land clearing and planting and the construction of barns and homes.[34] When Almont graduated from high school and was poised to enter the Oregon Agricultural College in 1911, Martha's family pulled up its Astorian roots to live in the valley permanently. The Columbia River still oriented their lives, but now they were cultivators of the land, not builders of Oregon's most important early city. They left a nineteenth-century city oriented toward river and maritime transportation to start anew in a valley opened to settlement by a new railroad, where an emerging fruit industry carried the characteristics of modern marketing and scientific agriculture. They were twentieth-century pioneers.

Even through the family was familiar with the valley, the move must have been disorienting. Everything inland, even the quality of the air, was different from Astoria. On the coast moisture clouded the atmosphere, a gauzy veil that softened the vista.

Verdant forests opened to wide stretches of sandy beaches. The moderately cool climate was occasionally punctuated by violent winter storms. Conversely, the Hood River Valley lay at the edge of the Cascade Mountain's rain shadow. While the valley was green, a few miles east, toward the Warm Springs Indian Reservation, one was suddenly in high desert and arid rangeland. Unlike the coast, the inland valley had distinctive seasons, with high winds and summer heat and winter temperatures that dropped below zero degrees. In their first valley winter, the Fergusons awoke one January morning to five feet of snow.[35] Spring orchard blossoms created breathtaking scenery, and each year at harvest everyone seemed to know the going price of the valley's fruit.

Hood River County had been carved from Wasco County in 1908.[36] The county's largest city and seat was the city of Hood River, near the banks of the Columbia River. To the south, Hood River and its three main tributaries watered the valley. Hills separated the lower and upper portions of Hood River Valley as well as the small communities of Odell and Parkdale. The small logging community of Dee sat between Odell and Parkdale to the west. Mount Hood National Forest (which was Oregon National Forest until being renamed in 1924) started at the edge of the upper valley, and Mount Hood could be seen from most vantage points in these small communities. The Warm Springs Reservation was located to the east of the valley in adjacent Jefferson County on the plateau's highlands.[37]

In the valley, underbrush covered everything. "Heavy willow and vine maple brush" were interrupted by "an occasional big fir or pine."[38] But clear the land a little and strawberries could be planted amid the unwanted vegetation. Clear it more and the land could be put to apples, pears, and cherries, high-value crops that found their way into West Coast urban centers, eastern markets, and eventually Europe. Orchardists "intercropped" strawberries between the rows of trees for a fast-growing cash crop as they waited for their trees to mature.[39] In a few short years, the valley's small orchards grew more apples than anywhere else in Oregon, rivaling those of Washington State.[40]

Between 1900 and 1920, the valley exploded with growth, attracting nearly five thousand new residents,[41] thanks in large part to the extension of the Mount Hood Railway in 1911. An orchardist who purchased his farm during this period remembered that "there was a land boom on in the valley and young men just out of college and even some from law schools were leaving their homes and heading west."[42] Martha's father and maternal uncle joined speculators, enthusiastic college graduates, and big-city retirees who sought the rural life, purchasing adjacent homesteads in the lower valley, a few miles south of the city of Hood River. Ferguson and Hawthorne located their farms in Pine Grove, near a recently developed railway stop, amid newly built warehouses.

This new wave of western expansion developed simultaneous to and with the assistance of modern technology and scientific agricultural practices. Newspaper reporters and community associations boasted that "the valley has become famous through premeditated plans. Nature has been supplemented by science in every possible way."[43] Strawberries grown in the valley, a variety called Clark Seedling, were developed for Hood River's climate and soil. Newspaper headline writers multiplied the clever monikers they used for the valley. "The University of Apple Culture" was a nod toward the educated men drawn to the area and their eager adoption of the most up-to-date scientific methods on their orchards.

The Oregon legislature had created a state board of horticulture in 1889.[44] State agents provided expert advice to valley growers who organized a three-day "Horticulture Chautauqua" in August 1912, the summer after the Fergusons arrived. In a tent city, four hundred valley residents discussed fruit varieties and the expansion of markets, attended lectures on the latest practices, and enjoyed local entertainment on an open-air stage.[45]

Growers brought scientific management and marketing to the valley's orchards. The industry was in the development stages from 1900 to 1912, with the largest harvest in that last year. As farmers cleared and planted land and waited for their trees to mature, they founded the Apple Growers' Union, which by 1907 "controlled 90 percent of the fruit of the Valley . . . the best organized district in the Northwest."[46] The fruit association made consolidated sales possible, steadying prices, and built the infrastructure necessary to the industry: "warehouse, storehouse, ice plant and storage plant where they are able to hold a certain quantity of apples handy for sale."[47] Valley growers became known for their innovative distribution of the fragile fruit, shortening distances and decreasing the frequency with which it was handled by shipping product in refrigerated containers to European cities rather than by rail to the Atlantic seaboard and then abroad. Stackable bushel-sized boxes filled with hand-wrapped apples and pears instead of the more common barrels of eastern orchards ensured that shipments were of the highest grade.[48]

Despite rampant boosterism, prices for apples plummeted in the first full year the Fergusons lived in the valley. A bumper crop in 1912 flooded an immature market. Orchardists dumped fruit and watched their profits drop. Months-old saplings on the Ferguson and Hawthorne acreage might have seemed a dubious investment. The Hood River Apple Growers' Union determined that inadequate shipping and marketing, not overproduction, were the cause. Growers started using refrigerated railroad cars on an expanding network of lines in place of river transportation, and they also developed a modern marketing campaign. They underwrote a 1912 pamphlet plugging "two hundred and nine ways to serve the apple" to increase consumer consumption.[49] During this period "an apple a day keeps the doctor away" and the less-remembered "every youngster needs an apple when his daddy needs a smoke" were coined.[50] National apple days became popular in many cities, and the dining cars of passenger trains featured "apple menus."[51] By World War I the federal government also publicized the health benefits of eating fruit, especially apples. The campaigns worked: Americans began to eat more apples and selected Northwest-grown fruit more often.

In the midst of rapid new settlement, Martha's family put down taproots. Although Martha's father split his time between the orchard and Astoria's Fisher Bros. Company, a "hardware, ship chandlery, grocery and cannery supply," he also joined local commercial and social clubs and advocated for development of the valley.[52] In September, the Fergusons were in a car accident when their "automobile was upset by a passing team" of horses.[53] While her parents and grandmother escaped unhurt, Martha suffered a broken arm. Perhaps it was this incident that drove her father to dedicate his time to championing road development in the county. In any case, the county's roads were hardly sufficient for a thriving fruit industry, nor did they accommodate the rising popularity of the automobile.

Martha's mother continued her voluntary civic work, taking leadership roles in the Daughters of the War of 1812 and the Daughters of the American Revolution. The family helped found Odell's Methodist Episcopal Church, which James designed and built in the summer of 1911. Almira plunged headfirst into the development of an associated Sunday school, attending a Sunday school convention in the city of Hood River in 1911 and holding her first class in her home less than a year later.[54] Although she was a Methodist, Almira declared the school "a community one" where all denominations were welcome.[55] By 1913, the "Ferguson Bible class," averaging a weekly audience of fifty-three and a membership of ninety, was "the largest organized rural Sunday school in the state."[56] Almira would be elected to the presidency of the Hood River County Sunday School Association for six consecutive terms.[57]

Martha's education included both the local public school and the club networks and culture cultivated by her mother and grandmother. The club meetings Almira held at her home introduced Martha to organizations she would contribute to as an adult. Almira also oversaw Martha's religious training, helping turn her into what the local newspaper called "one of this county's most zealous Bible students."[58] Martha was a diligent student who excelled at public speaking. At thirteen, she presented a solo ninety-minute program of recitations at Portland's Gillespie School of Expression to an audience of one hundred.[59] She turned her elocution skills to Bible verses, hoping to garner a "Helen Gould Shepard" Bible from the New York City philanthropist of that name. Winners of the coveted Bible had to be members of the YWCA and able to recite five hundred verses, in an order selected by Shepard, to a YWCA secretary.[60] After "applying herself closely," Martha achieved this goal in the summer between her high school graduation and enrollment in Salem's Willamette University.[61] She completed her high school studies in a remarkable two and one-half years, graduating at the age of fifteen. While in high school, she gave 125 talks and performances in the valley and Portland, to audiences of Red Cross members, YWCA members, teachers, and other groups.[62]

Martha's academic progress mirrored the celebratory environment of the valley. Hard work, evidence-based farming techniques, and robust civic organizations, it seemed, would ensure successful communities. One reporter described the valley's residents as "a sort of moral community with all the most glaring vices eliminated."[63] Newspaper columns celebrated the prosperity evident in the valley by pointing out the deliberate development of farms and infrastructure and describing the region as a model of Oregon resettlement. Optimism and a faith in predictable, even predestined, progress imbued the reporting. In a few years, with a rail line that "tap[ped] the heart of the Hood River Valley," the population and accompanying schools, churches, and stores expanded from the banks of the Columbia River to the feet of Mount Hood.[64] In the Fergusons' first summer in 1911, the *Oregonian* claimed that "more building has been done in the Hood River Valley than ever before in any one season" and used house types to track the evolution of the valley in a rewriting of Frederick Jackson Turner's 1893 "The Significance of the Frontier in American History" for the state.[65] In Turner's essay—whose narrative of American territorial progress set the tenor of western history for nearly a century—frontiersmen evolved into pioneers who were eventually replaced by entrepreneurs. Similarly, in the Hood River Valley "the tiny homes of the homesteader, unadorned with any luxuries" made the initial inroads until "plain but comfortable" larger houses replaced them "to accommodate an increased and maturing family." Finally came the "large mansions equipped with every modern convenience."[66]

The Fergusons made material their symbolic roots in the valley when they transplanted a Kentucky coffeetree from their Astoria home into their new yard in Pine Grove. Martha's grandmother had grown the tree from seed from George Washington's estate at

Fruit trees in bloom in the Hood River Valley with Mount Hood in the distance. Photo by Ralph Eddy, 1922. Courtesy of Old Oregon Photos

Mount Vernon. Almira arranged to have the DAR's Wauna Chapter, along with the Oregon Society United States Daughters of 1812, dedicate a bronze plaque at the tree "as a living memorial" to Martha Lupher Hawthorne in 1935, when Almira declared, "trees are living, growing reminders that our liberty and the welfare of our nation does not stand still. We either advance and build our nation and honor the men and women who left us a wonderful heritage or we destroy our liberty and natural resources that are so valuable to human and wild life conservation."[67] Almira's connection of patriotism and the nation's health to conservation was common among clubwomen during this time.

Perhaps not surprisingly in a land given over to orchards, Hood River Valley residents venerated trees. In spring of 1912, orchardists invited the state's motorists to view the spectacular blossoms that carpeted the valley in an annual Blossom Festival. The valley event, styled after *hanami*, the Japanese tradition of flower viewing, celebrated Oregon's fecundity. The festival adopted a Japanese tradition at a time when many white farmers relied on Japanese and Native labor.

Newspapers rarely mentioned the Indians who seasonally left the Warm Springs Reservation to harvest fruit or the important role Japanese workers and landowners played in the valley's orchards and timber mills. Japanese men brought their families to the valley to take advantage of opportunities for work and land, while for Indians, wage labor augmented fishing, hunting, and gathering, becoming part of the seasonal round. Both groups were necessary to the valley's burgeoning economy, and both faced exclusion from the valley. Farmers and federal agents alike assumed that Indians should reside within the boundaries of the reservation, while Japanese landowners were targeted with extreme discrimination as their numbers grew.

Most white farmers hired Issei (first-generation Japanese immigrants, who were prevented from becoming US citizens through naturalization) to clear land and sometimes to farm it as lessees. In 1908, according to the local newspaper, James Ferguson was busy "building one of the neatest little homes" for the Japanese man he hired.[68] The newspaper article—the only evidence that the Fergusons and Hawthornes used Japanese labor—did not include the hired man's name, and his relationship to his employers is unknown. But the circumstances of his life may have followed the general contours of many of the Issei in the valley. Many immigrated to the United States at the turn of the century as young bachelors, often first stopping in the Hawaiian Islands to work on pineapple plantations. Other jobs followed. For Dee resident Riichi Kiyokawa they included "sugar beets, salmon cannery in Alaska, railroad work in La Grande, falling timbers."[69] Kiyo-kawa met his wife in Seattle, but others returned to Japan to bring wives back to the States. They started families, purchased land, developed orchards, sent their children to local schools, and joined community organizations and started their own, like the Japanese Methodist Church, Japanese Community Hall, and the Japanese Farmers Association of Hood River. While they faced fla-grant discrimination in the valley, they were also able to pry open opportunities—especially to own land—unique in the valley.

Most Issei had previous agricultural experience, having devel-oped truck farms in eastern Multnomah County, between Port-land and Hood River, on land leased from white owners, often at exorbitant prices.[70] Purchasing land required funds and coopera-tion from sellers, who often boxed out prospective Japanese buy-ers. But Hood River Valley whites paid laborers in acreage as well as cash, an arrangement that meant that Japanese families could acquire their own land, even if they had little capital. In plots of five, ten, or fifteen acres, they planted fruit trees and berries and joined the Hood River Apple Growers' Association like their white neighbors. By 1910, there were 468 Issei and Nisei (the second-generation children of Japanese immigrants, who were citizens) living in a valley whose total population numbered 8,016.[71] Their growing communities—coupled with the profitability of their farming practices—became the target of Hood River Valley nativ-ists, who agitated to exclude Japanese immigrants.

The valley's white residents divided on matters of race, citi-zenship, and economic competition, with one local elected offi-cial arguing that people of Japanese heritage "are nice so long as they are in a minority."[72] In 1919, when Martha was leaving for college, community members founded the Hood River Anti-Alien

Association to prevent the sale or leasing of land to Japanese individuals. Local racism converged with anti-Asian activism up and down the Pacific Slope. Following California's lead, the Oregon state legislature passed the Alien Land Law in 1923, denying Issei the right to own land.[73] While anti-Asian sentiment was widespread, the Hood River Valley was the epicenter in the xenophobic battle to rid Oregon of "Japanese colonies." As elsewhere in the Pacific Northwest, racial hostility in the valley was directed both at Asian immigrants and their American-born children and at Native peoples.

Efforts to exclude Japanese families from the valley echoed the separation of Warm Springs Indians onto their reservation. Both were part of an effort to reserve the valley for whites by maintaining racially segregated spaces. Intolerance and exclusion would have been as much of the backdrop to Martha's childhood as the spectacular views of Mount Hood. But there were also models for racial acceptance and neighborliness in the valley, such as when Ralph Davies, an English immigrant, helped his Japanese neighbors thwart the Alien Land Law by acting as the guardian of their minor son, who, as an American-born citizen, could own land.[74] Likewise, Martha would come to the defense of her Japanese and Indian neighbors, rejecting intolerance and countering mainstream public opinion.

LA MOOSH CUSH-NEE-YI / FLORA CUSHINWAY

1898. No agent recorded Flora's birth date. Winter winds in the high desert may have battered the tule mat birth lodge. Or perhaps spring freshets cut through the packed soil just outside the lodge door. Martha Cushinway may have sweated

through a quiet August day to bring into the reservation world
a child who would go by "baby girl" well into her second year.
Martha may have constructed the lodge on land newly
allotted to her, siting it far enough from the family house for
privacy. Her mother, Pe las kow yai, may have brought her
food and water, told her stories about previous births, sung
prayers. Aunties, grandmothers, and perhaps a midwife might
have visited. In the final weeks of her pregnancy, Martha may
have made Flora's cradleboard, stringing beads from its
bow—made of "rose stalks as a protection against ghosts"—to
entertain her infant daughter.[75] If Flora was born in a birth
lodge, she came into a world characterized by female power
and authority in stark contrast to the assimilative reservation
space she also entered. The lodge, the songs, the knowledge
shared among women of a certain age encased her in cultural
and spiritual interdependence. Just as her cradleboard
protected her small and already growing body, the tule mats
made over months, sacred songs released into the desert air,
and grandmothers readied for the responsibility of raising
Flora were buffers against colonialism.[76]

Reservation agent A. O. Wright estimated that about one thousand Indian people lived on the Warm Springs Reservation in 1900. The population was divided between Sahaptin-speaking Teninos and Tyghs—the latter lived in the northern portion of the reservation—who were grouped together as "Warm Springs." Chinook-speaking Wascos, whom many considered the reservation's group most acculturated in American society, congregated in a community close to the agency near the confluence of Shitike Creek and the Deschutes River.[77] Paiutes, who were "the poorest, and need the most aid toward civilization,"[78] moved to the reservation beginning in 1879. Flora's parents were "Warm Springs" Indians, whom Wright described as wearing blankets and moccasins and keeping their hair long (whereas Wascos cut their hair).[79] Reservation activities centered on the agency where federal rations and government employment were disseminated, the two reservation schools, the Presbyterian mission and Shaker church building, and the small communities that developed in the valleys. Reservation life was a mix of significant change—in clothing, foodways, and schooling—as well as the persistence of tradition such as the seasonal round, naming practices, ceremony and spirituality, and the passage of ancestral knowledge from one generation to the next. When she conducted fieldwork in the 1950s, anthropologist Katherine French concluded that residents of the Warm Springs Reservation "had never learned to be ashamed of being Indians; in fact, there is some evidence that they think they have in certain respects, become less 'civilized' in the last century."[80]

Unlike the Hood River Valley with its acres of productive orchard lands, most of the Warm Springs Reservation was unfit for farming. The dry uplands were exposed to high winds and cut through with gullies that made traversing the reservation difficult. The reservation's economy was mixed: hunting, gathering, fishing, and the exchange of gifts and trade mixed with reservation wage work, treks into the Willamette Valley to pick hops and to the nearby Hood River Valley to pick strawberries, and the sale of salmon and huckleberries to non-Native buyers. By the time Flora was born in 1898, some Indian families augmented their seasonal rounds by raising cattle and sheep, but much of the rangeland was dedicated to the wild horses that tied residents to a recently past economy when herds indicated wealth on the Columbia Plateau.

Indian families relied on horses to move across and out of the reservation well into the twentieth century. Flora remembered her mother traveling from the reservation to Celilo Village by horse and buggy to purchase supplies and collect fish. High cliffs made it impossible to drive the wagons to the riverbank, so women packed salmon on horses or carried them on their backs uphill to the waiting wagons:

> The women were real strong in them days. . . . The Warm Springs [Indians] came down and bought flour and dried corn and they parked up here. They had to park their wagons up there on top of the cliff.
> *Interviewer: And walk down?*
> And walk down and pack their fish. Otherwise there is a trail way down there. They could bring a horse down and load it on horses and take it up on horses. Mama used to come down and park her wagon up here.

Allotment policy, designed to assimilate Indian families through landholdings and keep them tied to small farms so they wouldn't travel off the reservation, began on the Warm Springs Reservation in 1896. Jim and Martha Cushinway acquired an allotment in the Tenino Valley in the east-central portion of the reservation, near the agency. More than half their 160-acre plot consisted of rough terrain bifurcated by rimrock. Most of the tract was suitable only to livestock grazing, but a 70-acre portion was level enough for dry land farming. A natural spring provided water for cattle and horses. By the spring the Cushinways erected a one-room building, which they may have used as a home. By 1960, when their heirs, including Flora, sold the land, the structure was dilapidated. The surveyor described it thus:

12' × 15'—1-room frame shack with a 10' × 15' lean-to type addition. The construction is single with plank and batten siding, composition paper roof, soft wood floor, plank ceiling, and mud sill foundation.[81]

The couple also secured allotments for their young children, James (b. 1883) and Esther (b. 1885). James's allotment lay directly north of Jim and Martha's, extending his parents' rangeland. Esther's land lay nearby but not adjacent to the lots of her brother and her parents.

Flora Cushinway, who was born after the Warm Springs Reservation had been allotted and therefore did not receive an allotment, grew up in the valley, perhaps in the framed rooms at the spring but more likely in many different structures depending on the season. Anthropologist Katherine French observed that most families had "several houses, one in 'town' and one or more on outlaying farm lands."[82] Furthermore, "every year in August most of the Indians at Warm Springs move their homes in the hot, semi-arid eastern section of the reservation to a pleasant, wooded campground near the foothills of the Cascade Mountains."[83] While Indian agents desired that Native families "settle" in a single, ideally wood-framed home big enough for only a nuclear family, in reality, Flora's family and others had an enlarged view of "home" that included hunting and fishing sites, places where they harvested berries, roots, and other foods, and spiritually important places. Home, what Tenino Albert Kuckup called "our country," stretched from the basalt outcroppings of the Columbia River, to the Metolius and Deschutes Rivers, Horse, Cultis, and Paulina Lakes, Grizzly and Powell Buttes, and beyond, a region that encompassed but also surpassed the reservation boundaries.[84] With this definition of "home," a

George LaVatta (Shoshone Nation) took this photograph on the Warm Springs Indian Reservation in about 1938 when he visited as Bureau of Indian Affairs Organizational Field Agent. National Archives and Records Administration, Pacific and Alaska Region

single domicile made no sense, and Native families like Flora's continued to live in mobile structures like teepees and lodges, moving throughout the region as needed.

The family's "frame shack" survived decades of use, but other temporary buildings that would have been just as important in providing shelter to Flora's family were less likely to survive and are not documented in extant records. Martha likely erected canvas or tule mat teepees at berry-picking and hunting sites. She may have also erected a woman's lodge on her own property where she retreated during her menstrual cycle and birthed her children. Woman's lodges were so ubiquitous that anthropologist Verne F. Ray "identified them as defining characteristics of Plateau culture."[85] Though their use decreased by the beginning of the twentieth century, it is possible that Flora followed tradition by building her own lodge when she began puberty.

"A place of seclusion and ritual . . . of spiritual potential," the woman's lodge was "the center of Plateau woman's gender identification."[86] The lodge was the space in which young girls learned to be women on the Plateau. They made baskets, tule mats, and other women's supplies and learned lessons from their grandmothers and other elder women. Moreover, Mary Wright argues, "the woman's lodges established the blueprint for the larger structures of the people."[87] Flora, like Martha Ferguson, was born to a family of builders, but the architects in her home were women, not men. While Martha Ferguson's grandfather's and father's buildings would later be placed on the historic register, the building legacies of Plateau women would go unrecognized by preservationists and fall into decay.

Superintendents of the Warm Springs Indian Reservation described members of the Warm Springs bands, in which Flora's parents were members, as the most traditional on the reservation. Still, their lives were reshaped in significant ways by colonization. At the outset of the twentieth century, tribal peoples on the Warm Springs Reservation were under intensifying pressure to assimilate into mainstream settler society. As children, Flora's parents, Martha (*Hu leh*) and Jim Cushinway (sometimes identified in documents as Jim Cushny) lived in an Indigenous world transforming rapidly as they reached adulthood. Even traditional naming practices, which connected Indian people to their familial histories, were under assault, as agents demanded that families adopt American monikers and naming practices that conformed to the state needs to document individuals.[88]

Some colonial-induced changes invigorated Native cultures, such as the explosion of material culture and art associated with the seventeenth-century adoption of the horse or the integration of Christianity into new Indigenous religious practices. Yet change was also characterized by physical confinement, reduced access to resources, restrictions on religious and ceremonial practices, and attempts to eradicate Native languages. Moreover, Flora's parents were the survivors of decades of illness brought on by epidemics to which they had little immunity. They and their children were among the first generations to regularly attend reservation schools, where assimilative pressures aimed to disassociate Indian children from the lifeways of their parents and grandparents. To do so, Indian agents characterized traditional practices as shameful and celebrated any abandonment of them in favor of settler customs. While their overall effect is critical to understanding Flora's development and eventual leadership, the onslaught of identity pressures is nearly impossible to trace in extant records, most of which neither originate from Native peoples nor attempt to record their views.

Like Martha Ferguson, Flora Cushinway grew up in a household that included her widowed maternal grandmother, *Pe las kow yai* (sometimes referred to as "Old Lady Annie" in BIA records). Grandmothers, biological and otherwise, were essential teachers of Columbia Plateau Indian children and were therefore bulwarks against harmful alterations of Native ways. Warm Springs historian George Aguilar described them as "expert practical botanists. . . . master burn ecologists. . . . sometimes psychiatrists and priests."[89] He wrote, "they definitely were historians, whose wisdom and knowledge were held in high regard."[90] They sited the menstrual lodge and taught young girls "to be good [root] diggers, and how to make clothes, and do things like that." A Nez Perce man interviewed for a project in the late 1980s described the role of the grandmother: she "has all the knowledge of her years.

She probably has more experience than anyone else. And the grandmother was really, I think she was the core of the whole family group. She was the one who kept the family together, probably the one that had the most influence and directed the family, how that family acted. She probably had more effect on the family group than any other person."[91] Girls and boys who grew up with grandmothers observed their influence. As Kim Anderson argues, "In such families, Native girls witness both the social and the economic decision-making power of older women in their communities."[92] Flora may have tapped her memories of such female authority as she grew older and became a leader in her own right at Celilo Village.

While the role of elders was central in her life, Flora also had older siblings who likely cared for her as well. When Flora was born, her sixteen-year-old brother James and eighteen-year-old sister Alice were enrolled in the reservation's boarding school. Effie, who was fourteen, was also enrolled at the school and in adulthood would become one of Flora's most important companions.[93] Martha had one more child, Tommy, who survived into adulthood after Flora's birth. In 1906, within just a few years of Tommy's birth, Flora's father died. It would be more than fifteen years before the family would have the wherewithal to raise a cemetery stone for him. By the 1910 census, Flora's maternal grandmother no longer appears to be living with the family, so she may have died as well.

James and Effie appear to have made one of their homes on his allotment adjacent to their parents'. Included in the residence were James's and Effie's spouses and children, as well as some boarders. When Effie's first husband, Charlie Charles, died, she married William Sookoit, who was the brother of James's wife, Alice Sookoit. Effie may have just taken a liking to Sookoit or their marriage may suggest the importance of connections between families, rather than simply individuals, that marriage traditionally represented on the plateau.[94] After Alice died of influenza in 1920, James married Sowallus Jack. Effie focused on raising the children from James's first marriage when they weren't away at school. Many adults, not only the biological parents, raised children. Martha Cushinway also took in grandchildren and great-grandchildren. As an adult, Flora followed this practice, sending her children to live with relatives on the Yakama Reservation and bringing the children of others into her home.

The complexity of living arrangements on the reservation are revealed by census records and the annual Indian rolls recorded by the Warm Springs superintendent. Family members appear and disappear from these records, not because households were unstable but because mobility and extended family structures were so important to the community's welfare. Young adults moved from household to household to take advantage of work opportunities, to apprentice under elders, and to care for aging or sick family members. Wage work drew people from the reservation for periods of time, as did the annual harvest rounds and ceremonial gatherings that knit communities across reservation boundaries. Records indicate that Flora was living with her mother while she was also enrolled at the residential school. The snapshot in time that each record represents indicates that Flora alternated between the school and home, between the reservation, off-reservation huckleberry fields, and Celilo Village.

Flora entered the reservation boarding school on December 1, 1902, when she was four or five years old. According to historian Janice Clemmer, it was not unusual for children as young as three or four to be enrolled.[95] In Flora's case, her father's illness perhaps brought on an early enrollment. As with reservation boarding schools across the nation, the Warm Springs agency school focused on a curriculum that emphasized academic skills, vocational activities, and the alienation of children from Indigenous practices. Annual agent reports consistently criticized the lack of resources available to run the schools and indicated that dilapidated buildings and overworked staff were perennial problems. Students assisted with school operations by gardening, caring for stock, cooking, and cleaning laundry. These activities reduced the burden of federal employees and were meant to inculcate children to wage work and non-Native life. Agent John Smith demonstrated the strategy shared by many Indian agents in 1872:

> They should know how to prepare vegetables for the table. They do not know how to cook vegetables, and hence seek wild game, often leaving their crops to waste. They would soon abandon the chase and settle down to the quiet life of farmers, and would soon prove self-supporting, industrious, and happy.[96]

Smith blamed a reliance on wild game on a lack of kitchen skills, which could be remedied through schooling. In this scenario, if Indians knew how to cook the crops they were induced to plant, they would change their diets and thereby thoroughly alter the very way they conducted their lives, exchanging the seasonal round for "the quiet life of farmers." Lessons in cooking green beans, then, could resolve the conflict between Indians and agents regarding whether Native people continued their treaty-protected rights to procure traditional foods.

Flora attended school regularly but not consistently. At age sixteen, a BIA employee recorded that she performed at the fourth-grade level.[97] Periodic attendance was not unusual as children left school to participate in hunting, fishing, and gathering activities, to visit relatives on other reservations, and to attend ceremonies and funerals. Students also missed school due to illness.[98] The seasonal round shaped the academic year, with attendance lowest during the fall harvest and again as the weather improved in the spring.[99] School records indicate that Flora's brother James ran away for a week in the spring of his final year, probably so he could fish a Columbia River salmon run.[100] Like her brother, Flora attended boarding school until she was nineteen. She "deserted" on May 14, 1917.[101]

Boarding schools interrupted critical Indigenous gendered teachings, such as those lessons young girls traditionally received in the menstrual lodges and through puberty rituals. In May 1917, Flora was about two months pregnant, but it's not clear that the pregnancy prompted her to leave school. John Tewee, the father of her baby, was a few years her junior and also a student.[102] Their son, Edgar Tewee, was born on December 24, 1917.[103] Events that would not be shameful in prereservation Plateau communities, such as pregnancy before marriage (which indicated fertility and thus readiness for marriage),[104] were documented in government records through the lens of the dominant culture. Flora's infant son was listed at "illegitimate," but it's not clear that the designation was meaningful for her or her family.[105] In the first few days of January, John Tewee's parents may have consented to their son marrying Flora. An unsigned letter to the Jefferson County clerk in the BIA records provides consent for the marriage.[106] This may indicate that BIA employees exerted some pressure on Flora and John to wed. If they did, they were unsuccessful. Flora did not marry John but instead raised Edgar in her mother's home. Johnnie Tewee married nineteen-year-old Mable Henning on February 1, 1920, while Flora married Young Boise in 1921, a man two decades her senior and therefore a more stable prospect than

Tewee.[107] Young Boise's wife of twenty-three years had passed away in 1913, leaving him with young children. Flora moved to her husband's house, where she raised her stepchildren and son.[108]

KEEPING HOME

Just as boarding school matrons and teachers forced assimilation in educational settings, field matrons made interventions directly in Indian homes. Between 1896 and 1940, field matrons worked on reservations in the most intimate locations of assimilation, family homes. Promoted by the Women's National Indian Association, some of whose members worked as field matrons, the program complemented allotment policy, the refiguring of landownership, by inculcating Western values of land use and family structure. It valued nuclear families whose houses were organized in Western ways, with individual rooms reserved for single uses and with wage work and home life clearly delineated. Field matrons provided advice, evaluated whether Indian parents adequately supervised their children, modeled "suitable" housekeeping in their own homes, and recorded judgments about the Indian families they visited.[109]

During her employment at the Warm Springs Reservation, Minnie B. Holcomb oversaw 102 families living in 83 households.[110] In her general notes compiled in 1921 and 1922, Holcomb listed Martha Cushinway's as a home that was always sanitary.[111] In her notes covering specific visits to the Cushinway home, though, Holcomb wrote, "Martha has no education and is inclined to be lazy." Holcomb described Flora, who lived with Martha until she married Young Boise, as someone who "speaks very good English but keeps her baby and herself very dirty."[112] Later, when Holcomb visited Young Boise's home, she thought that Flora was a poor housekeeper and complained that their home, at the height of summer in July, was "full of flies."[113] Holcomb usually praised Effie's housekeeping and child-rearing, yet even Effie came under scrutiny when Holcomb declared the family home "not very well cleaned this year" after a designated reservation-wide cleanup day.[114] Holcomb described what constituted a well-kept house to Warm Springs superintendent Omar Babcock: clean walls, floors, and windows; white tablecloth on the dining table; decorative wall hangings; ordered yard and garden.[115] It's no wonder that of the thirty or so households she visited, Holcomb designated only two or three as suitably tidy.

Holcomb's record keeping may have truly indicated sanitary problems on the Warm Springs Reservation. She visited remote homes that had no garbage pickup and lacked electricity and indoor plumbing. In those ways, the homes she monitored were similar to others in rural America. What was different were the expectations, which she shared, that Indians would abandon Plateau lifeways to model settler lives. Not doing so was thought to reflect deficiency in character. On the Canadian Plains during this same period, "Indian reserve women were portrayed as slovenly and unclean in their personal habits as well as in their housekeeping," according to historian Sarah Carter.[116] Kim Anderson argues that descriptions of an Indian woman as "dirty and lazy," which became ubiquitous under settler colonization, "excused those who removed her children and paved the way for assimilation into mainstream culture . . . allow[ing] for the righteous position of those who participated in the eradication of Native culture, language, and tradition."[117] Holcomb certainly saw less than sparkling homes on the reservation, but expectations of filth may have also colored her observations.

Setting aside her commentary on Native women's housekeeping, Minnie Holcomb's notes provide an important window into how Indian families organized their lives. Holcomb's frequent visits reveal the continuing importance of the seasonal round, the integration of wage work, and the assistance individuals offered one another during illness and injury. Holcomb recorded when Martha, Effie, and Flora collected berries on Mount Hood, when they cared for sick neighbors and children, and when they worked for neighboring whites or the agency.

For example, on August 30, 1921, Effie alerted Holcomb to the fact that Dick Thompson, a neighbor, was sick and that his wife had left to harvest huckleberries on Mount Hood. For the next two weeks, Effie cared for Thompson until she and Martha were able to leave for the huckleberry fields in mid-September. They stayed in the fields for a couple of weeks. The following March, Flora and Martha traveled to Prineville, about fifty miles from the reservation, to dig sagebrush for a white rancher. Martha, and perhaps Flora, returned to Prineville in November with Martha's son James and his family to attend and perhaps perform in the Prineville fair. In the intervening months, Martha visited the agency and cared for a sick relative.

Because the field matron also provided elementary medical care, Holcomb's notes include information on illnesses and injuries. Flora and her husband lost a newborn son while they were on Mount Hood during the huckleberry harvest in 1921.[118] In March the following year, they lost another child, Charlie Boise, Flora's stepson. The bare details about these deaths are recorded; what is left undocumented is how these losses affected the family. Based on her recollections at the end of her life and records concerning other Warm Springs families, it is likely that in Flora's family, illnesses were "treated from a spiritual aspect" and not just medically.[119] Illness and death required ceremony, song, and prayer as well as the Western medical treatments that were slowly making their way onto the reservation.

Years after Young Boise died, Flora remembered that he once "took off with my first cousin." She asserted that it "didn't bother me one bit. I know he's always coming back, which he did."[120] They remained married until he died of a stroke in 1939.[121] Flora didn't deliberately describe her philosophy of marriage, but a contemporary of hers, Lucy Miller, did when anthropologist Katherine French interviewed her in 1953.[122] "They used to tell us, when we was getting married, not to be full of love," she explained. Elders warned, " 'You got a long time to love your husband.' " Instead, "You got to get out when you get married and just do what your old people taught you. You got to hustle. You got to dig roots and dry them and pick berries and dry them. You going to have to learn to rustle for yourself. No one is going to do that for you."[123] Marital love could develop deeply over time; the necessity to learn to work together as a couple was immediate.

Young Boise was a good provider, and Flora was proud of his hunting skills. She told an interviewer that Boise "used to even get them alive."

> He sneaked over there. He crawled and crawled and crawled. And those two deers, their ears would go like that. They know something was attacking them. When he got so many feet, I told him "You must have been just like a cougar . . ." The deer just kicked him around like an iron or something but he hung on. He just scuffled and the deer kept a kicking and kicking until it finally gave away. And he twisted the

hooves and he fell over and he jumped over and grabbed his neck and just twisted clear around, killed him—by hand. He was a really strong man because he was born hunter.[124]

The year before Flora married Boise, he was arrested for poaching deer off-reservation in August, when bucks were at their heaviest.[125] State hunting and fishing commissions considered Indigenous hunting and fishing activities that occurred out of state-imposed seasons and off-reservation as poaching,[126] and Young Boise, like many Warm Springs men, was arrested by officials who disregarded federal treaty-reserved rights. By 1931, Warm Springs men complained that white encroachment had destroyed hunting and gathering grounds while game wardens chased them away from off-reservation sites. Wasco Elijah Miller complained that whites "crowded deer out so we couldn't find anymore" and slaughtered antelope, mountain sheep, and other wild game.[127] He could no longer visit berry fields or hunt near Three Sisters or Horse Lake because "some officers get up and look at the book. They say 'You got no right to be there.' . . . Yes, Game Wardens and Fire Wardens and all kinds of Wardens chase me out."[128]

Boise's arrest may simply indicate that he was caught hunting out of season, but it might also signal that Boise resisted the limitations imposed on Indian hunters by the state. If the latter was true, it would have aligned Boise with Flora's third husband, Tommy Thompson, who spent his life railing against what he viewed as the illegal impositions of the state on the foodways of Columbia River Indians. Like the fishers at Celilo, many Plateau Indians viewed hunting regulations as unjustly limiting their treaty-protected rights. Hunting, like fishing, was instrumental to the survival strategies of Warm Springs people and, though often overshadowed by the midcentury fish wars brought on by dams and the decline of salmon, was part of a larger ability of Indian men and women to feed their families. Indians resisted encroachment and regulation by suing the state when it demanded they purchase licenses, and by hunting and gathering surreptitiously.

Treaties created new subregional spaces whose purpose was to segregate Indigenous peoples from white settlers and to isolate them from landscapes they viewed as within their home territory. The delineation of on-reservation and off-reservation spaces was relatively new to the generations of Indian women Flora lived with and to her husband, Young Boise. Flora's grandmother was old enough to have remembered a time before the reservation. Her mother would have grown up with those stories as well as the porous nature of reservation boundaries in the early years of its establishment. Attempts to keep Indians on the reservation caught traction by 1867 with the signing of the fraudulent Huntington Treaty, which devised a pass system to monitor and discourage trips. Despite the treaty, the reservation boundaries could not hold in people dedicated to providing for their families.

Leaving the reservation, though, was not only a means to physical survival. Periodic sojourns reconnected Indians with a landscape of great ceremonial and cultural significance, to the graves of ancestors, storied landmarks, and fishing and hunting grounds passed down through generations. Even wage work could bring relatives across the region's reservation system together in ways that mirrored gatherings of old. Furthermore, they connected with white neighbors who could act as allies.

While Young Boise navigated the legal system, white orchardists Gladys and George Struck met Tommy Thompson for the first time when they recruited workers for their farm in Parkdale, about ten miles from the Ferguson orchard. Gladys traveled to Celilo Village and met Thompson, who asked how much land they had available for horse pasture. "The following day," her husband remembered years later, "here came the Indians, horses, wagons, and . . . babies" to set up camp for the season. According to George, "Chief Thompson and I would talk things over and raise the picking price" until the harvest was over.[129] Wage work on the valley's farms and orchards brought Indians from Celilo Village and from the Warm Springs Reservation to the area. Into the 1920s and 1930s, Indians increasingly met with their white neighbors. It is likely that Martha Ferguson got to know Indian laborers, perhaps even Tommy Thompson, as they worked on her parents' orchard during this period. Notwithstanding novelist Frederic Homer Balch's predictions of Indigenous demise at the turn of the century, Indians persisted throughout Oregon. And despite efforts to segregate Indians from non-Indians, both Martha Ferguson and Flora Cushinway lived in overlapping settler and Indigenous worlds.

FOUR

Converging Paths of Leadership

... those individuals who stand at the margins of society
clarify its boundaries.

PATRICIA HILL COLLINS, *Black Feminist Thought*

FLORA THOMPSON STOOD BEFORE THE OREGON SOCIETY
of the Daughters of the American Revolution state board on a
pleasant October day in 1949. She was there to discuss how the
hereditary, patriotic organization might assist Indians, women in
particular, at Celilo Village.[1] Oregon's women's clubs took a special interest in Native American welfare, proclaiming in 1933 they
would unite to "back plans to aid Indians."[2] Like women in other
states, they believed that if Indians adopted Anglo-Saxon values
and lifeways they could enter the American mainstream as full,
participating citizens. Clubwomen formed subcommittees and
appointed Indian welfare chairs to encourage what they considered the betterment of Indian families and what looks now like
economic and social conformity. Flora's job was to navigate the
assimilationist terrain of voluntary associations to build political

and social support for Native rights. Pointedly ignoring how association chapters co-opted Indian names as their own and demanded a kind of simplified Indigenous "authenticity," she quickly established support with a presentation that at least one member called the "highlight" of the meeting.[3]

Martha McKeown, the newly elected state regent, had invited Flora to the meeting, which was followed by other speaking engagements the next day. The records do not reveal when the two women first met or the degree of intimacy between them, although Martha introduced Flora as her "very good friend." Tommy Thompson probably introduced the two women to one another in the early 1940s, when he married Flora. By that point, Martha had known the chief affectionately for two decades, insisting that Archie meet him before she and Archie married in 1923. By October 1949, the women were working closely together lobbying voluntary organizations to alter the state's proposal to widen Highway 30, which would dislocate several Celilo Village families. Maybe Martha picked up Flora, who did not drive, from her home at Celilo Village and they rode to Salem together, enjoying the fall weather and the chance to catch up on each other's lives. Both were great storytellers, and they had much in common that would have made the multiple-hour drive fly by—Chief Thompson, of course, but also their faith practices, concern for Indian welfare and community relations, their roles as mothers, and interest in regional history. Or perhaps Flora was already in Salem on one of her many visits to the capital and simply added the meeting to her agenda as a favor to her husband's friend.

In the years between 1930 and 1949, both Martha McKeown and Flora Thompson developed the skills and networks that they would rely on in the turbulent 1950s and that would make them influential leaders within the region's communities. Flora Boise started the period living on the Warm Springs Reservation with her husband Young Boise, their son Max, and other relatives. After her husband's death, Flora married a religious leader on the Yakama Reservation. The marriage didn't last, and within a few years she moved once again, this time to Celilo Village to marry Chief Tommy Thompson. Each marriage positioned her for increasing influence and allowed her to hone her leadership skills.

Martha Ferguson's mobility was driven not by marriage but by education, paid professional opportunities, and a network of club-women in the state. Martha and Archie McKeown anchored their lives in the Hood River Valley, eventually taking over her family's orchard. Martha earned a master's degree in English from the University of Oregon (she wrote a thesis about Henry David Tho-reau) and then returned to the valley to teach high school English.[4] In 1938, when her son David was eleven, she accepted a job in downtown Portland and became the dean of women students at Multnomah College, a two-year institution affiliated with the Portland YWCA.[5] While in Portland, Martha headed the Oregon Older Girls Association, continued her work with the DAR, and became a member of Zonta International, an organization of professional women that advocated for women's issues around the globe. She rose to leadership positions within the clubs, and when she returned home three years later in 1941—just as Port-land was transformed by the war—she had secured prominence both professionally and within the club networks that supported her activism.

By 1949 Martha had also become a distinguished author, hav-ing published a well-received book about her maternal uncle, with two more about him under way. *The Trail Led North* became a bestseller, and Martha and Archie traveled the Pacific slope for presentations and book signings.[6]

Flora, meanwhile, capitalized on her role as Chief Tommy Thompson's wife to participate in speaking engagements as well and accompanied her husband as his interpreter. The stories of these two women and the place that brought them together, Celilo Village, are separate in the 1930s, but by the 1940s they begin to converge. This chapter charts that convergence.

"I JUST LOVE TO SING"

The 1930s brought some difficulties to the Warm Springs reservation but they were less severe than elsewhere in Oregon. The reservation was always poor—arid land didn't support crops even in good years. The years that marked the beginning of the decade were drier than usual, and streams throughout the reservation dried up. Employment on the reservation was similarly always limited, and most Indian men found jobs as common laborers, although increased fire hazard due to dry conditions meant more work protecting the reservation's forested lands. As was typical, families spent months away from the reservation, especially in the summer and fall, to fish on the Columbia and its tributaries and to pick hops in the Willamette Valley and berries in the Hood River Valley. They also spent time harvesting traditional foods like the huckleberries on Mount Hood, some of which they sold for cash. Picking and fishing sites became more crowded as the Depression worsened and non-Native residents turned to harvesting the natural abundance of the region. Warm Springs superintendent F. E. Perkins reported that Native women ramped up their crafts to make up for the general lack of off-reservation jobs in the weakened economy. And families tended to keep more of their salmon rather than sell them in a market of depressed prices. But new construction projects—a hydroelectric plant, two new dormitories at the boarding school, and much-needed road improvements—funneled federal dollars to the reservation, where Indians were given preferential hiring.

Politically, residents at Warm Springs struggled with a superintendent who viewed them as intractable and indolent. Superintendent Perkins bitterly complained, "they could do much better for themselves, and live under much more desirable and sanitary conditions, if they could only be instilled with the proper ambition."[7] Between the lines of his narrative reports one sees a people living modernized traditional lives. Automobiles (the superintendent estimated that 60 percent of families owned them in 1931)[8] substituted for horses, and the annual migration to seasonal agricultural work augmented the traditional seasonal round practiced on the Plateau for millennia. Residents found ways to resist the supervision and judgment of their superintendent. They resented BIA efforts to eradicate wild horses; what Perkins described as "range destroying rodents" were symbols of the Indians' past wealth and prestige and provided more flexible transportation than automobiles when families ventured into the mountains for berries and to hunt.[9] So they delayed rounding them up, which made them less desirable to buyers. They also resisted registering marriages and divorces with the agency, preferring to keep their unions out of agency sight and oversight. And in meetings with the superintendent, they "continually reminded" him "that the reservation belongs to the Indians," much to his frustration.[10]

In 1930, thirty-two-year-old Flora Boise lived with her extended family in households that included, at different times, Flora's mother or her mother-in-law. The children living with the Boises included Priscilla (age eight) and Max (age five), as well as Edgar (age thirteen), Flora's eldest son, whose father was Johnnie Tewee. One of Young Boise's adult sons had moved to the Yakama

Reservation, while another from his previous marriage stayed with them. In February 1933, Flora and her husband added another child to their family when Flora gave birth to Nancy Brown Boise. Flora and Young Boise both worked various jobs to make ends meet in a difficult economy on a reservation remote from their traditional food sites.

Flora organized her days around spiritual practices and the care of her family. In two oral history interviews, Flora spent more time describing visions, songs, ceremonies, and how she and her husbands practiced their spirituality than on any other topic. Indian Shaker Church bells, longhouse ceremonies, the drums of Washat ceremonies, and especially Indigenized hymns and traditional songs peppered her recollections. Ethnomusicologist Chad Hamill writes that "the essential role of song in indigenous North American ceremonies is indisputable, for without a thing called song, there *is* no ceremony."[11] Songs, which were often transmitted by spirit guides, provided religious messages and connected singers to spiritual power. When Flora announced to one of her interviewers that she "loved to sing," she was declaring the importance of religious practice in her life; when she broke out into song during the interview, she recorded her religious teachings for future listeners.

The deaths of several close family members, including Flora's youngest daughter, marked the decade. Flora's religious beliefs shaped her understanding of this difficult time. Young and Flora Boise both lost their mothers just days apart from one another in April 1933.[12] Flora recalled her mother's death:

> She got sick Monday and she got real sick Wednesday and Thursday and they told me take her home. So I took her home Thursday. And I come to the store and I went in. I told

the storekeeper, I says, "My mother's dying. I don't think she's going to live."

"Oh, no Martha," he says. He ran out. Then she's in the wagon out there. I had to take her home. He went out and he patted her arm. "Oh, Martha, you're dying?"

"Yes, me dying."

"Oh, no."

And that was the last stopping at the store for her. And then we went on up and she says—my Indian name is La moosh—and she says "La moosh."

I says "yes, mother."

"You see these flowers?" She went like that. "You see these flowers different here, different there, different over there. All those pretty flowers, just different, just like that."[13]

Martha Cushinway was sixty-five years old when she passed. Despite the suffering she endured over several days of illness, according to Flora, Martha's death was good. When Flora said, "of course she died clean," she referred to her mother's spiritual state at the time. The many customs associated with death and burial and the dressing ceremony, wake, and funeral—as well as the songs sung at each—provided a period of communal mourning and purification.[14]

With the death of her young daughter Nancy, however, Flora described a frightening loss of faith.

I lost a little girl from the first husband. She's only between four and five. And she died sudden and I felt so bad. I thought, I'm not going to use this [longhouse religion] no more. She used to sing Indian songs like if she was taught but she wasn't. It just come to her and she sung it out like better than some of my older people or myself. So when I lost her I thought, I'm not going to sing no more.

When Nancy died unexpectedly, Flora stopped singing and attending longhouse ceremonies. According to Flora, "all the songs that you hear with words is a testimony what was sent back to this earth for us to teach one another and make one understand one another."[15] To cease singing was to turn away from the religious life of her family and community. Her rejection of sacred practices was complicated by Nancy's close connection to the spirit world, as evidenced by her ability to recite songs she had not been taught and to sing with a strong, confident voice that rivaled those of adults. When Nancy visited Flora in spirit form and reminded her to sing again, she helped her mother emerge from a deep grief.

Well, instead several weeks later she come to me up in the air. She says, "Mother, I don't want you to be like that. You will never catch up to me in glory. You must arise, look at yourself." And I looked at myself. And we used to wear loose hair. We used to wear loose hair while in mourning for our children or husband. And I looked up like that and my hair was over that way, all full of dirt and ashes. And she said, "arise now and go take a bath." So I went down and I took a bath. And I came back and I changed my clothes. I took my dark clothes off. And then I made fire in the heater in the kitchen. And I started combing my hair. And I began singing. And even though my tears are slowing down but I just try to be brief, just singing. My husband was laying over there just mourning, couldn't keep still, and so I went in and I got to cook breakfast. While at the table, we have a dinner bell we use every Sunday. I rang that bell and I sang one verse. And I says, "my dear people, I have to bring this up. My little girl come to me in glory up in the air but in glory, up in the air and she told me this and that and now I have to continue singing from now on."[16]

At her daughter's urging, Flora removed her dark clothes and cleaned her body and hair, purifying herself and physically leaving behind the despair she felt after Nancy died. Young Boise was also overcome by grief, but Flora revived him with breakfast and, more importantly, by ringing the family's bell and singing. "The individual," Hamill explains, "and the spirit realm are two parts of a dynamic whole, at the center of which sits the song—the very thing that binds them."[17] Flora and Nancy rebalanced the family by initiating healing through song.

Flora's faith was centered in song, the personal testimony that she shared with a community of Native believers. Sacred traditions on the Columbia Plateau took forms that altered over time, place, and practitioner, all of which were bound to "indigenous epistemologies shaped through centuries of spiritual practice."[18] Some of the songs Flora sang had been handed down for generations, while others represented more recent teachings and still others were Indigenized hymns, songs "absorbed, reconstructed, and re-sung as expressions of Native identity."[19] Flora spoke extensively about her religious beliefs and practices but did not claim membership in any single church and did not distinguish between introduced Christianity and Native religions. Instead she described participation in the Indian Shaker Church, the Mormon Church, and Celilo Village's Washat ceremonies. The sacred simply infused every aspect of Flora's life.

Flora often assumed that others had similarly inclusive religious worldviews. Flora praised a Baptist minister on the Warm

Springs Reservation who she remembered recognized their common spirituality: "You could just see him standing amongst the Indians. He could just feel the spirit in the singing."[20] When an interviewer puzzled over whether her husband was a Christian or a "medicine man," Flora graciously described what scholars now consider the Indigenization of Christianity. "Lots of people think that we worship the sun and the moon and different images," she said. "But we all know Christ was crucified, and he has risen." She followed this with a description common to Native Plateau societies of how prophets received teachings through death followed by revival: "Well, so that's the way Indians got their religion—people had died and then they come to and they brought the message, what was in glory."[21]

Missionaries, Indian agents, and anthropologists frequently misunderstood how people like Flora adopted and transformed Christianity to fit Native lifeways and beliefs. Often, they maligned Indigenous religions and, like Flora's interviewer, sought to distinguish between traditional believers and Christians. The Indian Shaker Church that Flora attended was controversial among non-Native BIA employees because it combined Protestant and Catholic practices with Indigenous ones, and because sick practitioners submitted themselves to group healing ceremonies performed by church members rather than to Western medicine. Although missionaries and agents endorsed church prohibitions of alcohol, smoking, and profanity, Warm Springs superintendent Omar Babcock restricted the use of ceremonial healing, forcing members underground while they protested to his superiors.[22] The Indian Shaker Church received media interest in 1912 when newspapers across the country reprinted an *Oregonian* article in which Yakama minister—and Flora's

Indian Church, Lone Pine Tree Village, 1959. Gladys Seufert Photograph, OrHi 104926, Oregon Historical Society

second husband—Timothy George explained that followers were "good Indians" who "help one another."[23]

Young Boise died in 1939 at the age of sixty-seven while the couple was in White Swan, Washington, on the Yakama Reservation.[24] Ten months later, Flora married Timothy George and moved to the Yakama Reservation, where her son Edgar Tewee and his young family also lived. Flora brought to the household Max Boise, who was about fourteen at the time, and six-year-old Josepha Meanus, the daughter of Flora's sister, Effie. Flora would eventually raise Josepha's daughter, Linda, as her granddaughter.[25] Into his seventy-fifth year, George was much older than forty-year-old Flora.[26] The relationship was short-lived, ending in an acrimonious separation after a few years. After Flora moved out of George's home, she would never live on a reservation again for an extended period. Instead, she and her son Max moved to Celilo Village, a place that reflected modernity and traditional Indigenous lifeways both, just as she did.

TEACHER, WRITER, CLUBWOMAN

In 1930 twenty-seven-year-old Martha Ferguson McKeown lived on her family's orchard with her husband, Archie, her three-year-old son, David, and her widowed mother. Martha's brother, Almont, his wife, Viola, and their five children also lived in the household (until the couple divorced and Almont moved to Alaska while his ex-wife and children remained at the family farm). Archie worked as the orchard foreman and Martha taught English at Odell High School.[27] By 1937 Martha accepted the position of dean of women at Sherwood High School in the Willamette Valley, about eighty-five miles from the family orchard.[28] While there, she enrolled at the University of Oregon, earning a master's degree in English in 1938. The degree helped her secure a position at Multnomah College in Portland as the school's dean of women, and Martha moved to Portland at that point. She stayed for just three years, returning to the Hood River Valley and its school district in 1941. Her life was shaped by her commitment to education, her work to document regional history, and her club activities, all of which drew from her relationships with and sometimes assisted her Native neighbors.

When she became a schoolteacher, Martha joined a profession that had been dominated by women since the Civil War.[29] Her long career as a teacher and school administrator was nonetheless remarkable during a time when most white, middle-class, married women with children did not work outside the home (in 1930, only 10 percent of white married women worked for pay).[30] Although women increasingly entered the workforce during the period of Martha's career, doing so for reasons other than economic necessity was controversial until well after World War II.[31] Moreover, Martha simultaneously dedicated herself to two career paths—teacher/administrator and published author. Unpaid work in club activities was often as time-intensive as her other pursuits. Although there is little evidence of how Martha's work affected her home life, Archie appears to have supported his wife's ambitions, accompanying her on research trips, taking photographs of her subjects, and joining her on publicity tours. Shortly after her first book was released, Martha credited Archie with helping her realize her dream of becoming an author.[32]

Martha attended to writing and voluntary service during school breaks, weekends, and evenings. "I am a teacher," she declared in a 1940 guest editorial for the Oregon Daily Journal. "I believe that the main purpose of any school is to teach people to think; that progress should be made through education; that standards are raised only by individual development."[33] In the classroom, Martha drew from her experiences in the Hood River Valley and her interest in local history to enliven her curriculum. One student remembered her as "a storyteller par excellence" who arranged field trips to the Native American artifact collection at a nearby museum and brought Chief Tommy Thompson to speak at school assemblies. He remembered that she made up for a lack of classroom management skills with "a background that was so much richer than the average teacher."[34]

Martha's introduction of "Indian lore" and culture to her students had a lasting impact on them. But as a club member and educator, Martha also frequently participated in celebrations that romanticized a Native past that had little to do with actual Indian residents of the state. When she was at Multnomah College, Martha instigated the election of Princess Tamahnawus (purportedly meaning "luck" or "magic") at the school's annual Tyee dance.[35] Historian Philip Deloria calls the use of such symbols "costumed mimicry," examples of which were likely familiar to Martha through organizations like the Camp Fire Girls and the Girl Scouts.[36] Rather than reflecting "traditions of any native society," young white women performing as "Indian princesses" or "Indian maidens" in such organizations were practicing "white, middle-class feminine ideals."[37] Multnomah College's "Indian Princess" also echoed the colonial-era costumes McKeown herself wore as a DAR member, with the "Indian" and "Settler" mirroring one another in a supposedly shared history.

Some of Martha's activities clearly fell within the "playing Indian" trope described by Deloria, while others suggest a more critical approach to regional race relations likely influenced by the intellectual turn to cultural pluralism in educational and religious institutions as well as in the voluntary organizations with which McKeown associated. At the time that she oversaw the Multnomah College dance, Martha was also involved in the Oregon Older Girls Association, a regional extension of the national Sunday School Association that Martha's mother cofounded in 1913.[38] The interracial and interdenominational Oregon Older Girls Association sought to "develop leadership among girls and give girl leaders an opportunity to exchange ideas."[39] It reserved its most important ethnic connections for Native Americans, appropriating Indigenous-appearing words—*akita, wanji, wichota,* and *onspikiye*—to designate leadership roles within the organization. As a result, it provided ritualized moments of growth for young mainstream women on the threshold of adulthood that were framed by Indigeneity.

In a photograph that may have been taken to market one of her books, Martha McKeown is dressed in the clothing typical of a Daughters of the American Revolution member. Chief Tommy Thompson stands next to her dressed in full regalia. Undated photo by Archie McKeown. Special Collections and Archives, Eric V. Hauser Memorial Library, Reed College

Martha presented a talk titled "Down Memory Lane" when the association held its annual meeting in Portland in 1937.[40] The next day, girls from the African Methodist Episcopal (AME) Zion Church in Portland addressed the audience. Also on the program was a five-part pageant, "Gifts of My People," "written and presented at THE COURT OF GIRLHOOD by girls of Indian, Chinese, Negro, Japanese and Caucasian heritage." The conference program reflected the interracial and interethnic environment organizers wanted to foster. The focus was not an unusual choice for the organization. When the conference was held in homogeneous Corvallis three years earlier in 1933, the program included presentations such as "The Gifts of the American Indian" by the Chemawa Indian School's religious studies director and some of her pupils, "The Afro-American Brings His Gifts" presented by the pastor at Portland's Bethel AME church, and a presentation by member Ruth Nomura, the first Issei woman to attend Oregon State College, who spoke about a trip to Japan.[41] Moreover, although most elected offices were held by white-appearing women, Chrystalee Maxwell (second vice-president, 1933) and Geraldine Williams (first vice-president, 1938) were both African American women from Portland.

The Oregon Older Girls Association reflected the racial and ethnic diversity of the state's Protestant believers at a time when many of the nation's churches were segregated, including those in the Hood River Valley, where Japanese and Japanese American Methodists attended their own church. The role of race and racial justice became one focus of many Protestant denominations during Martha's adult life. Historian David Hollinger points to the decades between 1940 and 1970 as a period when "ecumenical Protestants played [a role in] diminishing Anglo-Protestant prejudice and embracing the varieties of humankind."[42] Ecumenical Protestant leaders (which he distinguishes from evangelical Protestant leaders) supported human rights platforms at United Nations conferences, argued that unified world institutions could combat nationalism, critiqued the role of American Christians in the nation's racial injustices, and rethought the assimilationist aims of foreign missionaries. Many Protestant leaders advocated for an acceptance of racial and religious diversity, "attacking the ethnocentrism and sectarianism they professed to find all around them."[43]

In contrast, historians rightly characterize the DAR as reactionary, especially in the interwar period.[44] While the American

Protestant leadership began a process of self-critique in light of the emerging civil rights movement, by the time Flora spoke to the Oregon Society of the DAR, the organization's national leadership was notorious for excluding African American musicians from performing in Constitution Hall, its building located on the mall in Washington, DC. While the organization would turn away performers before and after, the singular event that brought the organization much unwanted scrutiny was its 1939 decision to reject a performance by contralto Marian Anderson before an integrated audience. In 1942 DAR leadership reversed its stance and invited Anderson to perform at Constitution Hall, but not before First Lady Eleanor Roosevelt resigned her membership and arranged for Anderson to sing at the steps of the Lincoln Memorial on Easter Sunday 1939.[45]

Oregon's DAR leaders defended their national society's decision, arguing that the singer was turned away because the hall's schedule was full. What most contemporary observers understood to be a matter of prejudicial policy, local DAR leaders excused, chalking it up to a simple matter of unfortunate timing.[46] In response to a similar incident five years later, when jazz vocalist Hazel Scott was barred from playing at Constitution Hall, the state society voted on a resolution that would have "urged their national society's board to strike out the restrictions 'to white artists only' in the rental regulations governing their Constitution Hall" at its annual meeting in 1946. The resolution was defeated by a vote of forty-seven to thirty.[47]

While the DAR excluded African Americans from its membership and characterized the emerging civil rights movement as communistic, DAR views toward Native Americans were moderated by a desire to connect an American past to an Indigenous one. Oregon DAR chapters celebrated Oregon's "pioneering" past in plaques, memorials, and the preservation of historic houses. They were also intent on legitimizing American settler claims to the Northwest by signaling ties to an Indigenous past, which they did in the selection of chapter names.[48] If Native histories were a target of co-optation, Indians themselves were the objects of DAR charity. The Oregon Society of the DAR began assisting Native families at Celilo Village in 1931, a few years before the national organization established a subcommittee on Native American issues in 1936. It was during this time that the state society intervened in federal Indian policy as it was implemented in Oregon.

Bureau of Indian Affairs commissioner John Collier was intent on closing federal boarding schools and placing Native children back into their reservation homes. Oregon's DAR chapters opposed the bureau's proposed closure of Chemawa Indian School in Salem. Buoyed by the support of the DAR, Portland's Chamber of Commerce, and several tribal officials, Senator Charles McNary blocked the closure.[49] In 1941, the national DAR made permanent the subcommittee on Indian welfare and designated Chemawa one of two Indian schools in the nation selected for support from the national organization, a relationship that continues to this day. This mirrors a long tradition of women's organizations intervening in federal Indian policy that dates back to the 1880s with the founding of the WNIA. Given the DAR's conservatism, it would be easy to read the Oregon DAR's challenge to Commissioner Collier as a repudiation of his support for cultural pluralism and a reinforcement of assimilationist policies of the turn of the century. But local members seemed to have been motivated by a practical issue when they argued that shuttering Chemawa would leave Alaskan Natives without access to schooling.

Chemawa Indian School students were also the recipients of annual holiday gifts from various Oregon DAR chapters. In some years, DAR members traveled to the school to observe students and determine what their material needs were. Indians at Celilo were also the recipients of DAR Christmas gifts in some years, according to newspaper coverage. Chapter interest in Native peoples spiked in the late 1940s and through the mid-1950s, perhaps due to Martha's influence when she directed activities as the state regent. Her interventions in the organization suggest that Martha may have been among the more politically moderate or even progressive members of the state DAR.

For example, the year before Martha moved back to the Hood River Valley, the Oregon State Society of the DAR held its annual meeting in Hood River, hosted by the Wauna chapter, where Martha and her mother were members. Martha provided one of the key talks, "Education in Our Democracy," a personal reflection that indirectly rejected the DAR's illiberal position in the nation's battles over public school curriculum.[50] Approximately one hundred attendees from around the state gathered for the meeting, which included a program dedicated to "Indian Contributions to Life in the Northwest" and promised the participation of unnamed "outstanding Indian men and women."[51] Martha's mother, acting as program committee chair, explained the focus of the State Society: "The conservation of human life, Indian as well as of our own race, is stressed."[52]

In her speech, Martha drew from years in education to reflect on the world newly graduating students were to inherit.[53] She worried about their prospects in the Depression-era economy and the growing inequality among the state's students. But she also argued that their search for answers to society's problems was patriotic, reflecting their ability to think critically, an important characteristic in a democratic nation. "In my own work," she stated, "I am deeply impressed with the sincerity, the ambition, and the self-sacrifice of the great majority of our students. . . . If they weren't thinking, we would question their intelligence."[54] While she did not directly address the growing antiradicalism within the national DAR society, Martha asked her audience to consider dissent as a form of freely expressed patriotism. This would not be the last time she urged a more liberal and expansive approach to the often racialized and politically charged atmosphere of the wartime Pacific Northwest.

Martha's approach to Christianity and her views on race have to be pieced together. Martha did not align neatly with either the reactionary politics of lineage and patriotic societies or the ecumenical Protestant liberalism of the period. She was a proud DAR member, but sources don't reveal how she felt about some of the organization's most important controversies regarding race, nationalism, and, after World War II, anticommunism. Beginning in the 1920s, when Martha's teaching career was just getting started, the DAR and other patriotic societies urged school boards to adopt history curricula that emphasized conservative, celebratory interpretations of the American past. Martha celebrated her own family's history and that of the nation, but she often viewed the past with a critical eye. She gently pushed DAR members to consider political dissent, especially among young people, as patriotic. She also introduced them to residents of Celilo Village and asked the DAR to intervene on their behalf.

Perhaps just as important as her work in the DAR was Martha's commitment to other associations that reflected her Protestant faith and identity as a female professional. Martha's membership in the Oregon Older Girls Association, whose purpose was to bridge racial and ethnic boundaries in a fellowship of Protestant Christianity, lasted for decades, as she moved from young member to adult leader and organizer. Martha also held membership, of unknown duration, in Zonta International, an association of female professionals who promoted professionalization among women and provided an outlet for service among women professionals.[55] Memberships in organizations that emphasized global women's economic rights and intercultural unity provide a counterpoint to Martha's leadership in the DAR.

Complicating an interpretation of Martha's political views are the archival records themselves. Available records best describe her activities in the Daughters of the American Revolution but are silent about her views of the organization's various platforms. The society pages of the *Oregonian* reported on DAR state conferences and chapter meetings with regularity and in good detail but dedicated far less ink to the Oregon Older Girls Association or Zonta International. At the close of World War II— when she joined her neighbors to oppose racial prejudice directed toward Japanese Americans and Native people and began to write about her observations—Martha's progressive views on race relations and education become easier to track.

IN DEFENSE OF NEIGHBORS

When Martha returned to the Hood River Valley in 1941, she began to write in earnest. As a freelance contributor, she published lengthy "local color" articles in the *Oregonian*, which Archie often illustrated with his photographs, beginning a long collaboration between the two. She spent three years interviewing her uncle and conducting research that would culminate in three books about his life. As with other women regionalist authors, Martha's writing crossed boundaries. She played the role of journalist when she wrote full-page articles for the *Oregonian*. Her writing was also historical in the sense that it was imbued with the past, but despite its careful reconstructions of the past, her writing did not fit the criteria of professional historical writing at the time.

Although in her writing Martha constructed implicit arguments about the role of women and domesticity and the place of Native people, she wasn't often overtly political. An exception came in 1945, when she wrote a full-page *Oregonian* article to express her dismay at the treatment of returning Japanese American veterans. The article highlighted the wartime contributions of her former student Frank Hachiya. Responding to federal policies, which she felt were unjust, and to the prejudice of her fellow Oregonians, Martha rooted the article in her personal relationship with Hachiya. It established a model that Martha would use when she eventually wrote about the Thompsons and others at Celilo Village.

The incarceration of Japanese and Japanese American residents depopulated the Hood River Valley. In 1930 Hood River County's population included 514 Japanese immigrants and their children, second only to the state's most populous county, Multnomah.[56] Removal of these families to detention and then internment camps began in 1942. Some families found white neighbors who agreed to tend the farms and homes they were forced to leave. Draft-age Japanese American boys from the valley volunteered for armed service despite their families' imprisonment. The War Department initially classified Nisei volunteers and draftees—citizens of the United States—as IV-C, aliens not acceptable for service, a policy reversed after several months, at which point Nisei were accepted into the service, in segregated units.[57]

The return of Issei and Nisei to their Hood River homes after the war resulted in some of the most serious racialized violence the valley had seen since the 1920s. Scores of white residents fought to keep Japanese and Japanese Americans from returning. The Hood River Chapter of the American Legion made national headlines and epitomized the tension in the region when it removed the names of sixteen Japanese American soldiers from its World War II memorial in 1944. A veteran of World War I, Archie was an active member of the valley's American Legion, perhaps propelling Martha to enter the debate to protect the rights of Japanese and Japanese Americans neighbors.[58] As with the Indian families at Celilo Village, Martha counted many of the Japanese immigrants in the Hood River Valley as neighbors, and their American-born children were her students.

A scattering of white residents organized to quell the discrimination and harassment directed at returning Japanese and Japanese Americans, with much of the valley's oppositional activity centered in several churches. Sherman Burgoyne, pastor at the Ashbury Methodist Church in Hood River city, cofounded the League of Liberty and Justice, which sought to protect Japanese neighbors by making purchases for them, helping them sell their agricultural products, and speaking out against the harassment they faced. It was the first organization Martha joined with an explicit social justice mission. Martha also drafted a public letter with other members of the Odell Methodist Church, which her parents founded, demanding that the American Legion reinstate the names of the Japanese American soldiers it had removed.[59]

In the *Oregonian*, Martha provided the details of Frank Hachiya's biography and death.[60] When he was sixteen, Hachiya and his parents left the valley for Japan, where he attended high school and became fluent in Japanese. When Frank was nearly ready to graduate, he returned to Hood River to brush up on English before he started college. During his final months of high school

Frank stayed with a white family for whom his father had worked. Hachiya enrolled at Multnomah College, where Martha was the Dean of Women, before the war and then eventually transferred to the University of Oregon, where he was taking classes when the United States entered the war. Hachiya immediately enlisted, moved to Minnesota for training, and then visited his father at the Tule Lake Interment camp in California before he was shipped out to the Pacific theater as an interpreter, where he was killed.

Martha drew from Hachiya's writings—letters to her and other friends and family and an autobiographical essay he wrote as her student—to paint a portrait of a stalwart and loyal American. Martha's article was a meditation on citizenship, especially in times of war. She used Hachiya's words to question the actions of a democratic government toward its citizens and their immigrant parents. To her, he had written of being relieved that the military lifted its ban on Japanese American service on the front lines but also regretting that he would not be allowed to return home during leave because home lay within the boundaries of the exclusion zone: "I do wish I could come out that way." To a friend back home in Hood River he wrote, "Our position in this nation is not too agreeable, but I hope that it is nearly at its worst." "The source," he suggested, "of all this ill treatment being forced upon us is the inconsistency between the theory and the practice of democracy."[61]

Martha spoke at Hachiya's memorial service, which was held in 1948, three years after his death. In the period between his death and the service, Hachiya had become a cause célèbre, and the Ashbury Methodist Church in Hood River overflowed with friends and prominent Oregonians. Martha spoke as a result of her relationship with the young man as well as her public activism on

Frank Hachiya, Martha McKeown's former student, in uniform. All rights reserved, Defense Language Institute Foreign Language Center Archives

behalf of returning Japanese and their families. Ray Yasui of the Hood River Japanese American Citizens League wrote that he was "proud to be a Nisei because then it is possible to number such persons as Mrs. McKeown . . . as a friend."[62] Martha's aid to Japanese Americans in the Hood River Valley was part of a larger effort among "Progressive Christians" who fought xenophobia with "education and personal interactions between Nikkei and white Americans, utilizing American and Christian tropes of tolerance and democracy."[63] And it positioned her to speak out later against unjust federal policies directed at her Indian neighbors.

The debates regarding Japanese immigrants and their American-born children hinged on the issue of citizenship. Federal law prohibited Japanese immigrants from naturalizing, but the Fourteenth Amendment meant that their American-born children were automatically granted citizenship. To revoke their citizenship, virulently anti-Asian politicians in the American West unsuccessfully called for a reversal of the Fourteenth Amendment.[64] Martha and others countered by pointing out the many ways in which Japanese Americans were exemplary citizens. This debate was critical to valley residents, but there were other debates about the meaning of citizenship that occupied those living on the mid–Columbia River.

Just as it did for Japanese Americans, the meaning of national citizenship for Native peoples shifted dramatically as a result of the war. On the whole, Japanese American activists and organizations called for the United States to treat them as citizens, equal to other citizens of the nation. The extension of full citizenship to Japanese Americans and their Issei parents was an enhancement of their otherwise limited rights. In contrast, in addition to US citizenship, Native peoples also held citizenship within their tribal nations, entities that had certain rights vis-à-vis the federal government, including at least limited sovereignty. Congress extended citizenship to all Indians in 1924 through the Indian Citizenship Act, with congressional representatives pointing to Indian involvement in World War I as a motivating factor. Prior to 1924, Indians became citizens only as they visibly shed Indigenous identities to assimilate into the American mainstream.[65]

Indians volunteered for military service at the onset of World War II in numbers out of proportion to their populations.[66] For Indians enrolled on reservations of the Northwest, World War II military service was a twofold responsibility: to the United States *and* to their tribal nations. Umatilla William Minthorne spoke to the protection of traditional and reservation lands and resources when he told a congressional committee reviewing the damming of the Columbia River that "our sons made fine records as soldiers in World War II, and many of us worked in shipyards or ordnance depots. But we do not know that it is necessary for national defense to destroy our centuries-old salmon fishery at Celilo."[67] While Hood River's sympathetic white residents fought to include their Japanese neighbors in an enlarged bond of citizenship, Indian leaders reminded the nation that membership in tribal nations made them more than US citizens. When regional and national politicians advocated for the termination of Indian tribes' federal status after the war, many Natives saw it rightly as a diminishment of their standing because it would eliminate tribal citizenship.

Quieter controversies over citizenship were visible within Celilo Village itself. If national citizenship secured belonging in the nation-state, adoption created kin—with all its attendant rights— of strangers within tribes. Tommy Thompson extended tribal membership to non-Native people occasionally. Before the treaties of the 1850s, someone of his authority would have had the right (and at times the obligation) to extend kinship rights in such a manner. However, in the twentieth century, adoption of non-Native people became controversial, especially if adoptees were granted rights to treaty-protected resources. The Yakama tribal government and the BIA stepped in at least once to contest Thompson's adoption of a non–tribally affiliated neighbor to whom Thompson had extended fishing rights.[68]

At some point, Tommy Thompson adopted Martha McKeown into the Wyam, which appears to have gone uncontested by other tribal members or Celilo Village residents, and for good reason.

Although important to Thompson and McKeown, the adoption did not explicitly reallocate resources. Martha had no intention of living with the people at Celilo Village, nor did she raise her children in the community, and she made no claim on fishing rights or any other material resources. But she did attend ceremonies and meetings, and she interviewed and photographed Celilo families, especially the Thompsons, in her home and at the village site. Perhaps the adoption recognized the intimacy of Thompson's relationship with Martha, which went far beyond that of subject and scholar. Martha, who had lost her own father in her twenties, referred to Thompson as a parental figure and supervised his care like a daughter as he aged. Thompson's adoption of Martha suggests a familial friendship. It was also smart of him to secure a close relationship with a powerfully connected and sympathetic white woman. Thompson knew that relationships mattered, and bringing strangers into the realm of kin could strengthen the community he guided.

FLORA MARRIES A CHIEF

Flora was unhappy in her marriage to Timothy George, whom she married in 1939. In an interview decades after she left him, Flora complained that George accused her of adultery. "He was an elderly man like chief," she said, "but he was a witch doctor so I divorced him." After she married Thompson, George "came down and he tried to send word to me to go back." Exasperated, she asked, "He signed our divorce papers, what's the matter with that old man?"[69] Despite the lapse of time between their divorce and the interview, Flora's remarks—which questioned the legitimacy of his faith work—indicate her animosity toward George, a respected religious leader. Although they separated in 1943, the marriage dragged on.

Chief Tommy Thompson and his wife Flora Thompson getting ready for the salmon feast in 1943, the year following their marriage. Courtesy of Old Oregon Photos

In 1948, the BIA alerted Flora that she was still legally married to George because Yakama records misidentified their last name as Joyce, which confused employees of the county court. Other official records muddied Flora's marital status as the time. BIA records, which identified her as Flora Boise after she filed for divorce from George, indicate that Flora was single between 1943 and 1948, although she clearly stated in later oral histories that she and Thompson began living as husband and wife in 1943.[70]

Chief Thompson's grandchildren arranged the marriage when they convinced Flora to keep company with the newly widowed chief. Thompson had been married for decades to his wife Ellen, who died in 1943 during the cherry harvest. Flora knew the Thompsons through family connections and because she traveled seasonally to the Hood River Valley and the south side of the Columbia River for work and to harvest traditional foods. When Chief Thompson's grandchildren asked Flora to stay through the summer, Flora responded: " 'Well, I got to haul my fruit home first before I can come back.' . . . So I went home and I came back and I stayed here all through July, August, September. September I began to get married to him, big Indian trade, so I lived here since the early 40s."[71]

Although the sources are largely silent on the quality of their relationship, Flora and Tommy seemed to share a lighthearted approach to their marriage. Nearly a half century separated them, and Thompson would sometimes pass off his much younger wife as his daughter. When Gladys and George Struck, Hood River Valley farmers, visited the couple in February 1948, Thompson "introduced [her] with a smile, saying, 'This is my daughter.' " Flora assured the Strucks that he was joking.[72] According to Flora, Tommy had engaged in plural marriage when he was married to Ellen, as was the tradition for a man of Thompson's status. "As a chief he

Leading Ladies Meet

Mrs. Douglas McKay (right) called at home of Mrs. Tommy (Flora) Thompson (left) at Celilo before speaking at luncheon meeting in The Dalles. In background is picture of Chief Tommy Thompson of Wy-am Indians, husband of Mrs. Thompson. Chief is patient at nursing home in Hood River.

On October 6, 1955, the *Oregonian* newspaper published a photograph of Flora Thompson accompanied by Governor Douglas McKay's wife, Maude, with the headline "Leading Ladies Meet." An article did not accompany the photograph. Courtesy of Barcroft Media

could have as many wives as he wanted," Flora insisted. "He wasn't married once or twice. He was a handsome looking man and he used to have a dozen wives in one lump sum." As a result, "he had a lot of children."[73] When Tommy asked Flora, "'how would you stand it if I had two other, three wives like I used to?,'" she retorted, "I wouldn't mind it. I'd be getting rest through them.'"[74]

The union would change both in dramatic and public ways. Flora's marriage to Thompson elevated her status and made her into a public figure. "I had a chance to get a chief husband this time," she stated. The *Oregonian* dubbed her a "first lady" when it published a picture of Flora with Maude McKay, wife of Oregon governor Douglas McKay.[75] The *Oregonian*'s white audience recognized Flora as Thompson's spokesperson and representative. The marriage elevated Flora's status among the region's Native people too, making her a woman of increased authority at a time of great upheaval at Celilo Village.

Flora arrived in the midst of several ongoing conflicts in the community over its governance, which came from several directions. BIA supervision of the village site shifted from the Umatilla Reservation to the Yakama Reservation, neither of which sat well with many residents. Thompson was suspicious of the power the Yakama wielded at Celilo and thought that they sought to undermine his authority on the river. Moreover, the BIA appointed a field agent to The Dalles in 1939, increasing federal oversight of the community. Within a year, The Dalles Chamber of Commerce and other business interests began petitioning the federal government to clean up the community and proposed various ways to make it more attractive to tourists, including developing a store for Indian crafts, a museum, and a service station and motel for visitors.[76] Proposals for the redevelopment of the village periodically gathered steam but didn't garner the concern at Celilo that other threats did. Oregon wanted to widen Highway 30 by acquiring village land, and Washington and Oregon fish and game agencies continually impeded treaty-protected fishing rights on the river. For Celilo residents, the marketing of Indian crafts was far less important than land retention and access to their fisheries.

If Flora's status improved by marrying a chief "this time," Tommy Thompson's life got much easier when his grandchildren urged the union. Flora took on the work of corresponding for her husband, removing the need for him to rely on individuals who might rival his authority. Not only did Flora not undermine Thompson, she made every effort to bolster him. She insisted that Thompson's authority as hereditary chief be recognized, and even dated some of the more radical fish conservation efforts on the

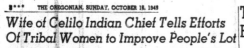

Wife of Celilo Indian Chief Tells Efforts Of Tribal Women to Improve People's Lot

Mrs. "Tommy" Thompson, wife of the chief of the Wy-ams at Celilo on the Columbia river, shows off the service record of her father, Jim Cush-ny, who was an Indian scout for the United States government during the Modoc wars. Mrs. Thompson was a guest at last week's state board meeting of the Daughters of the American Revolution; asked the Daughters' help in meeting some of the needs of the women's society of her little community on the river.

BY FREDA MOWREY

This photograph of Flora Thompson accompanied an *Oregonian* article about her presentation before the State DAR meeting in 1949. Courtesy of Barcroft Media

mid–Columbia River to his becoming chief. Wife of Celilo's salmon chief was a demanding position, and Flora's correspondence to friends in the years after her marriage reveals frequent exhaustion. Flora came to rely on her older sister, Effie Cushinway, as well as other women at Celilo Village, to meet the role's various demands. As Thompson aged, Flora's responsibilities multiplied. Her relative youth helped.

Flora Thompson's marriage linked her to Martha McKeown and led her to the Oregon State Society Daughters of the American Revolution meeting board in October 1949.[77] Flora signaled her ethnicity with neatly braided hair pulled away from her face and strands of beads encircling her neck. The DAR women shared with

Flora a veneration of veterans of American wars and military service. After a brief presentation, Flora pulled papers from her own beaded bag documenting her father's participation in the Modoc War as a member of the Warm Springs Indian Scouts, a subdivision of the US Army. Before she left the meeting, an *Oregonian* staffer snapped her photograph, posing with the federal document.

Flora Thompson's presence before the Oregon State Society of the DAR board in 1949 was striking, a brief convergence of two worlds made possible by cross-cultural friendships that connected the orchards of the Hood River Valley to the fishing platforms of Celilo Village. The meeting was notable, so much so that the state's largest newspaper covered it. According to the paper's society reporter, Flora asked the DAR women to help women at Celilo Village collect the deer hides and beads they needed to craft the moccasins, bags, and belts they made for the non-Native market. She might have told them that hides were increasingly hard to come by due to diminished habitat and increased pressures on deer populations from recreational hunters. She may have mentioned that hides were necessary for ceremonial regalia too. Flora's request for deer hides was part of a larger effort to build actionable sympathy among Oregon's decision makers regarding issues facing residents of Celilo Village. It was an easy one for the women around the table to fill: several hunting organizations could be tapped for hides that had little value to white Oregonians.[78]

As the *Oregonian* photograph deftly captured, Flora Thompson and the state leadership of the DAR held values in common. Carefully recorded and preserved lineage placed a woman, whether white or Native, in a progression of generations that tied her to the heroic actions of her forebears. Because other Native people would have used Flora Thompson's lineage to place her geographically and socially, she could probably recite her genealogy in her sleep. Bloodlines created kinship networks and were as important to the tribes and bands along the Columbia River as they were for members of the DAR. Both the DAR and tribes carefully kept membership rolls that connected a current generation to past members and provided benefits associated with membership. The past was mapped and recalled through genealogies, the family trees and kinship networks that rooted people in place.

The DAR inscribed a patriotic narrative onto the landscapes that also held importance to the state's Indigenous peoples. The DAR used preservation, Americanization committees, and its nationally disseminated magazine to broadcast the success of American imperialism. Their chapter names, borrowed or stolen from Native peoples, announced the success of colonization and obscured its legacies. But landscape also held the memories of Warm Springs and Wyam peoples. Stories rooted in specific geographies documented how Native people came to live in the region and have rights to its resources.

Their commonalities also suggested deep differences between the women in the conference room on that October day in 1949. Both Flora and Martha relied on systems of nonbiological kinship, the close social ties of obligation that developed between friends and neighbors over time. In their celebration of civic nationalism, the DAR traded on the currency of the imagined kinship of citizenship and supported its extension to Indians. When Tommy Thompson adopted Martha, he recognized an enlarged citizenship among the Wyam. While Martha could bring Flora into the web of clubwoman sisterhood, her lack of biological connections to the American Revolution would keep the relationship temporary, at least in the space of the conference room. Due to an Indigenous tradition of extending kin relationships beyond blood, Martha could be Wyam. But because her bloodlines precluded a connection to a colonial past, Flora could never be DAR. Nonetheless, it was remarkable that Flora was even there, standing before the DAR women. She may have gained admittance to the state society meeting as part of their validation of American expansion into Oregon Country, but Flora did not squander the opportunity. She harnessed the energy and social networks of white clubwomen in support of the Native community at Celilo.

Alliances with non-Native people would become increasingly important to the region's Indian people as dam construction on the Columbia River quickened. The Dalles Dam, which would inundate Celilo Falls and part of Celilo Village, became a lightning rod for whites concerned with the status of the region's Indians. Nontribal resistance to construction came from all corners—from Portland with artist and bird lover Jimmie James at the helm, from Yakima Valley where retired newspaper editor and sculptor Click Relander worried about the loss of tribal fisheries, and from the Hood River Valley, Martha McKeown's home. Their efforts converged and overlapped with other regional activists like Columbia Gorge conservationist Gertrude Jensen. Collectively, they illustrate the spectrum of assistance that outsiders presented to Native communities in a time of potential crisis. Set against the efforts of tribal members and Celilo Village residents, they also illuminate the limits of cross-cultural alliances in the mid-twentieth century.

FIVE

Protecting Home

The U.S. Engineers could decide to cut Mt. Hood off at
its base and dump [it] into Crater Lake to make an
International Golf Course, they could even start before
we knew it—and who would you go to, to get the thing
stopped? . . . This sounds ridiculous I know and if you
had been told that Celilo Falls would have been covered
by water by building a dam five years ago we would have
been aghast—but just such a thing could happen over
and over again until our state would be stripped of all of
its beauty.

JIMMIE JAMES TO MARTHA MCKEOWN, January 21, 1953

MORE THAN ANYONE ELSE BEFORE OR SINCE, MARTHA
McKeown shaped how non-Native Oregonians understood Celilo
Village and the Thompsons. She eventually wrote two children's
books, published in 1956 and 1959, that invited Oregonians—who
knew the community next to the falls only fleetingly as they drove
by on Highway 30 or because they stopped to watch fishers haul

salmon onto their wooden platforms for an afternoon—into the community's homes and longhouse. Even before the publication of her books, which would remain in print for decades, she wrote several full-page articles that highlighted various aspects of Northwest history, including one about the Thompsons and Celilo Village. "Celilo Indians: Fishing Their Way of Life" came out in October 1949 to contextualize the threat widening Highway 30 posed to village homes.

By the time of the article's publication, the highway was not the only hazard the community faced. Proposals to build The Dalles Dam made clear that portions of the village would be inundated by the dam's reservoir and that the picturesque Celilo Falls, which drew tourists to the area, would disappear under its man-made lake. Indians throughout the basin, especially those with familial fishing rights, were alarmed but faced the proposed dam as part of an ongoing struggle to access the river's resources and doubled down on efforts to maintain their treaty fishing rights on the river. The potential loss of the falls, however, energized non-Native people in Oregon and Washington—and eventually from farther afield as well—who rallied to stop their inundation. Activists interested in Indian cultural persistence joined efforts with conservationists, at least for a short time, to protest river development that would abrogate treaties and reshape the gorge landscape. The "Save Celilo Falls" campaign brought together a variety of people who hoped they could, through letters and other forms of lobbying, influence federal policies in one of the most scenic sections of the state.

At the center of these activities was James J. James, a retired Portland Port Authority employee who offered his services as the tribe's "press agent" to Yakama tribal chairman Alex Saluskin in 1950.[1] James would eventually count Flora and Martha among his friends. James, who lived in Portland, relied on occasional visits to the mid-Columbia as well as typewritten letters to connect him to Indian and non-Indian friends upriver. His copious correspondence quilted the threads of opposition into a concerted and organized effort. James's typewriter briefly brought together Portland clubwomen conservationists eager to protect the Gorge, like Martha's associate Gertrude Jensen; politicians like Oregon senators Richard Neuberger and Wayne Morse; and Indian advocates and regional writers like Martha herself and Click Relander, the city editor for the *Yakima Herald* in Washington State. James also wrote to Indian leaders—his press agent designator Alex Saluskin, Flora and Tommy Thompson, Yakama tribal council member and fishing activist Wilson Charley, and many others.

James wrote thousands of letters over a period of about two decades. Over time, his letters became more personal, asking after spouses and children, speculating on the activities of mutual friends, and disclosing the health struggles of his wife and silent partner, Maude. Senator Neuberger became Dick. James's correspondence with Martha McKeown extended to her husband Archie, and James worried when his letters went unanswered. As it became increasingly clear that dam construction would proceed, James turned his energy to termination policy and strengthened his relationship with the Thompsons at Celilo Village. Years later, Flora Thompson would describe James as being "just like a son."[2]

The letters Jimmie James left behind make visible the political and social networks briefly forged among Indians, their allies, and conservationists attempting to halt construction on The Dalles Dam. They also reveal ruptures in those networks, which often hinged on competing conceptions of time, the scope of opposition, and the very meaning of citizenship. White advocates held a spectrum of views, with some focused on Indian fishing rights and self-determination and others, like Gertrude Jensen, primarily interested in preserving the scenic Columbia River Gorge, including Celilo Falls. The white allies who opposed the dam and who were brought together through James's efforts illustrate the variety of approaches offered by advocates to Indian communities in the midst of crisis. One particularly negative experience with a man who went by "Chief Rising Sun" made James cautious and perhaps appreciative of Martha's focused interventions in issues at Celilo Village, as well as her careful documentation of the community through her writings.

This chapter charts the lobbying that Martha, Flora, and Chief Thompson embarked on in 1949 to mitigate changes to Celilo Village as a result of road development. Their campaign did not stop road expansion, but it did familiarize Oregonians with the Thompsons and Celilo Village. Martha shifted gears by 1952 when she successfully reversed a case of land fraud perpetrated by BIA employees against Indians living in the Hood River Valley. Thanks to her investigation, two employees were fired and sent to prison, and one victim received fair market value for the timber on his land. During this period, Martha and Flora also cared for an ailing Chief Thompson, eventually placing him in a nursing home. Defending village homes in BIA meetings, following up on suspicious Indian land sales, and locating suitable housing for elderly Indians provide a counterpoint to the rush of activity among white allies to stop The Dalles Dam.

James's isolation from the mid-Columbia at his home office in Portland limited the strategies available to him and meant that he sometimes misjudged those who promised to help. His efforts— though fraught with missteps—also brought advocates and Native leaders into a network of his own making as he disseminated correspondents' personal news along with information related to dam construction, and recruited potential advocates in other regions. He also forged lasting personal relationships with Martha and Flora that continued until his death in 1967.

PROTECTING CELILO VILLAGE, DOCUMENTING A NATIVE HOME

When Flora Thompson spoke before the Oregon State Daughters of the American Revolution board, it was one of many talks she, her husband, and Martha would deliver in the last months of 1949. The day before the DAR meeting, Flora had translated Chief Thompson's statements at a Portland Chamber of Commerce luncheon. The Thompsons also joined Martha McKeown when she spoke to more than three hundred people gathered for a banquet at the Fifty-Fifty Club, an association for businesswomen. The following month, Flora Thompson spoke to the Salem Council of Women's Organizations, among others. Together, Martha McKeown and the Thompsons engaged in direct advocacy as they appeared before audiences at luncheons, libraries, and even department stores. In a mere six weeks at the end of 1949, they used public presentations, publications, and testimony before BIA officials to slow the relocation of Celilo Village homes necessitated by the widening of Highway 30. At the campaign's onset, McKeown wrote a lengthy illustrated article published in the *Oregonian*. As a result, the trio reached government officials, Portland's decision makers, and the general public all within a matter of weeks. They employed these strategies to protect Indigenous homelands, honing techniques they would use later to address changes wrought by The Dalles Dam.

The lobbying in 1949 gathered steam around three primary issues: support for an autonomous tribal council of River Indians,

The Fifty-Fifty Club of Business Women's annual banquet, October 18, 1949, Multnomah Hotel, photographed by Gladys Gilbert Studio. *From left to right*: Charles Quintoken, Martha McKeown, Tommy Thompson, unidentified woman, and Flora Thompson. Courtesy of Thomas Robinson

restructuring of the Celilo Fish Committee, and alternative designs for new home construction slated for the village. The first two issues were perennial, part of broader concerns over who carried legitimate authority on the river. The Thompsons argued that river communities should form a federally recognized River Indian tribal council separate from and equal to reservation governments, instead of being treated as subsets of federally recognized tribes like the Yakama or Umatilla. Moreover, Chief Thompson called for changes to the Celilo Fish Committee, an intertribal board that mediated fishing disputes, complaining that it distorted traditional forms of Indigenous leadership such as his.

A more immediate concern that demanded quick intervention was the physical changes to the village residences. The Thompsons argued that plans to relocate homes to allow for the widening of Highway 30 were poorly orchestrated and based in miscommunication between village residents and federal authorities that disrespected them personally. Flora told the audience at the Portland Chamber of Commerce luncheon that the new houses lacked privacy, and Chief Thompson complained that the engineers "did not listen to me on how we wanted the houses built after pleading with us to move and promising they would build them as we wanted them."[3] Their efforts were rewarded when the Portland Chamber of Commerce organized an investigation of conditions at the village. The *Oregonian* newspaper reported that the Thompsons arrived at the meeting "to plead for the white man's help . . . and won it."[4]

A month later, Martha McKeown and Tommy Thompson used the talking points they developed before Portland audiences at a Celilo Village meeting with local BIA representatives and engineers. Chief Thompson and E. Morgan Pryse, director of the BIA's Portland Area Office, had met previously. Letters between the two followed, with Pryse attending the November conference in the hopes of coming to a final understanding that would precipitate families moving into ten new BIA homes. Thompson's persistent requests for clarification of the conditions of relocation at the Celilo meeting, however, suggest he was suspicious of the bureau and its agents and reluctant to finalize any agreement. Among other items, he asked who would pay for the electricity in the new homes. Pryse equivocated over what may have seemed a minor issue, and then "replied that it would be only a small amount for the lights anyway."[5] But Thompson knew that for the cash-poor families of Celilo, an electric bill could be overwhelming. Moreover, the new costs were not part of the original deal between residents and the BIA. According to C. G. Davis's notes:

> Chief Thompson argued that he may have no money with which to pay for lights, and accused the Director of at first declaring that the houses were free to the Indians and now announces that there will be lights to pay for; that prior to re-building, his people never paid for electricity, and had been encouraged by the government to accept remodeling of Celilo Village; that his people feel that they should be free as before even though the houses had been modernized; that the two things—light and water—to pay are becoming an obstacle in the way of moving into the houses.[6]

When Director Pryse pressed Thompson about who paid for the electricity used in the longhouse, James Dyer, an adopted member of the community, pointed out that he personally paid that bill.

Thompson, McKeown, Dyer, and others presented the BIA officials with a laundry list of issues, many of which had no easy resolution. McKeown asked about access to a strip of land in the village site and who had authority over it, and complained about the incursion of the Celilo Fish Committee into matters pertaining to the community itself, which she claimed they had no jurisdiction over. The issues were wide-ranging, and it quickly became apparent that those in attendance would not agree to the terms of relocation that day. Well into the meeting, Pryse tried unsuccessfully to excuse himself to return to Portland. Another white advocate demanded that the director stay to hear further complaints. Pryse and others from the BIA eventually pried themselves from the discussion, having resolved little in regard to the meeting's original purpose.

Nonetheless, Thompson and other leaders at Celilo impressed upon BIA representatives the real and critical problems they faced at the off-reservation community. Of course, attention did not automatically lead to action, and it is likely that Pryse left the meeting aghast at the myriad issues he was asked to address and the divisions between residents of Celilo and reservation-based Indians. While BIA representatives sought to narrow the day's discussion to the relocation of ten families to new homes, Thompson and others focused on the community's long-term functioning. The modern homes—in the eyes of BIA employees, clearly improvements over the dilapidated housing typical of Celilo—threatened to upend the careful balance of authority in the village. While Pryse may have thought the meeting was about replacement housing, the Thompsons and other Celilo residents knew it was a test of their inherent sovereignty over their community and individual lives, and what kinds of homes they would live in.

Martha McKeown narrated the governmental and economic issues at Celilo Village through a personal tour of the Thompsons' home in an *Oregonian* article, "Celilo Indians: Fishing Their Way of Life." Using a method she had used when writing about Frank Hachiya and would employ in subsequent writing on Celilo, Martha provided *Oregonian* readers with "an intimate view, from the homeside" of village life that was indelibly shaped by fishing controversies and struggles for self-determination.[7] In doing so, Martha domesticated the policy discussions at meetings like the one described above. Moreover, the piece insisted on Indigenous belonging outside reservation boundaries at the resource sites so important to the Thompsons and others. Because it reached a statewide audience, the article had the potential to alter public opinion about Indians, their homelands, and their regional status.

Although an important figure in the article and in the home, Chief Thompson was silent. It was Flora who welcomed her guests. "She came to the door of the low, weather-beaten house, under the high, overhanging cliff . . . and said, 'I am Mrs. Chief Tommy Thompson. Won't you come in?' "[8] Flora was the "youthful, slender, erect figure" beside Chief Thompson, who "whether in beautiful ceremonial garb or at her household duties in a simple, worn, work dress, with a double strand of wampum at her neck and dangling coin earrings, is a woman of rare distinction and intelligence."[9] Martha's description was echoed years later by Barbara MacKenzie, a social worker hired by Wasco County to supervise the relocation of Celilo families whose homes were going to be inundated by The Dalles Dam. "Flora was very dignified," MacKenzie recalled in an oral history interview. "I never saw Flora flustered or at a loss. Usually she wore the calico but her hair was always combed and you knew that she was the lady of the house, you knew that she had to be consulted."[10] Martha declared that "no woman could be more loyal to the man whose name she proudly bears, or more eager to share his burdens" than her friend.[11]

Martha brought readers into the Thompson home and thereby showcased domesticity, kinship connections, community relations, and the gendered work necessary for the fishery. In phrasing that echoed Frederic Homer Balch's description of Wallulah's longhouse, Flora's home was "typically Indian, remind[ing] one of the pictures of Oriental interiors."[12]

There are two large rooms. The front one, opening onto the porch contained four neatly made beds; one in each corner. There were no bedsteads: the bedding was placed directly on the floor. In the center of the room was a round, highly

Minnie Charlie Johnlee talks to Martha McKeown in the Celilo Village
longhouse as (*left to right*) Davis Thompson, Black Braids, Henry Thompson,
Flora Thompson, Max Boise, and Tommy Thompson listen. Special Collections
and Archives, Eric V. Hauser Memorial Library, Reed College

ornate, antique iron stove. There was no other furniture. At
the windows hung simple, green draw curtains. The walls
were lined with pictures; most of them were of the chief,
others were of his children.[13]

In contrast to Balch or the field matrons of Flora's childhood
and early adulthood, McKeown did not seek out evidence of "civilization," nor did she evaluate the household against assimilative
standards of cleanliness and order. She made women's labor in the
fishing community visible but did not judge it or seek to reform

the lifeways of the women about whom she wrote. She thereby reversed the long tradition of women's organizations targeting Native women for assimilative transformation. While she may not have recognized it at the time, her rejection of the WNIA-styled homemaker hierarchy signaled a turn toward what Amanda Zink calls "domestic sovereignty."[14]

Women's contributions to the Indigenous salmon industry took place in the home and in nearby drying sheds, where women hung filleted fish out "like great scarlet fans."[15] Flora related to Martha the process of constructing dip-nets with traditional materials, when women pulled the bark of a roselike bush until it stretched like twine and could be knotted into netting. As Martha and Flora chatted, another Celilo woman, Effie Smith, who was related to the Thompsons through marriage, flaked dried salmon onto a tule drying rack, the first step in producing *chelae*, the powdered salmon that was a treasured trade item. Despite the article's subtitle—"Fishing Their Way of Life"—the picturesque and public platform fishing performed by men, which often dominated white-led discussions of Celilo, was integrated into the private domesticity of kinship in a way that mirrored Indigenous conceptions of work and life.

It was a domestic life that Martha presented as closed to most outsiders except for the rare "privileged, trusted guest."[16] Martha and Flora's shared history in the region and Martha's grandfather's treatment of Indians "swung open wide the door of the chief's home."[17] The welcome allowed Martha to position herself as the mediator through which other Oregonians could virtually visit the community. She directed her readers to approach their stay with respect for the village's rich heritage. But she also addressed shared sacrifice when she included the wartime experiences of Steve Boise, Young Boise's son and Flora's stepson, who was quick to downplay his service record in order to return to the more immediately pressing treaty fishing rights, a reminder that sovereignty and the struggle for it organized the Thompsons' domestic space. Martha's sympathetic portrayal and the speaking tour came at the close of a difficult decade, which opened into the challenging period of the 1950s, when, among other things, the widening of Highway 30 would proceed.

OREGON, 1950

Nineteen fifty was a bad year for returning salmon and for the Indians who relied on them. Since the closing of Bonneville Dam in 1938, Indians had marked the diminishing returns of the salmon runs and blamed river development. US Army Corps engineers plotted ahead, mapping the riverscape they aimed to create. They did so within the context of the Cold War, which internationalized the flow of the Columbia River, as well as the Indian-held treaty right to fish in its waters, by framing the river's "work" as beneficial to the nation's military readiness.

The persuasiveness of arguments that linked redevelopment of the Columbia to the global conflict of the Cold War threatened to overwhelm any other consideration. Nonetheless, according to historian Thomas Borstelmann, "There was no greater weakness for the United States in waging the Cold War than inequality and discrimination."[18] Indians and their non-Native allies grasped this and peppered opposition to river development with references to America's international reputation as well as their own patriotism, lest their protests seem anti-American. Countering Army Corps claims of the greatest good for the greatest number, dam opponents argued that within the context of global conflict, treaty promises—as long as they were upheld—represented the best of

American democracy with the nation's most vulnerable peoples meriting federal protections. Upheld treaty provisions could strengthen the nation's moral standing within the Cold War. The breaking of treaty promises, however, portended a nation that trapped its minority populations in abject poverty and denied them full citizenship rights, and would weaken the nation's international reputation. Indians pointedly argued that protection of traditional territories and the treaties that recognized their rights to them motivated their national military service and that of their sons, fathers, and grandfathers.

Nineteen fifty was also the year when governors in sixteen western states, including Oregon's Douglas McKay, formed the Governors Interstate Council on Indian Affairs, an organization that promoted termination policy, promising to finally accomplish the settler aspiration of Indigenous assimilation. If the governors got their wish and the federal government carried out termination policy with each tribal group in the nation, tribally held resources like land would be liquidated and the proceeds divided among those formally enrolled in the tribe. Rights to off-reservation resources, like the salmon of the Columbia River, and off-reservation sites, like the land at Celilo Village, as set aside in the 1855 treaties, would cease to exist. In 1952, President Eisenhower appointed McKay to direct the Interior Department, where he energetically oversaw the policy's rollout.

Advocates of Indian rights and Indian people themselves were often ambivalent about the program that would sever the nation-to-nation relationship between the federal government and the nation's recognized tribal groups. By the 1940s and '50s, "'reservation' became code for confining space, othered or racialized space, and even emasculated space," where Native adults were forced to navigate and conform to BIA paternalism.[19] Some reservation governments, like the Colville in Washington State, were sharply divided on whether accepting termination would liberate tribal members from federal supervision or constitute a significant diminishment of their rights.[20] The termination crisis, coupled with dam construction, crystalized an Indigenous "hybrid patriotism that embraced national service to strengthen both Native American identity and the 'democratic way of life' that protected it."[21] While terminationists assumed that participation in World War II would bring Indians into the national mainstream, Indian leaders in the Pacific Northwest used military service—stretching back to the Modoc War for members of the Warm Springs Reservation—to demonstrate a patriotic dual citizenship within nation and tribe. These strands converged in opposition to The Dalles Dam.

JAMES JAMES AND BUILDING OPPOSITION TO THE DAM

Congress's allocation of funds for dam construction in 1952 drew many potential allies within the region to the struggle to save Celilo Falls. Perhaps one of the most important was James "Jimmie" James, a contemporary of both Martha and Flora, who had worked at the Port of Portland ridding the warehouses of vermin.[22] In retirement, James, self-described "Painter of the Gorge," created realistic images of Indians and the Columbia Gorge landscape.[23] After contacting Alex Saluskin, chairman of the Yakama Tribal Council, in 1950 offering to act as a "press secretary" for the Yakama Nation, James spent most of his time churning out correspondence on his typewriter in his home office, rooting his motivation in a deep-seated patriotism.[24] As a veteran of World War II, James declared, "I'd fight for my country at the drop of a hat." On the other hand, "I am ready to fight against the way our Indians are being treated."[25] "My skin may be white," he professed, "but my heart is red!"[26]

James helped galvanize a campaign against the dam that rested on his writing numerous letters about the dam every day. His efforts contextualize Martha McKeown's work with the Thompsons at a time of environmental and social transformation. His letters went to politicians in Oregon, Washington, and Idaho, and three or four press releases at a time hit the local papers. James also kept voluminous correspondence, carefully numbering each letter, with anyone he thought might help in the opposition of the dam. He kept carbon copies of everything he wrote, including magazine subscription renewals, and carefully preserved incoming letters as well. In an understatement, James acknowledged to a friend in 1953, "letter writing has been a big part of my life this year."[27] Opposition to the dam was James's most pressing concern, but his letters also disclose an agenda of his own making: James believed that Native peoples could reverse the long course of injustice by founding a new national pan-Indian organization (of James's design) and by focusing on the creative arts as a bridge to mainstream society.[28] Nonetheless, James was circumspect in advocating his ideas to the tribal leaders he knew. His letters depict a man who desperately wanted to help, with clear ideas about strategies, but who was careful to take a backseat to those who truly had authority, the chiefs and elected leaders on the reservations. Others weren't so careful, and one of James's tasks was to wrangle, to the degree he could, white allies who acted without consulting or getting approval from the Native leaders they purported to help.

For James and other whites, opposition to the dam was expressed in a flurry of letters and actions over the course of a couple of years. For the Native peoples to whom they were allies, opposition to The

Jimmie James placing miniature teepees in Mill Ends Park ("the world's smallest park") in downtown Portland, Oregon. Undated photograph courtesy of Cascade Locks Museum

Dalles Dam was embedded in generations of struggle to maintain land, resources, and economic and cultural autonomy. Many sympathetic whites viewed the movement as one to save the spectacular Celilo Falls on the Columbia River. For Indigenous leaders, the struggle was much broader and based in opposition to resettlement of the region itself. White allies grounded their opposition in democratic citizenship and advocated that Indians do the same, citing the recent extension of rights to them under the Indian Citizenship Act, passed in 1924. Indians pointed to alternative models of citizenship by animating tribal nationhood. Nonetheless, Indian leaders and white friends developed sincere alliances during this period and the shared experiences of opposing The Dalles Dam, creating real sites for intercultural cooperation.

Jimmie James's first task was to determine public opinion regarding the dam. Beginning in 1951, James surveyed more than thirteen hundred Oregonians in "man on the street" interviews. Apparently not worried that a leading question would skew the results, he asked, "Do you believe it would be right, to build a dam just below Celilo Falls, that would cover it up, and to the depth of at least 40 feet? And by doing this, break another treaty given in good faith, that is to last forever?"[29] Overwhelmingly, participants voiced objections to the dam. James figured that 70.3 percent said "No," while 18.1 percent claimed that dam construction was too far along to stop.[30] James used these figures as evidence of widespread disapproval of river construction, eventually claiming that "70.3 percent of us all are *fighting this loss*," data that seem dubious but that reflected his optimism and drive.[31]

By 1952, James disseminated his findings in letters written to every organization he could think of that might aid in protecting the Native fisheries on the mid-Columbia. A letter to the Oregon Federation of Women's Clubs was rebuffed by its president, Leona Weatherford, who lived in Arlington along the Columbia River (a city that would be moved in 1963 to accommodate the backwaters of the John Day Dam). Weatherford told James that the plans were simply too far along to be stopped: "because I live in the close proximity of Celilo I happen to be very much aware of the organizations and lobbies that have worked for years toward the completion of this dam, and I do not believe it is possible to stop its construction at this late date."[32] But letters to the Portland Women's Forum met with more success. The forum's president and friend of Martha's, Mary Arnest, was a former state DAR regent and a conservationist.[33] With realtor Gertrude Jensen, also a forum member and conservationist, Arnest had formed a "Save the Columbia Gorge" committee the year before she heard from

James, and placed Jensen as its chair.[34] James's call to save Celilo Falls converged with the group's mission to protect the scenic Columbia River Gorge, at least briefly. Soon James was reporting an organized effort among Oregon's clubwomen: they "are calling each member and telling them to write and work directly with Mrs. Jensen."[35] Jensen spearheaded the effort, activating networks of clubwomen, including Martha. Jensen credited conservationist and state political leader Marshall Dana, who would become Martha's second husband in 1960, as her mentor. In 1952, the three of them participated in a conference organized by the Portland Women's Forum to call attention to preservation of the scenic Columbia Gorge.[36]

Efforts to halt the dam complemented those to protect the Columbia River Gorge, which were then just emerging. As the chairwoman of the Portland Women's Forum "Save the Columbia Gorge" Committee, Jensen negotiated elaborate swaps of privately owned timbered lands in the gorge for more remote and less scenic tracts of state-owned land in other parts of the state. Her work in the Portland Women's Forum garnered the attention of Governor Paul Patterson, who organized the Columbia River Gorge Commission in 1952 and appointed Jensen as its first chairperson, a position she would hold through three governors until 1969. Over the course of her career, Jensen helped preserve more than three thousand acres of the gorge, lands that included Chanticleer Point, now known as the Portland Women's Forum State Scenic Viewpoint.[37] But those efforts were piecemeal and required the cooperation of many state and federal partners, some of whom were quite unsympathetic to conservation. Jensen dreamed of protecting the gorge wholesale by designating it a national park. James's inquiry, and the historical and cultural significance of the Native fishery, gave Jensen and conservationists another rhetorical strategy to add to those that emphasized pristine beauty. After all, not only was Celilo Falls the site of a traditional Native fishery, it was also Oregon's most spectacular waterfall.

James plotted to put Yakama tribal chairman Alex Saluskin in direct touch with Jensen, a meeting that finally took place in Washington, DC. Just months after her appointment to chair the Columbia River Gorge Committee, Jensen took a weeks-long trip to DC and New York to solicit support for a national park in the Columbia River Gorge. As she stepped out of Oregon representative Homer D. Angell's DC office, "I noticed these Indians sitting in the office of the congressman from Washington. I went in and asked them, 'Are you from Celilo?' . . . I told them it was terrible that this dam was going to cover up Celilo Falls and that I wanted to help."[38] Jensen introduced herself to six Yakama tribal leaders, Alex Saluskin, Eagle Seelatse, Wilson Charley, Watson Totus, Dave Eneas, and William Winnier, who were in Washington to participate in Eisenhower's inaugural parade and were waiting to meet with her.

The group traveled to New York City, where Jensen took the men to the Madison Avenue Baptist Church to meet with a Baptist minister with ties to Portland who was then officiating there. The church hosted a reception for the Yakama leaders and "wanted so much to help," a vague commitment despite the warm welcome. Determined to spend more time with the Yakama leaders, Jensen hired "a limousine with a chauffeur to pick them up and bring them to my hotel, and I took them all over New York City on a sight seeing trip."[39] Jensen reported to James that she had "done everything I could and am hopeful of 'Saving Celilo Falls'" as she wrapped up her trip in early February, but she returned to Oregon disillusioned about the prospects of saving the falls.[40] Representative Angell wrote to James, "From what I can learn, and even Mrs. Jensen admits it, too, Celilo Falls cannot be saved. While the money has not been appropriated for the project, it has developed to a point where it is almost certain to go through."[41]

Despite the setback James forged ahead to publicize the trip.[42] He asked Marshall Dana to interview Alex Saluskin on KEX radio out of Toppenish, Washington, but Dana withdrew at the last minute. James suspected that Dana wasn't willing to associate himself publicly with the dam's opposition and alerted others that Dana had "visited Salem in the interest (of the dam being built, I believe). . . . I believe he asked the [Portland Women's] forum to lay off, so I heard." Detecting an erosion of support, James speculated that "perhaps there is a greater undercurrent against us here than was supposed."[43] James tied Jensen's declining interest in opposing the dam to Dana's influence, later also complaining that Dana influenced McKeown's withdrawal from antidam activism.

It is likely that James misunderstood Marshall Dana's opposition to The Dalles Dam and more generally to river development. Like Jensen, Dana sought legislative protections for the scenic Columbia River Gorge. But Dana also advocated for river development and reclamation, having worked on such issues for more than four decades. Moreover, he did not view support for gorge protections as contradicting advocacy for river navigation. As a founding member of the Pacific Northwest Regional Planning Commission in 1934, Dana "shared regionalists' focus on small cities, rural prosperity, and the conservation of natural areas."[44] In his view, navigable rivers and the protection of scenic lands were compatible strands of a strong regional economy. The Celilo Canal, a precursor to The Dalles Dam built in 1915, was, according to Dana, "a monument to and an evidence of one of the finest exhibitions of persistent patriotism and untiring public spirit in the memory of the West."[45] Dana distanced himself from those who opposed construction of The Dalles Dam, yet he maintained an interest in aiding Indians at Celilo Village affected by dam construction. Jensen also distanced herself from James's projects, eventually halting her correspondence with him, perhaps at the insistence of Dana. But fallout with an acquaintance she and the Yakama made while in New York may have also contributed to her reluctance to remain involved.

CHIEF RISING SUN

Despite writing eventually thousands of letters, Jimmie James struggled to turn philosophical opposition to the demise of the falls into real action that could halt the dam. The view that construction was inevitable kept many potential allies from putting much energy into opposing the dam. That tribal opposition was not unified across and between reservations turned others off. James's faith that his letters would make a difference in the face of such realities may explain why he was so quickly drawn to the charismatic and theatrical figure of Chief Rising Sun. The episode with Chief Rising Sun could be understood as a brief diversion from the real work of opposing river development that continued after Sun faded from the scene. But the episode also threatened to undermine non-Native oppositional work entirely. Moreover, once James regained his footing, he reoriented his efforts toward people whose knowledge about river politics was deeply local— Martha McKeown, Tommy and Flora Thompson, and Click Relander, an editor at the *Yakima Valley Herald* in Washington State who, like McKeown, was dedicated to regional Indigenous rights.

Chief Rising Sun met with Gertrude Jensen and the Yakama leaders at the Hotel Houston in New York City on February 2,

1953. The octogenarian flaunted seven-sixteenths Cherokee blood, three chieftainships, and eighteen educational certificates and diplomas. Rising Sun claimed also to be a Baptist minister, psychologist, psychoanalyst, and naturopath and to hold a PhD. But his true gifts were of "the spoken word!" and "healing!"[46] Rising Sun connected with James thanks to his meeting with Jensen.

From New York, Rising Sun quickly took on the cause of saving Celilo Falls as his own, striking up an intense correspondence with both Jensen and James. He offered to fly to the Pacific Northwest to preach a sermon on treaties and then return to Washington, DC, to see President Eisenhower and Vice President Nixon on behalf of the Yakama. James was taken in by the possibility of this help. An audience with the nation's top leaders could turn the tide against the dam, and Rising Sun convinced James that he could secure it. James exclaimed in a letter to Alex Saluskin, "this seems to be the answer to our prayers." He urged the Yakama leader to authorize Rising Sun to speak for the tribe and "give Chief Rising Sun power of attorney."[47] When he wrote to Rising Sun, though, he cautioned that only the tribal leaders could authorize Rising Sun's proposals. He advised Rising Sun to be patient and then concluded, "I enjoyed your letters, and admire your accomplishments, and attitude towards your people, and I can assure you there are many others like my self who are trying to help and believe in you."[48] Rising Sun followed up by asking that James and Saluskin endorse him for a position at the Interior Department of his own making, "Commissioner of Indian Spiritual Welfare and Public Relations." With apparent scant understanding of the internal workings of federal agencies, James thought the appointment a good idea and told Saluskin that "it could hurt nothing and then we would have someone back there who would be conscientious and could help a lot."[49] James was taken in by Rising Sun's energetic promises, but Saluskin and other Yakama leaders proceeded with caution.

James pushed on and within in a few weeks further legitimized Rising Sun by asking that Oregon's senator Wayne Morse notify Rising Sun of any senate appropriations committee hearings on The Dalles Dam.[50] As a result, Rising Sun testified at a hearing in May. *Life* magazine devoted a full-page spread to his appearance. An accompanying picture showed Rising Sun angrily animated in his testimony, his finger pointed at listeners.[51] In another photograph Rising Sun danced on the grounds of the capitol building. In both, he wore what one critic would later describe as "garb approaching regalia."[52]

His performance further alienated Yakama leaders, who were also present at the hearings. Two weeks later a devastated Rising Sun wrote to James, "Chief Alex Saluskin denies me as Peter denied Jesus Christ."[53] Saluskin and other Yakama leaders characterized Rising Sun as an outsider who offered his services, which were declined well before the May hearing. National press coverage of his testimony led the *Oregonian*'s Wallace Turner to dig into Chief Rising Sun's past, calling him an "old acquaintance" to the paper's readers. Turner exposed Rising Sun as the same man who went by the name Alzamon Ira Lucas in Portland in the 1910s, where he practiced a variety of "healing arts" until drummed out of the city in 1919 by bad publicity.[54] At that time the press reported that Lucas was an African American passing as a white man.[55] The charges were noteworthy in a state where until 1926 the constitution included language that excluded African American citizens from residing within its borders.

On July 22, 1953, a syndicated columnist wrote a damning rebuke of Rising Sun's testimony based on the *Oregonian* coverage that portrayed politicians as fools for granting an audience to

Picture of 'Chief' in Magazine Spread
Recalls 'Healer's' Career in Portland

The *Oregonian* reprinted this photograph of Chief Rising Sun speaking before a Congressional subcommittee in 1953. Courtesy of Barcroft Media

a faux Indian. Dozens of papers across the nation published variations of the article, which noted that the Yakama did not sanction Rising Sun's performance. Instead of the Native spiritual and political leader he claimed to be, Rising Sun was just "an over decorated, negro ex-bellhop" who dazzled naive congressional leaders with an "indian [sic] costume."[56]

Rising Sun repeatedly contacted James and Jensen, promising to travel to Portland to publicly defend himself and "clean up this mess." Both urged him to remain back east, and when Rising Sun did finally make it to Portland in the winter of 1954, neither saw him. By that point, James declared that the cause did not need "glamor, we need friends we can work with I believe."[57] The widespread negative publicity hurt non-Native opposition to the dam in Oregon and elsewhere. Jensen distanced herself from Rising Sun and pulled away from her energetic organizing to protect Celilo. Far worse was the possible split between the Yakama, who had not granted Rising Sun authority to speak for them, and James, who had urged Yakama leaders to cooperate with Rising Sun. Rising Sun didn't just mock Indian culture and steal the spotlight, he attempted to usurp the authority of the region's actual Indian leaders, aided by James. The entire event cracked open the fissures that were always present but mostly submerged in the coalition to oppose the dam, called into question the authenticity of claims on authority, and exposed the racial politics of the period.

The loss of two seemingly important allies in the battle against The Dalles Dam must have been hard for James, but the experience with Chief Rising Sun clarified his views on how best to aid the region's Native peoples. From that point forward, James placed authority squarely in the hands of Native leaders, either elected or hereditary, and recommended that other allies do the same. Moreover, James oriented himself toward a clubwoman who was much more knowledgeable about River Indians and their histories, Martha McKeown.

"THEY SHOULDN'T BE OBJECTS OF CHARITY"

While Jimmie James was wrapped up in the drama created by Chief Rising Sun, Martha McKeown was caring for some of her elderly Native friends and tracking down the sale of Indian fee patent land that she worried was fraudulent. This was the kind of direct local aid that James could not provide from his home office in Portland, and it led to an investigation into sales of Indian land in the Hood River Valley and the Warm Springs Reservation. Unlike James, who would work with the elected tribal chairs of the Yakama Nation and the Confederated Tribes of the Warm Springs Reservation, Martha came to the aid of individual Indians with whom she shared a friendship. Yet more so than James, Martha identified the problems that Indian people faced within a broad context of federal-Indian relations. Although she participated in and helped organize acts of generosity to the impoverished Indians she knew, she regarded charity as insufficient to correct government-perpetuated injustices in Native communities and used her time and publications to call for better federal policies.

Yakama enrollee James Slim Jim told Martha and their mutual friend Arline Moore that he sold the timber on his 80-acre fee patent land in the Hood River Valley for $1,000. The women were shocked at the price and concerned that the elderly Slim Jim, who didn't write or read English, may have been ripped off. They looked up the exchange in the Hood River Courthouse records, where the paperwork raised some red flags, and got an estimated value of the land's timber from the county assessor's office. The land was valued for tax purposes at $2,000, but a timber buyer thought the lumber, some 770,000 board feet, was worth at least $6,000 and maybe as much as $9,000.[58]

Martha contacted the *Oregonian*'s Wallace Turner (the same journalist who exposed Chief Rising Sun) and complained to Senator Wayne Morse, who called for an investigation of the Portland Area Office of the Bureau of Indian Affairs, which facilitated the sale.[59] Martha and Moore secured the services of a lawyer who sued the buyers to cancel the sale. It turned out the same two men

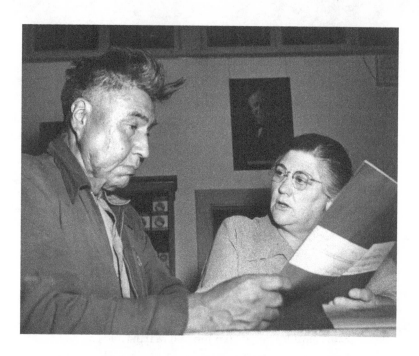

Arline Moore and James Slim Jim in a photograph taken by Archie McKeown, 1954. Courtesy of the History Museum of Hood River County

had purchased other plots of Indian-owned timber, including 160 acres on the Warm Springs Reservation. Turner's reporting and pressure from Congress revealed a series of fraudulent sales beginning in 1950 that all originated within the Swan Island offices of the BIA, Portland Area Office.[60] Clyde Flinn, land officer for the BIA, identified timber allotments that his partners would then purchase, often for a song, from their Indian owners, many of whom, like Slim Jim, did not realize the value of their holdings.

The 160 acres on the Warm Springs Reservation was under private ownership and appeared to be coming on the market. The tribal council and Superintendent Elliott notified the area office that they were interested in purchasing the land. Flinn's role as

BIA land officer would have been to manage the sale to the tribe, but instead he lied to Superintendent Jasper Elliott, telling him the land was not for sale. He proceeded to facilitate the purchase of the land by the Warm Springs Lumber Company, a reservation-based mill that was privately, not tribally, owned.[61]

E. Morgan Pryse, the director of the Portland Area Office, suspended and eventually fired Flinn and his assistant, who later received prison sentences and fines for their roles in the conspiracy. Slim Jim's suit was settled in his favor in an out-of-court settlement because the provenance of the land patent was unclear.[62] The lawyers that McKeown and Moore hired appointed Moore as James Slim Jim's guardian, and she arranged for a public auction to sell his timber. When it was held on the Hood River Courthouse steps, the auction brought Slim Jim nearly $19,000, well over even the highest previous estimates of its worth.[63]

Clyde Flinn, the land officer at the Portland Area BIA office who orchestrated the land fraud, was potentially much more dangerous to Columbia River Indians than someone like Chief Rising Sun, whose antics were often absurd. Together, though, they suggest a spectrum of threats that River Indians faced and that friends like McKeown and James could intervene in, ranging from charlatans and thieves to federal policies that usurped Native-owned resources and left Indians vulnerable. The land case also indicates the importance of and problems with federal wardship. The elder fraud, which was common in many communities, was compounded by Slim Jim's inability to read English. Slim Jim was a highly competent fisher well versed in the Indigenous politics of the mid–Columbia River, but like many people, he had little experience with American legal language or land patents. Moreover, because he would likely only cut the timber on his allotment once during his lifetime, leaving future harvests to subsequent heirs, he probably could not estimate what the timber was worth on the open market. Men and women like Slim Jim—elderly, illiterate, and impoverished—were easy targets of fraud, made worse by the machinations of the abuse within a paternalistic system that was meant to protect them.

McKeown had a complicated response to federal wardship of the Indian people she knew. She argued that the federal government should provide assistance to elderly Indians so that they would not have to rely on private charity, writing, "They shouldn't be objects of charity. Those people deserve care from special funds."[64] In a letter to the editor published in the *Oregonian,* Martha noted the displacement of Indians "who lost their homes and food" with the construction of Bonneville Dam, including Slim Jim's sister, Alice Slim Jim Charley. "Wouldn't it seem logical," she asked, "to make some provisions for these Indians before proceeding with the construction of The Dalles Dam that will displace more of them?" She added that the Swan Island BIA employees "when one does travel the necessary miles to visit that spot . . . appear to be comfortable and well housed—and the offices seem to be more than adequately staffed."[65] Like Indian advocates before her, Martha indicted the federal agency for misdirecting funds that should have gone to Indians.

McKeown faced the limits of federal wardship in this instance and others, when federal employees defrauded Native people or when they intervened in Native lives in ways that denied individuals agency and disregarded their needs. For example, when Chief Thompson professed at a meeting with federal agents that the "Celilo Fish Committee was organized to carry out the wishes of the white men and to abolish the rights of the Celilo chief," McKeown introduced documents that she claimed limited the power of the CFC.[66] At the same time, McKeown herself intervened in those same lives by arranging medical care, providing transportation, halting land sales that she felt were unfair, and raising funds and collecting goods through private donation to be distributed at the village—providing the very charity she felt they shouldn't be made to rely on. Intervention, even when offered as help, exposed the tricky balance between neighborly assistance and paternalism, both bureaucratic and intimate.

Striking that balance became necessarily personal when Martha helped elderly Indians find long-term care. Martha arranged for James Slim Jim's sister, Alice Slim Jim Charley, with whom she was close, to stay at Hanby Nursing Home in Hood River. Martha would also make arrangements for Chief Thompson to stay at Hanby periodically when he was ill and it was hard for Flora to care for him. He spent the last two years of his life living at Hanby, eventually treating the lobby as a longhouse. Martha complained that she and Archie saw "so much poverty."[67] She wrote, "Old Alice is cared for and comfortable and so is Chief Thompson. We see them often and provide little extras for them. But they wouldn't be at Hanby's if a friend hadn't moved in on the situation."[68] Flora at times asked Martha to bring Thompson back to their home at Celilo Village, but Martha refused, arguing that Flora wasn't well enough to nurse Thompson and that he was well cared for at the professional facility. But the carless Flora had to rely on friends to drive her to visit Thompson and worried that he wasn't getting the traditional foods that would heal him.

Chief Thompson spent much of 1953 fighting pneumonia or recovering from surgery. He was growing increasingly feeble as he neared what many thought to be his one-hundredth year. Nonetheless, in February, using a dollar that a Portlander had sent him to fill their gas tank, he caught a ride with friends to visit Martha at her home as she recovered from flu, telling her he had "missed his friend."[69] The visit may have brought on Thompson's next bout of illness, as later that month Martha reported that Thompson was too sick to join her in a presentation she was to make at a women's club meeting in Arlington.[70] By April, Thompson was still not well, and during the First Salmon Ceremony, Flora welcomed guests and spoke in his stead.

The ceremony that year represented the persistence of the Native river community in the face of tremendous, disquieting change. Construction at the dam site, which had begun a year earlier, was plainly visible by that April. Moreover, the widening of Oregon Highway 30 changed the layout of the community by necessitating the removal of some Celilo Village households, including the Thompsons, to new homes on the south side of the highway, interrupting their pathways to the Columbia.[71] The BIA's Clyde Flinn, the same employee eventually convicted of land fraud, oversaw the process. That Thompson had difficulty standing at the ceremony must have portended an unsettling future for the Indians who gathered to welcome the salmon runs back to the river. In the press coverage of the ceremony from the previous year, a reporter announced that Chief Thompson's only concession to his considerable age was "partial deafness."[72] But by 1953, the chief's health mirrored the changes on the river, and the end of an era seemed close at hand.[73] In the midst of that, Flora Thompson and the ceremony itself ensured that persistence and tradition would sit beside transformation.

Perhaps Jimmie James felt the changes that were visible to participants in the First Salmon Ceremony. In April, the same month in which the ceremony always took place, James wrote a pleading and desperate letter to Alex Saluskin. "This is a hard letter to write, because I have felt for some time something was wrong up there—It has come to me several weeks ago at night, that things were not going well with your people," wrote James. Despite the foreshadowing of trouble, James assured Saluskin that "today there are over 300 thousand men sitting for most every city in the United States shaping resolutions asking that the Government stop construction at The Dalles and restore the treaty to you." James then turned to a packet of seven letters of protest that he arranged to be delivered directly to President Eisenhower, an act that would "be a hollow gesture if I thought you and your people had changed your thoughts." James pleaded with Saluskin to "realize by this time that the Indian People are backed by several million white people, the Legion and Vets alone represent several million alone let alone churches and individuals and organizations."[74]

These hundreds of thousands of supporters who grew to millions in the course of a paragraph were supposedly rallied to the cause by James's copious and strategically directed letters over the last several years. The inefficacy of James's assistance was made plain in his very argument, which was meant to sustain Saluskin and other Yakama as they considered finalizing negotiations on a monetary settlement for their fishing stations. The number of supporters was too vague and their support not explicit enough to make a difference in the construction of the dam. Seven letters, no matter how persuasive, would not interrupt the progress made on the river's redevelopment. The plan to deliver the letters, through the use of a distant relative of the president's who lived in Portland and would hand them off to Mamie Eisenhower, was as naive as the thought that they would stop the large federal project.

Unlike his appointed press agent, Alex Saluskin had spent decades protesting the incursion of Washington and Oregon states into Indigenous fishing rights. It was within the context of the Celilo Fish Committee, of which he was a Yakama representative, and the decades-long work of the Yakama and other Columbia River tribes to maintain their treaty-protected rights to fish, that Saluskin opposed The Dalles Dam. His protests of the dam were deeply personal—Saluskin was a fisherman whose very ability to fish the falls was in peril—but much of what was recorded in the historic record he did on behalf of the Yakama Nation, as one of the nation's elected leaders, not for himself individually.

Saluskin spoke before the very first meetings having to do with the dam at The Dalles, held in 1946.[75] The Yakama and other Columbia River tribes had been through this process before with the Army Corps of Engineers' development of Bonneville Dam. In 1935 the Yakama entered into an agreement for compensation for fishing stations lost because of that earlier dam. Because the tribes understood how every dam slated for construction on the Columbia River was a threat to the Indigenous fisheries, Saluskin and other Yakama later sued to stop construction of McNary Dam.[76] They were unsuccessful. Saluskin spent several days testifying before a congressional subcommittee in Washington, DC, in 1951 and again in 1953. In 1953 Saluskin was as busy as ever. As Yakama tribal chairman, he penned a thirty-seven-page denouncement of the damming of Celilo Falls. In that same year he was a founding member of the Affiliated Tribes of Northwest Indians (ATNI), whose membership included tribes in Washington, Oregon, Idaho, and Montana.[77] In form and function, the intertribal organization mirrored the organization that James himself conceived and promoted, with one important difference: with bylaws, formal agreements with tribal councils, and regular meetings, Native leaders brought ATNI into existence.

When James lamented to Saluskin, "things are not going well with your people," he did not understand how right he was. But not in the way he suspected. Federal dams were one critical threat the region's tribes faced. But they were one threat among many. The ATNI focused on the unfair taxation of Indian people and on termination policy.[78] Saluskin saw fishing and hunting rights within a broader cultural context as well and sought to record the four Yakama dialects he spoke in a dictionary and curriculum for Yakama children. Saluskin and the Yakama did not easily relinquish the battle against the building of The Dalles Dam. As Yakama tribal council member Kiutus Jim exclaimed, "We fought it to the last ditch." Tribal leaders did not give up when they signed agreements for monetary settlements to compensate for the loss of their fishing stations. It's more instructive to think of them as pivoting within a larger struggle, within a context well beyond what James and other whites could see. If friends saw Celilo Falls as a few years' fight characterized by appeals to a handful of congressmen, the region's Indians saw the whole river basin, generations of conflict brought on by settlement and forced assimilation, and a political system meant to erase their very existence.

SIX

New Narratives in an Ancient Land

... look at the engineers. Covered up their Celilo fishing grounds, the biggest fishing industry. And not only that, the biggest scenery along the Columbia Gorge. We have so many people, even today they come over and visit me and have sympathy with me. Why did they have to build this dam? They could have built it further up. They had enough dam down here at Bonneville, one up there at McNary. Why did they have to build this one?

FLORA CUSHINWAY THOMPSON

ONCE THE WARM SPRINGS, UMATILLA, AND YAKAMA SIGNED agreements with the US Army Corps of Engineers, obstacles to the construction of the dam cleared and the inundation of Celilo and the mid–Columbia River became inevitable. In many ways, life went on as communities along the river warily watched the progress of construction and waited for the dam closure to permanently reshape the river. Celilo Village was awash with change because a portion of it would be inundated by the dam's reservoir. Residents kept busy in meetings to organize the village's relocation, echoing the period a few years prior when families moved to accommodate the highway expansion. The Thompsons also met with engineers to discuss their own monetary compensation for the fishing stations they would lose. Some village residents, including Tommy Thompson, weren't enrolled with the area reservations and therefore did not fall under the agreements negotiated by tribal committees. Instead, these residents secured the help of a local lawyer and worked out compensation on an individual basis.[1] Flora and Martha, who would both be widows by the end of the 1950s, experienced this period as one of intense personal loss.

PATHS TOWARD RESISTANCE

Chief Tommy Thompson's birthdays were often big celebrations, but in the run-up to the completion of The Dalles Dam, they also offered an opportunity to shine light on conditions at Celilo Village. Although Thompson's exact date of birth was not recorded, Celilo residents often threw a party near the end of December to coincide with the start of the Christmas season and the raising of a tree in the longhouse. In 1955, Thompson's 102nd birthday was celebrated in stunning fashion with a formal dinner at the community longhouse. Martha McKeown baked a chocolate cake, a tradition she had kept for several years. This time it needed to be large enough to hold more than one hundred candles. Flora's son, Max Boise, alerted Jimmie James about the upcoming party with a plea to "notify your friends as well as in Washington D.C."[2]

James threw himself into the task, writing thirty-three letters in ninety minutes, including notes to President Eisenhower and

US senator Richard Neuberger from Oregon.[3] James collected letters of congratulations for the chief, which he hoped would bring "joy to the old fellow's heart" and "keep the Indian name before the public."[4] Senator Neuberger sent a message by Western Union telegram, as did the president.[5] Clarence Adams of the Indiana Council for the Appreciation of Poetry wrote a poem for the occasion, which read, in part, "You met earth's joy and strife / with zest to win the right to live among your own in peace."[6] At the dinner, Archie McKeown snapped a photograph of Chief Thompson surrounded by Flora's granddaughter Linda and Martha, who lit the candles on the cake before him. The photograph appeared in press coverage of the party, and Martha McKeown used it as her author's photo on the back of her first book about Celilo Village, *Linda's Indian Home.* James's efforts were worth it. Martha professed that the best part of the party was "the card from THE PRESIDENT" that James had arranged.[7]

Newspaper coverage of Chief Thompson's birthdays in the early 1950s highlighted his occupation in two worlds: one dedicated to carrying forward traditional Indigenous practices, another embedded in the modern manifestations of settler culture. In the coverage his 1954 birthday, much was made of Thompson's use of "Indian" and English. With encouragement from McKeown, the chief recounted Sahaptin words for "one hundred" and "years" but then also shot a "cheese" at the newspaper's photograph "to prove he also knows paleface slang."[8] The article concluded by drawing parallels between the aging leader and what seemed to be the inevitable demise of the wild Columbia River, a comparison that was typical at this point. Such depictions echoed the trope of the "Vanishing Indian" and turned the advanced years of a single person into a parable of a people destined to disappear before the onslaught of American modernization. Flora Thompson tirelessly countered that comparison in the years to come by emphasizing Thompson's refusal to "signature away his salmon" in the fight against the dam.

For his part, Jimmie James, refusing to believe that the fight for Celilo Falls was over, engaged in correspondence with Click Relander, Wilson Charley, and Alex Saluskin about the future of tribal resistance in the region. Relander and James pushed the Indian leaders to engage in electoral politics. They generally agreed that Indians of the Northwest would do well to elect representatives friendly to and knowledgeable about local Native issues. Relander also advocated homegrown politicians: "they must start bringing up some men of their own for state offices—legislators— because unless they do this, they will be unrepresented in the future."[9] Both James and Relander were clear about how tribal leaders like Saluskin needed to guide their people: interview candidates, vote as a bloc, elect sympathetic officials, change policy. Relander pointed out, "They have plenty of votes and it is time they were using them." He had offered "to get stickers printed up for windshields, showing that the car driver has registered and the way the cars get around, it would certainly set the politicians to thinking." But, he grumbled, "they don't seem to want to do that."[10] Relander worried that Indians were their own worst enemies, too consumed with tribal politics and infighting to recognize the true power they had in local and federal elections.

While inspired by a deep sympathy for Native people and their rights, the strategies James and Relander proposed were often naive. Moreover, their emphasis on off-reservation politics ignored the importance of self-governance through tribal politics, an area of tremendous power and influence, for those enrolled in federally recognized tribes, to shape their immediate lives. The two men argued for strategies that hinged on their own experiences of citizenship and voting as white-identified, middle-class men. Those experiences were often at odds with the rights and obligations of citizenship conferred to Indians in the Pacific Northwest. They also ignored the complicated ways in which Congress had granted Native people citizenship rights (some thirty years before in 1924) and how many states, including Washington, had denied voting rights to Native people through World War II.

Oregon became a state in 1859, the same year that Congress ratified the treaties derived at the Walla Walla Treaty Council. Yet Indians within Oregon's borders were neither citizens of the state nor citizens of the United States. Many state and federal leaders saw Native people as belonging to separate, if internal and dependent, nations. The reservations established in 1855 represented "foreign cultural space," although they were located within the nation's states.[11] Reservations, which policy makers originally envisioned as incubators for citizenship, were the homelands of Indigenous nonnationals who could only become American citizens through a process of assimilation by which they eventually left the reservations.

But assimilation did not necessarily mean one would become a citizen. William McKay—grandson of Hudson's Bay Company chief factor of the Columbia District John McLoughlin, who faced his own citizenship issues in early Oregon—found this out just twenty-five years after Congress ratified the treaties. McKay, who was of Scottish and Chinook descent, sued to register to vote, arguing that he had abandoned tribal affiliations to live as a white man. The US District Court of Oregon "ruled that because of his Indian blood, he had not been born subject to the jurisdictions of the United States; therefore, he had not met the qualifications demanded by the Fourteenth Amendment and was not a citizen."[12] When the Supreme Court weighed the argument in 1884, it decided that the Fourteenth Amendment did not apply to Indians, who could be granted citizenship only through an act of Congress.[13] When Congress passed the Dawes Allotment Act three years later, they created a pathway, albeit a problematic one, to citizenship for Indian people.

Allotment was meant to break communally owned tribal landholdings into individually owned private property, after which remaining reservation lands were placed on the public market. In addition, working the land for twenty-five years, applying for the fee patent, and beginning to pay property taxes opened the way to citizenship. The act was grounded in an assumption of gradual assimilation culminating in national citizenship. Together, landownership and citizenship would "civilize" tribal people. By 1905, about half of all Indians in the United States were citizens.[14] Because it accompanied Dawes-era land allotment, Native citizenship was predicated on ownership of real estate. The connection was unique: no other group was required to own property to "prove up" citizenship in the United States (white male suffrage did not require property ownership after 1856).[15]

In fact, for the second largest nonwhite group in the Columbia Gorge, the inverse was true. Oregon passed legislation that prohibited Japanese immigrants from owning land *because* they could not become naturalized US citizens.[16] In 1924 Congress passed the Snyder or Indian Citizenship Act, which conferred citizenship to all Indian people born in the United States. Naturalization would not become an option for American Indians born outside the United States until 1940, although thousands of Indians became naturalized citizens before 1900 simply by leaving their reservations.[17] Congress opened naturalization to Japanese immigrants in 1952. Race, nationality, and citizenship played out along the banks of the Columbia River in a mix that was deeply exclusionary. As a result, active use of the franchise was not the universally accessible strategy that James and Relander assumed.

Even with citizenship, "Native Americans were not allowed to vote in city, county, state, or federal elections; testify in courts; serve on juries; attend public schools; or even purchase a beer, for it was illegal to sell alcohol to Indians."[18] In 1910, the Washington state legislature passed a law declaring, "Indians not taxed shall never be allowed the elective franchise," language that was not amended until the 1970s.[19] In 1936 the state's attorney general issued a statement in support of Indian voting, citing the Fifteenth Amendment and the 1924 Indian Citizenship Act, but it's not clear what difference it made for individual voters.[20] In 1938, seven states, including Washington, did not permit Indians to vote. Historian Willard Rollings points out that with the implementation of the franchise firmly in the hands of states until the passage of the 1965 Voting Rights Act, "western states were successful in their efforts to prevent Indians from voting" by "using poll taxes, literacy tests, English language tests, and refusing to place polling places in or near Indian communities."[21] Oregon, for example, passed a literacy test in 1924, the very year that Indians were granted citizenship.[22] Whether the franchise extended to all Indian adults in the nation was not fully resolved in the courts until 1974.[23] Decisions issued by the courts, however, still required meaningful implementation by local governments.

Click Relander and Jimmie James used the pen and their unchallenged right to vote to affect state and federal policy, even if marginally. Because they were advocates of Indian rights, they were active civic participants, likely more so than many of their neighbors. But in urging Indian leaders to use the off-reservation vote, they missed how intensely active their Indigenous friends and acquaintances were in the political process each and every day. Self-governance was at the heart of political activity for the region's Indians, and the struggles to maintain Indigenous control over the fisheries through imperfect mechanisms like the Celilo Fish Committee are a key example.[24] Because state and federal agencies were the locus of colonial domination, Indians viewed them with suspicion. They were not so much invested in being included in colonizing governmental structures as they were in protecting themselves from those structures.

Moreover, while voting would become an increasingly important tool among Indian activists as they forced the franchise open after World War II, Indians had a much more powerful weapon than the individual vote available to them. Directly lobbying politicians and the public was a well-practiced, successful strategy with a deep history in Indian-white relations. From the delegation of Northwest Indians who journeyed to Saint Louis to meet with William Clark in 1831 to Sarah Winnemucca, Toby Riddle, and Chief Joseph, whose rounds on the lecture circuit and in popular publications roused the interest of sympathetic whites after the so-called Indians wars at the close of the nineteenth century, direct and often personal contact was a proven effective mode of shaping policy and public opinion.[25] In meetings with BIA and other federal officials, in the offices of their senators and congressional representatives, Indian leaders had access to federal and state leaders well outside the experiences of James and even Relander, the newspaper editor. In public appearances before women's clubs and community organizations and in performances in rodeos and theatrical pageants, the region's Indians lobbied directly to the general public.

Direct lobbying was a powerful tool. Washington senator Warren G. Magnuson recognized this when he said that the state's Native people were "an effective voice in legislation which concerns them" who "make their needs known by writing and paying calls *in person*, even to come to the Nation's capitol."[26] Tommy Thompson understood this when he traveled to Salem and kept up a strenuous schedule of meetings with agency representatives in The Dalles and Celilo Village. Alex Saluskin understood this when the Yakama Nation repeatedly approved funds to send their leaders to address congressional subcommittees in Washington, DC. And Flora Thompson understood this as she traveled the state, accompanying her husband and Martha McKeown, outfitted in regalia, to translate for Thompson and speak before audiences of influential clubwomen.

Despite direct lobbying's ability to influence policy makers, it is difficult to measure its impact—which might not be immediate. McKeown and the Thompsons were ultimately not successful in stopping the expansion of Highway 30, and the Bureau of Indian Affairs persisted in their demands that Indians relinquish the homes in its path. Indians balked at moving and staved off the transition but could only do so temporarily. The Thompsons' efforts were likely more successful in the area of public relations. Certainly, they shaped the views non-Native Oregonians had about Indians. Audiences were interested in hearing from and seeing Native people, as evidenced in the many presentations the Thompsons gave. These performances of Indianness often placed the Thompsons in the role of racial informant, but they also prompted sympathy and understanding in audience members. Civically minded northwesterners were interested in providing material, if not direct political, assistance to their Indian neighbors, which was apparent through the works of the Oregon state DAR, among other organizations.

"THE D.A.R.S HERE IN OREGON
ARE DOING A GREAT DEAL"

Martha wrote to Jimmie James that "the D.A.R.s here in Oregon are doing a great deal for Celilo and Chemawa."[27] Oregon chapters of the DAR continued the charity work they had started in the 1930s with Chemawa Indian School near Salem, Oregon, and Celilo Village. Canned food drives, the collection of clothing, and gifts at Christmastime were regular offerings. Chapters also invited Native musicians and dancers to entertain them at their meetings. For example, the regent of Portland's Wahkeena chapter brought Chemawa students Irma Peplon and Lonnie Racehorse as well as others from the school's choir to perform a holiday program in December 1954, after which the singers were "treated to candy and ice cream."[28] "The D.A.R.s sent up a car and trailer loaded with food and clothing [to Celilo] at Christmas. We had over fifty warm coats but we could have still used more for the larger women," she reported to James. "The D.A.R.s did buy three huge turkeys and about a hundred dollars['] worth of other food stuffs for the Christmas dinner. But there are always so many needs at the village that we never seem to have enough for the Indians who gather at Chief Thompson's longhouse."[29] Eventually Jimmie James would likewise organize truckloads of food and household goods to be delivered to Celilo Village, and to the Warm Springs and Yakama Reservations.

Members of the state DAR chapter took their most political action regarding The Dalles Dam at their annual meeting in 1955, when they passed a resolution calling for monetary compensation for nonenrolled Celilo residents for damage to their fishing sites associated with the project. The resolution supported a restitution bill that Senator Wayne Morse submitted to Congress the previous month. Although extant documents do not point to a direct connection between McKeown and the resolution, it carries her imprint. Reflecting the grievances she raised elsewhere, the resolution insisted that the Wyam be dealt with as a legitimate tribe, similar to other federally recognized tribes in the region, in addition to asking that they be compensated. The resolution read in part,

> WHEREAS, The resident Indians have received no payment of damages nor has any provision been made for housing, rehabilitation, care of the aged, education of the children, or any way left open for future subsistence or livelihood expect to become objects of charity, and,
>
> WHEREAS, The resident Indians are the descendants of Army Scouts, who served as guides and friends to the early settlers and were never moved from their long abiding places to any reservation,
>
> BE IT RESOLVED: That the Oregon State Society of the National Society, Daughters of the American Revolution, hereby deplore this grave wrong against a helpless, loyal people, and call upon the Congress of the United States to make prompt and substantial amends for this act of rank and unjust discrimination against the Indians whose homes are in the Columbia Gorge . . . [30]

Given the mission of the organization, it's not surprising that the state DAR highlighted the connection residents had to the nineteenth-century US Army and in the settlement of Oregon State. Even though Celilo Village residents shared a history of both resistance and aid to American settlers, it was politic to describe them as allies. The state society of the DAR sent the resolution to their US senators and congressional representatives and to Secretary of the Interior and former Oregon governor Douglas McKay.

After passage of the resolution, the Willamette and Multnomah DAR chapters, both of which were located in Portland, continued to follow the unfolding events at Celilo. At the end of 1955, the two chapters held a joint meeting to view a twenty-minute film of the purported "last salmon feast" at Celilo produced by the Oregon Historical Society, featuring Martha McKeown, a society board member. The film began with the society's young director, Thomas Vaughan, speaking with McKeown, who wore a strand of wampum and clutched a flat twined bag in front of the roaring falls. Most of the film, however, took place within the longhouse and depicted the day's feasting and dancing. McKeown secured permission for the society to film a religious ceremony that was seldom documented in visual media.[31] She described her contribution: "I was much involved that day in our attempt to get some interior pictures of the longhouse" where the ceremony took place.[32] The Oregon Historical Society organized many public showings of the short film, having, according to McKeown, "shown the film to a number of school and civic groups."[33]

Martha McKeown and Marshall Dana attended the chapters' next meeting, in January 1956, as representatives of the Oregon Historical Society's "Indian Committee."[34] Dana spoke on the resettlement process of about thirty Celilo families brought on by the flooding that would accompany the completion of the dam, information he gathered as a member of a community board charged with overseeing relocation (although he rarely was present at the meetings). At the end of the year, Portland's Wahkeena chapter of the DAR brought in Don Foster, the director of the BIA's Portland Area Office, to speak on issues facing the region's Indians. The chair of the chapter's American Indian Committee organized these programs and prepared annual reports that documented the activities of their chapter related to Native Americans. Gladys Struck, who hired Chief Thompson and other Celilo residents to pick fruit at her family's orchard, was the chairwoman of the Native American committee at Hood River's Wauna chapter, where McKeown was a member. Struck documented her correspondence related to the village and sent copies to both McKeown and Dana.[35] Despite the 1955 resolution, the state DAR limited its activities to monitoring the effects of dam building rather than intervening in them.

As tribes settled for compensation for the fishing sites the dam would inundate, vigorous vocal opposition to the project petered out. Jimmie James continued a less-intense correspondence about the dam yet still wrote letters every week to Wilson Charley and others. Gertrude Jensen turned her energies to protection of the Columbia River Gorge, chairing the Oregon Columbia River Gorge Commission, which the state legislature established in 1952. Tribal leaders and those at Celilo continued their fishing battles unabated, determined to enact their treaty rights long after the dam was completed.

"YOU WRITE, I THUMBPRINT"

The pattern that McKeown and the Thompsons developed of shared speaking engagements continued and was strengthened in the mid-1950s when Martha published a children's book that took place at Celilo Village and featured Flora Thompson's granddaughter Linda Meanus. According to McKeown's count, fifteen hundred children turned out for a reception for *Linda's Indian Home* at Portland's Multnomah Library that included a presentation by McKeown and attendance by Linda and her grandmother

Martha McKeown and Flora Thompson listen to Tommy Thompson in a photo taken by Archie McKeown in the McKeowns' Hood River Valley home. Special Collections and Archives, Eric V. Hauser Memorial Library, Reed College

Flora, Chief Thompson's daughter Ida Thompson Wynookie, and Leroy George, who appeared in the book.[36] They dressed in regalia and entertained the children and their parents with drumming and dancing. The *Oregonian* published a brief editorial that praised the book as "mighty instructive,"[37] and the DAR sold the book at a benefit for Celilo Village.[38]

By the mid-1950s, Martha McKeown was a celebrated author of pioneer tales. Her three previous books, based on the recollections of her maternal uncle Mont Hawthorne, "saw a lot, took nothing from anybody, and [had] a flair for remembrance in detail in keeping with his methodical mind," according to one reviewer.[39] The first in the trilogy was *The Trail Led North* (1949), which recounted

Hawthorne's trek to the Klondike goldfields in 1898. The second, *Them Was the Days* (1950), preceded the first volume chronologically to follow the Hawthorne family's migration from Pennsylvania to Oregon in the 1870s. Another reviewer described Martha's prose as having "the same quality of authenticity that is in the speech of such writers as Willa Cather, James Boyd, and recently of A.B. Guthrie."[40] In 1951 *Alaska Silver* rounded out the series by examining the period between 1899 and 1906 when Hawthorne developed the modern salmon industry along the Washington Coast and Alaska's Cook Inlet. Reviews in regional scholarly journals made much of the books' authenticity and faithfulness to Hawthorne's vernacular, denying McKeown's authorial interventions. Archived manuscript pages from the works demonstrate her organizational hand as well as the degree to which McKeown made her narrator increasingly colloquial over several drafts.

Macmillan publicized the books heavily in local newspapers and organized book signings and lecture tours in California and the Pacific Northwest. The first book, *The Trail Led North*, sold unexpectedly well, "the fastest selling book we have had in years," exclaimed a Macmillan manager who arranged to have the fourth printing air-freighted to the Pacific Northwest in mid-December for holiday sales.[41] The *Oregonian* published an illustrated spread on the author and her uncle written by *New York Times* journalist and eventual US senator Richard Neuberger, and published a notice for each new book in the series as McKeown sold the manuscripts.[42] Libraries from Illinois to Alaska featured McKeown's books in their newspapers' "library corners."[43] The books were even featured in a Portland department store's "salute to Oregon products," alongside Pendleton blankets.[44] A year after the publication of the final book, Mont Hawthorne, McKeown's uncle, neighbor, and muse, died. Calling him "a rugged character, physically, mentally and morally," an *Oregonian* editorial mourned the man who was "an inspiration for years to come to a less hardy generation."[45]

But Martha also wanted to write about Celilo Village and the Thompsons. She complained that when she approached her editor about it, she "found the reaction discouraging." Her editor "wishes I'd forget the Indian situation because Indian books, telling their side of the story, aren't very popular."[46] She grumbled, "Indian books have been hard to sell. My McMillian editor said most people don't want to hear about the way they had been treated."[47] Despite being unable to attract a press with national reach to the project, McKeown pushed ahead. She eventually published two children's books with the region's largest publisher, Portland's Binford and Mort, whose catalog promoted regional history and literature. McKeown was pleased with the regional press, writing that "naturally they have to make enough money on books to run a business but they feel deeply about Chief Thompson and his people."[48] Binford and Mort publicized the book and donated copies at wholesale rate for the DAR benefit.[49] The entire experience may have driven home for McKeown the value of working with a local press for such an important regional message. Collectively, McKeown's books strongly suggest that there could be no pioneers, whose adventures appealed to a national audience, without Indians, whose stories unfortunately reached a far smaller, regional audience.

Unlike her earlier historical works, the two books Martha wrote about Celilo Village have a contemporary focus. The Mont Hawthorne books were marketed as "told-to" tales in which Uncle Hawthorne spun out stories of his past to a note-taking Martha as they sat before many evening fires in his living room.[50] Martha repeated this method with the Thompsons as she collected stories from Celilo Village residents gathered around the longhouse's wood stove. Her methods diverged from her earlier books, though, because she also based them on her own observations and interactions with the community. Martha's Celilo books, though marketed as children's stories, aligned with a tradition of non-academic ethnography. McKeown followed the conventions of other regional settler observers who documented their Indigenous neighbors, often with a sympathetic view of the cultural, political, and economic changes they faced.[51] As with the Mont Hawthorne books, Martha shaped the narratives of her Celilo books, but she also hewed more closely to ethnographic depictions of the community, detailing their physical and ceremonial structures while eschewing the dialect and homespun character-driven narratives of her earlier publications.

The McKeowns collaborated with the Thompsons to create the books. Archie's pictures, which illustrated both books, depict the intimate interiors of the Thompson home as well as longhouse ceremonies that few had permission to photograph. Martha credited her family's history with Indians of the Gorge for her access to Celilo Village. She attributed her husband's approach to community members for making his documentation possible. On the back of a photo of Archie in which he is crouched down to gently pet a fawn, Martha inscribed, "Archie W. McKeown who took the pictures for *Linda's Indian Home* and *Come to Our Salmon Feast* took time to make friends. When Archie made an Indian picture he returned a print so that he 'took nothing away.' These people were his friends and not just distant figures against a huge backdrop of dashing cataract."[52] She wrote that Chief Thompson's directions to her were "You write, I thumbprint," and both books include the chief's thumbprint on its first page. Martha claimed to "never write anything except from their point of view," minimizing her

Archie McKeown with a fawn. Unknown photographer, date unknown. Special Collections and Archives, Eric V. Hauser Memorial Library, Reed College

authorial interventions at the expense of a sincerely felt claim for authenticity.[53]

Martha McKeown cast herself and her husband as documentarians who simply recorded life at Celilo Village as it was, and only with the permission of their subjects. But in actuality, their books and photographs constructed a particular set of truths about the village and its residents. As historian Carol J. Williams states, "between parties of unequal status, looking was not an innocent act."[54] Even while he willingly cooperated with the McKeowns, Chief Thompson was not fully in control of representations of him or his family, nor how those representations would be produced and reproduced over time. The McKeowns had the wherewithal to tell Celilo stories: the time, camera equipment, writing ability, and connections to publishers. As white, educated observers, they mirrored anthropological and ethnographical constructions of Indigenous peoples by scholars who also believed that they were representing Native communities and people as they were. The McKeowns intended to correct a record they felt was in error, but they were still caught in the asymmetrical power dynamics that colonialism constructed, in which non-Natives reported to others on Indian lifeways while Indians remained largely silent, the subjects of settler tales, not the authors of their own stories.

McKeown wrote *Linda's Indian Home* for third-grade readers and their teachers after a group of educators asked her to recommend materials about Indian cultures appropriate for elementary-level curriculum. At seventy-six pages, the book is fairly long. Each spread includes one page of text with a photograph taken by Archie McKeown on the opposite page. The book tackles a central question: What is an Indian home? Initially, Linda's Indian home was the cradleboard she lived in as an infant. McKeown homed in on the material details of the cradleboard: how it was crafted from canvas and wood, the shells that formed the top and could rattle for the immobilized Linda, and the lacing that Linda's mother Josephine used to bind her daughter into the "little Indian home."

McKeown also focused on other Indian homes. Summer and winter homes at Celilo Village housed the community's residents. Winter homes were small, which made them easy to heat with firewood, while summer homes were spacious, faced the river, and were open to the gorge winds necessary to properly dry salmon. Tepees round out the book's architectural examples; they were the temporary housing used in the mountains when residents gathered huckleberries and other foods away from the river. Summer and winter homes and tepees were all shared housing, and the book follows Linda's transformation from individual resident of a cradleboard to member of a household who must learn to live with others.

The Indian home was not just the residence, however, but also the wider environment. The rock outcroppings that constituted the community's fishing stations were also part of the Indian home, as were the huckleberry and camas fields. Because food was central to the household and because so much food production happened in the home, it was also central to McKeown's narrative. The summer home was also a drying shed, where women hung butchered salmon to dry and interrupted their sleep to tend to them. Archie's photographs captured the halved salmon heads, made batlike in their splitting, and the baskets of dried eels, both of which would become winter soup. Another photograph depicted Indian women sitting on the floor processing roots for a meal. Still others show Flora bent over a half-finished beaded belt that she would sell for groceries. Rather than home as refuge from labor, it was the very location of subsistence and market-oriented work.

Seemingly a simple story of one Indian girl's development into a member of the community, *Linda's Indian Home* radically tackled one of the most important sites of assimilation during a period of intense domesticity in the nation.[55] By the 1950s, the typical American home was a modern, plumbed, and electrified single-family dwelling organized around "a generic house plan containing five to six rooms with bath, including a living room, dining room, kitchen, two or three bedrooms and bath."[56] For Indian people, "home" long represented a metric by which their assimilation was measured, but for middle-class, white Americans, the normative home was also politicized private space. This was especially true in the aftermath of World War II and during the Cold War, when the American home was cast as sacrosanct protection against a volatile geopolitical environment.[57]

If the postwar suburban American home was supposed sanctuary, Native homes had been the site of aggressive reformist intervention for decades. Many in the BIA viewed Native forms of housing, like the multifamily residences with workspaces but lacking dedicated rooms for sleeping and eating common at Celilo, as undesirably "traditional."[58] Bureau representatives often assumed that the modern homes the agency offered to Celilo residents ousted by the expansion of the freeway were improvements over the "shacks" in which most families lived. BIA employees held that modern homes were advancements over older structures and "naturally" more appealing than "traditional" Indian homes (which, of course, had undergone many changes themselves over the generations). That assumption helps explain why non-Indian government representatives had such trouble understanding the protests of Indians who demanded suitable buildings in which to dry their salmon and raise their families. When McKeown explains to her young readers that "drying sheds" the BIA officials wanted to consolidate and relegate to the community's periphery were actually family-owned summer homes, the importance of Indigenous architecture and organization in the community becomes clear. Yet the idealization of modern single-family homes persisted among BIA officials, who replaced Indian homes with them during the expansion of the highway and after the dam inundated a portion of the community.

Hierarchical beliefs about proper housing and homemaking—what historian Jane Simonsen calls "domestic ordering ideologies"[59]—undergirded much of the federal assimilationist policy that shaped Flora's early years. Nineteenth- and early-twentieth-century reformers accepted a framework of social evolution that plotted cultural norms, including common residential structures and homemaking practices, on a spectrum between savagery and civilization. Allotment policy contained within it the assumption that by introducing structures suitable to nuclear families, reformers could change Native social structure. In 1910 the federal census contained a section, "Special Inquiries Relating to Indians," that documented whether Indian families lived in "traditional" or "civilized" housing. (Flora's mother, Martha Cushinway, was listed as living in "civilized" housing.) The reservation school Flora attended emphasized domesticity for female students, while off-reservation boarding schools implemented the "outing" system that placed Indian girls in non-Indian homes to work as domestics.

Domesticity was central to the education of Indian girls, but agency-run schools focused on stripping them of the domestic lessons of their mothers and grandmothers.[60] The field matrons who visited Flora's mother's home and then her own passed judgment on their cleanliness and thus on the progress Indian families were making toward complete assimilation. The conformity of a home to mainstream, white standards was proof of assimilation within a family. In this way, assimilation was the purview of Indian women, whose commitment to mopping floors, dusting, and purchasing modern furniture indicated cultural advancement.[61] McKeown, therefore, reinterpreted the Native home for her non-Native readers.

Toward the end of *Linda's Indian Home* McKeown recounts a friend's gifting of a white-skinned doll to one of the girls of Celilo. The gift prompts Flora to buy her granddaughter a "white girl costume," in effect making her a living "white" doll. Linda, of course, was still an Indian child, whether ensconced in a cradleboard or in a lacy dress from a department store. The technologies of whiteness—clothing or household goods, automobiles or milled lumber—were not always the technologies of assimilation.

Instead, Indians transformed them to meet their own needs. This is echoed again in McKeown's second book about Celilo Village, *Come to Our Salmon Feast*, which was published in 1959. In that book, McKeown describes some of the materials that comprised regalia at a salmon ceremony: "a red taillight reflector, from an old truck," goat hair, and "shredded cellophane."[62] Materials, dances and songs, and even food changed, but the sacred ceremony remained constant.

Just as *Linda's Indian Home* focuses much of its narrative on one little girl, *Come to Our Salmon Feast* follows two preteen boys, Chief Thompson's grandsons Davis and Richard Thompson, as they engage in the ceremonial drumming and dancing that could commence because Richard caught the first salmon of the spring run. The book details his catch, preparations for the following feast and the ceremony itself, and the traditional ceremonial dances, including a portion dedicated to the day's courting practices. The narrative is loosely organized around "layers of dawn," the day that slowly emerges after a night of feasting and dancing.

Embedded in the narrative is a muddy discussion of Plateau gender roles that suggest they elude tidy analysis. Traditional Indigenous ideas about what it meant to be male or female entwined with contemporary mainstream concepts to produce a mixed performance of gender. Moreover, McKeown brought her own lens to what she observed and how she wrote about it. McKeown did not set out to define gender roles for her young readers—although she did so in intriguing yet limited ways. Her record of the activities of the evening interpret the roles of Indian men and women in the longhouse. While the Native home at Celilo brought together marketable labor and domesticity, the longhouse, which was the community's most important interior space, physically divided men and women along two sides of a floor kept clear for dancing and other ceremonial activities. Men and women sat separately throughout the First Salmon Ceremony, participated in single-sex dances (but not exclusively), and contributed to the ceremony in gender-specific ways.

The physical division of the longhouse into male and female spaces reflected long-held Indigenous ideas about gender roles on the Columbia Plateau. According to anthropologist Lillian Ackerman, men and women engaged in different but complementary activities to complete the tasks necessary to sustain life before and well after encounters with Europeans and Americans. Indeed, she argues that gender *equality* was "a necessary component of Plateau culture."[63] Moreover, her fieldwork on the Colville Reservation in Washington State in the 1970s and '80s showed that gender roles were sometimes modified by but largely withstood the transformations wrought by colonization and continued into the contemporary period.

Ackerman and some of her consultants pointed to men's and women's differing economic roles for the origin of their separation.[64] At the annual First Salmon Ceremony, men with status like Chief Thompson and his son, Henry, welcomed guests and attended to the spiritual needs of the community. Women like Flora Thompson and her niece Catherine Cushinway cooked the feast but ate only after the guests were fed. Because people stayed for an extended period, more meals would need to be planned and prepared. Flora Thompson maintained her husband's status by ensuring that no one left Celilo hungry. For the 1951 feast, she sold "a bundle of beautiful beadwork" to pay for groceries. "During the summer, she will pick cherries. It will take all and more than she can make to pay for the groceries that are being served at this feast in Chief Thompson's longhouse."[65] McKeown's text details the labor Flora contributed to the ceremony:

beading, marketing her craftwork, and engaging in seasonal farm labor in addition to the preparations required to ready the longhouse for guests and to cook several meals. Flora led Celilo women into the longhouse, carrying the first salmon so that it could be blessed.[66] The procession was a critical part of the ceremony and recognized the importance of women to the community.

According to McKeown, Chief Thompson valued tradition above all else, only grudgingly accepting at the insistence of the fire marshal the electric light and new door affixed to the longhouse through which the women marched that spring day.[67] In the third and fourth layers of the night, when the fire marshal's new light would be particularly noticeable, young men and women participated in social and courting dances. Young Indian women wore buckskin dresses that "cost far more than a white satin wedding dress"—the most important dress in most young white women's lives—to attract the attention of potential suitors. Young women, McKeown informed her readers, needed older female teachers to provide both the ceremonial garb and essential lessons "in the old way of the river people."[68]

According to the text, Chief Thompson, who provided a special blessing for the young women present, viewed the role of Indian women as deferential to the needs of their families. In contrast to a brief courting period, "Chief Thompson says that an Indian woman should not attract attention to herself when she is married. She must forget herself and serve others first. She must always dress all of her family in beaded buckskins before she makes anything new for herself."[69] By the time they are full adults, "Indian women have been taught how to work and to serve. They know how to make buckskin. They make baskets and cornhusk storage bags. They dry fish and dig roots and gather huckleberries up in the mountains. An Indian woman never sits down to eat at the table until the men and children in her family have eaten."[70] Much of the work Indian women performed was invisible to outside observers—beading, cooking, and preparing for guests occurred out of sight of tourists and journalists. As a result, non-Native guests could overlook their important roles (even while other Indians recognized and honored them). Thompson emphasized that Native women must humbly deflect attention and forget themselves. Yet Martha made sure her readers could not ignore their contributions, which were of equal importance to the more visible activities of their husbands, brothers, and sons.

Far from being subservient, Flora derived her authority from tradition, including traditional gender roles. Men and women who were accomplished in the gender-differentiated tasks they performed were considered excellent marriage partners and members of the community. Leaders turned to skilled hunters, gatherers, and traders for counsel. Successfully accomplishing her tasks would likely have been more important to Flora than anything approaching midcentury mainstream notions of equality, which would have been as much an anathema to her as they were to her high-status husband.[71] Flora and Chief Thompson shared a conservatism that the preservation of Indigenous culture in the midst of assimilation required.

McKeown's children's books were not reviewed as widely as her books written for adults, with one notable exception. The *Pacific Northwest Quarterly* published a review of *Come to Our Salmon Feast* by noted anthropologist David French, who conducted extensive fieldwork at the Warm Springs reservation with his wife, Katherine (whose field notes have augmented this text). He concluded that the book—written by a nonprofessional who had borrowed the methods of his discipline—"merits neither unqualified criticism nor wholehearted praise."[72] French complained about sloppy English renditions of Sahaptin words and a slippery chronology, which marked McKeown's work as amateurish. But he thought that her perspective, which, although not scholarly, adopted a respectful, nonjudgmental tone, balanced these deficits. The "details," he wrote "are in no sense white stereotypes," and the book contained "careful . . . biographical details about particular Indians."[73] Although it did not offer full reviews of the books, the *Oregon Historical Quarterly* included both volumes in its recommendations for young readers.[74] A writer for the *Oregon Journal* assumed that "the story may not intrigue adults" but that with the completion of The Dalles Dam at hand, McKeown had given Oregon's children "a final and understanding look at Celilo and its Wyams."[75] McKeown did not explain why she turned to children's literature instead of an account meant for adult readers for her explorations of Celilo Village, yet the set remains the most accurate and sympathetic depiction of Celilo Village at midcentury.

CLOSING THE GATES

As the *Oregon Journal* writer indicated, the timing of both books was fortuitous. They provide bookends to the struggle over the building of The Dalles Dam, a way to frame the devastation of the community and to document it as it once was. The completion of the dam in 1957 was a crushing though slow-moving blow to those who saw the loss of Celilo, the Long Narrows, and other fishing locations as an irrevocable and heartrending loss whose implications would be far-reaching. The books also bounded a period of extreme loss for Flora and Martha that reached beyond the reconfiguration of the river and into the most intimate aspects of their lives.

Illness and death surrounded Martha and Flora during this time. Archie McKeown suffered his first heart attack in the early spring of 1955 and then was diagnosed with lung cancer. In a letter she wrote to Jimmie James in March, Martha warned him that "because of illness in our home, I am having to curtail many of my outside activities." Martha limited her work with Celilo Village and in her various women's organizations. Nonetheless, she and Archie "continue[d] to help out the home folk in any way we can."[76] By early summer, Archie was still sick, and although he visited with Celilo residents and began his own correspondence with James while Martha was away at the high school, he was unable to help as she arranged a place for Chief Thompson in a nursing home in Hood River.[77] In the midst of that transition, Flora lost her adult son, who lived with her and the chief, to a senseless accident. In the early hours of Sunday, May 6, 1956, twenty-seven-year-old Max Boise's car collided with a Consolidated Freightways trailer near the village on Highway 30.[78] Flora mourned her son intensely.

By June 1956, Martha McKeown had arranged for Tommy Thompson to reside permanently at Hanby Nursing Home in Hood River, but Flora was uncertain if removing Thompson from her care in favor of a nursing home was the right thing to do. She worried that such places were "allergic to Indians." But Flora was sick too, and Martha wanted her to go to a hospital. Finally, they agreed that Martha would "keep an eye on Chief at the nursing home, and Flora will go to the hospital Monday morning." Ida, the Chief's daughter, would care for Linda, Flora's granddaughter, temporarily.[79]

Flora's concerns about Hanby Nursing Home were soon dispelled. When the Hanbys had remodeled an old motel into a nursing home a few years before, they'd donated truckloads of furniture they no longer needed to Celilo Village.[80] Martha credited the Hanbys' religion for their interest in their Indian neighbors and the care they offered to the Celilo elder. As Mormons, they "believe that the Indians have a special blessing. They are deeply saddened to see them in this condition and are doing all they can for the chief."[81] Martha was "grateful to the Hanbys. Chief is a very great care but they all treat him with the greatest respect."[82] Years later, Flora agreed and even described herself as Mormon, probably because of her association with them. McKeown regularly visited Chief Thompson:

> Sunday I went down with my Sunday drum and he played
> and sang for me. I put him in a wheel chair and took him out
> in the yard so we would not disturb the patients. Soon the
> ones who could get there and also the nurses were out to join
> us in our Indian prayer service.[83]

In the fall of 1956 she exclaimed that "keeping Chief happy has been the big job" of the summer.[84]

As the holidays approached, Flora struggled with her health (Martha described her as "shockingly ill" but provided no details).[85] Martha was busy with a whirlwind of activity: "putting on a big Christmas for my flock at school, going down with my drum so Chief Thompson could sing to the carolers, and taking a load of gifts and clothing my youngsters and I had gleaned to Celilo." Once the tasks were completed she "folded with the flu."[86] Compounding matters, Chief Thompson couldn't always remember where he was. In his old age, his imagination turned the nursing home into a longhouse, oddly reversing federal efforts to transform Celilo structures into modern American ones.[87]

Things had grown even worse at Celilo Village as the dam project was in its final stages. McKeown complained, "most of those old people can't read or write, they don't have cars. They don't have licenses to drive the ones they own. The young people are away, every pressure is being brought to bear to have them relocate."[88] McKeown's letters to Jimmie James don't mention the eventual inundation of Celilo Falls and a portion of Celilo Village with the completion of The Dalles Dam on March 10, 1957, although she wrote him a brief letter three days earlier. Jimmie James watched the television coverage of the gates closing but "did not have the heart to go up there."[89]

The closing of the gates of The Dalles Dam changed everything and nothing. The river took on a new and different shape and the falls fell silent. The very sound of the world changed. For the first time, the roar of traffic—not of the river—accompanied those who spent their days at the village. When Jimmie James visited Flora in early May, the sight made him sick.[90] New homes dotted the village site to house families displaced by the reservoir. Some people moved away from the village entirely, enticed by county funding made available for that purpose or pushed out by the lack of fishing sites and overwhelmed with sorrow. A few families stayed, witness to the wild, living river laid waste.

But in the fall, school started as it always had. Chief endured under the care of the Hanbys. Indians returned to the now quiet river to fish the fall salmon run. After the loss of her son and with the chief in Hood River, Flora felt incapable of caring for her granddaughter Linda, who moved into The Dalles to live with a foster family and then eventually to Portland to attend a Catholic boarding school. By May, Martha reported that Archie had suffered another heart attack, and the progression of his cancer landed him in the hospital again in September.[91] Martha had cared for her husband over the summer, but once school started the couple relied on a neighbor to stay with him while she worked.[92] Archie passed away in November of 1957.

The records Flora Thompson left behind are silent about where she was and what she was doing when Army Corps of Engineers employees shut the dam gates and the Columbia River slowly rose over the falls. She may have been in Hood River sitting with her husband, who did not, in life, return to Celilo Village after the dam inundated the falls and was said to have never set his eyes on the river's obstruction. Chief Tommy Thompson died on April 12, 1959, as the spring salmon began their run upriver. His body was moved from Hood River to the Celilo Village longhouse in the dark of night so that he would not have to acknowledge the dam even in death.[93] Jimmie James prepared a press release and typed a letter to President Dwight Eisenhower that very evening, announcing the passing of the hereditary salmon chief.[94] People from around the world, including the president, wrote notes of condolence to Flora.[95]

Flora rejected efforts to make Thompson's death a coda for the wild Columbia River. Instead she worked to secure a proper cedar casket from the Warm Springs Reservation and planned a traditional burial for Chief Thompson.[96] The expense would be enormous for the five-day ceremony. The chief would be buried in new, ceremonial buckskin, his remains "wrapped in some 10 fine Pendleton blankets."[97] The undertaker and gravedigger required compensation. Everyone who arrived to honor Tommy Thompson would need to be fed, and Flora and the rest of the family probably provided gifts to elders who attended the ceremony. "That way," Linton Winishut explained, "the chief would be respected." In the mid-1950s, Winishut recalled working "for wages for three years before [he] was all paid up" on his own father's funeral expenses.[98] Like Winishut, Flora had gone into debt to pay Max's funeral expenses three years prior. By the 1950s, Warm Springs enrollees could count on their tribal government for small grants to offset funeral costs, and it's likely that Flora received such help when her son died, but her husband lacked enrollee status.[99] Jimmie James attempted to secure the federal compensation owed to Tommy Thompson to pay for the funeral on Flora's behalf.[100]

James spent an evening at the longhouse, where guests slept and ate from the tule mats arranged near the chief, who lay in state. In a letter to Senator Neuberger, James complained about the intrusion of outsiders who did not know the funeral protocol and acted in offensive ways. "It was a little hard to believe that his white brothers would come in the Longhouse with flash bulbs and walk in the middle of the floor during the services and take flash after flash, blinding the singers," he wrote. Moreover, reporters misrepresented the Washat ceremony, with some newspapers mischaracterizing the bell that was "used as signal of a song to be sung" as a way to ward off "evil spirits." James explained that Washat was "older perhaps than the white man's [religion]." The songs were "some of the most beautiful music . . . rendered there that night."

When they sang the Chief's song that was buried with him, you could hear the coming of dawn, the wind coming up, blowing the sands of his birthplace, awakening sounds as life stirred. Common things they were, distant river flowed again over the flooded rocks that made Celilo Falls, the falls roared as the day broke. Calmness came with midday as the warm Sun warmed his Mother Earth. Evening again came as sound of life prepared to sleep, winds died down, the sand stopped blowing, it was the end.[101]

SEVEN

Aftermath

While we do our good works let us not forget that the
real solution lies in a world in which charity will have
become unnecessary.

CHINUA ACHEBE, *Anthills of the Savannah*

FLORA THOMPSON LOOKED EXHAUSTED IN THE THIRTY-MINUTE
documentary of her husband's funeral that ran on Portland's
KGW television station.[1] As the camera panned the doorway of her
home, she stood just outside its wooden frame, flanked by Thompson's adult children, in a wing dress and neat braids, her eyes downcast. The days running up to the five-day funeral were a rush of
activity. After spending three days crafting his funeral regalia in
plain buckskin, Flora "went down to Portland and . . . put in both
[news]papers that each and every one was welcomed to come and
attend his funeral," while Martha contacted the television station.
When Flora was done in Portland, Martha drove her back to
Celilo Village. Flora recalled that difficult day: "I called her up

Martha McKeown consoling Ida Wynookie, Chief Thompson's daughter, at his funeral. Photograph by Allen DeLay, the *Oregonian*. Courtesy of Thomas Robinson

and she came down and she brought me home. She just about hold me in her lap all the way up."[2]

Flora lived at Celilo Village until her death in 1978, while Martha McKeown remarried at the end of 1960 and moved to the town of Milwaukie on the outskirts of Portland, where she continued to teach and kept a busy speaking schedule. Flora dedicated her time to monitoring treaty fishing issues on the ever-shrinking salmon runs of the Columbia, making public appearances to speak about the treaty rights, solidifying her husband's legacy in the region, and doing community work at Celilo. According to Martha's granddaughter, the two women often visited one another until Martha's death in 1974.[3]

The factors that brought the women together in the 1940s and '50s shifted significantly by the 1970s. With the exception of Jimmie James and the Anselm Forum, a midwestern interfaith organization whose leaders corresponded regularly with James, most non-Native interest in the effects of dam building on treaty rights evaporated (only to rebound a few decades later with the recognition of a basin-wide salmon crisis). Although her literary contributions continued to shape how Oregonians understood their past, the networks of clubwomen that sustained Martha's work in the 1940s and 1950s lost traction as the emerging women's movement forced open new paths to authority for women. Flora also lost authority in this period as community leadership moved from the Thompson descendants to other River Indian families. Moreover, the letters that documented their work and relationships stopped with Jimmie James's death in 1967.

Martha's second marriage altered the direction of her final years and may have been the most important event in her life after the completion of The Dalles Dam. Flora faced two important events in that same period, the loss and rebuilding of Celilo Village's religious and cultural center, the longhouse, and the removal of her granddaughter, Linda George Meanus, from her home. The events recounted in this final chapter, which all take place between 1959's completion of the dam and Flora's death in 1978, do not follow a linear chronology. Like river-born eddies, the final years of Martha's and Flora's lives swirled and overlapped, engulfed one another and gave way, part of the larger currents of the region itself.

A NEW LONGHOUSE

In 1960, the longhouse in which Tommy and Flora Thompson prayed and hosted the annual salmon ceremony burned to the

Flora and Tommy Thompson at Celilo Village. CN018928, Oregon Historical Society, courtesy of Barcroft Media

ground. The community had gathered for the funeral of John Whiz, who had died on July 24 of that year.[4] Henry Thompson, who succeeded his father as salmon chief, was burning trash several yards away from the longhouse when winds kicked up and spread the fire through the summer's dry grasses. The longhouse burned quickly, as did two other buildings.[5] No one was hurt, but the destruction of the ceremonial building left a fissure in the community. As soon as the embers died, members began to make competing plans for the construction of a new longhouse.

The community had already been agitating for funds to build a new longhouse for several years. Jimmie James wrote to the Bureau of Indian Affairs and state agencies on behalf of the Celilo leadership, asking for funds for a new structure. Official responses directed community members to raise money independent of the BIA; James thought this might be the best strategy to keep control of the sacred building in the hands of the Indians who worshiped there. But the community had little success raising money. Nonetheless, the destruction of the old longhouse necessitated the building of a new one. The questions, however, were how and when.

The destruction of the old longhouse presented an opportunity to re-envision what a new building would look like and how it would operate. James recommended an A-frame structure built on a cement foundation that could help prevent the loss of the building in the event of another fire. Flora worried that a new longhouse wouldn't allow for some of the religious practices essential to Washat. A cement floor would separate dancers from Mother Earth, while an A-frame structure deviated from the traditional shape of a Plateau longhouse. Celilo Village resident and community leader Maggie Jim asked about siting the longhouse closer to electricity so that evening ceremonies could be lighted and the kitchen modernized. Relocating the longhouse would also allow for the construction of a parking lot that could accommodate up to one hundred cars. But Flora and Henry wanted to replace the longhouse where it was originally sited. Such issues would slow progress and indicate a transition in leadership in the village from Flora and Henry Thompson to Maggie Jim and her husband Howard, a hereditary river chief and fisher.

It would be five years before Celilo residents formed a committee to tackle the construction of the new longhouse. Maggie Jim was elected to lead the committee, while Henry and Flora Thompson served as ex-officio members. Jimmie James remained engaged in the developments at Celilo Village, including the longhouse.

Jeanne Hillis, an artist who volunteered for the Wasco County Dalles City Museum Commission, also got involved, taking notes at the committee meetings, which she sent to James. Hillis brought the project to The Dalles Jaycees, the local branch of the United States Junior Chamber, a business-oriented civic organization for young men. In the spring, The Dalles area Jaycees hosted a salmon feast to raise money, organized dancers to publicize the event in Portland, secured donations of materials, and offered their own labor to build the structure.

But the question of location interrupted the "bright and bustling" progress of the Jaycees.[6] The *Oregonian* covered the conflict, disparagingly describing Flora as "the spritely and loquacious little widow of the chief" and the primary instigator of the slowdown.[7] Flora's ally and the current Wyam chief, Henry, was ill with ulcers and often absent from the village. Moreover, he seemed less inclined to community work than his father, opting to spend his time beading and making regalia instead. James gently noted that Henry Thompson "has not the know how as yet like the Old Chief Tommy."[8] In a letter to Flora, he commiserated with her, writing, "it is too bad that Henry does not step out and fight for those up there, and take care of things that is needed."[9] Henry's lack of leadership impinged on Flora's influence in the community, and she stood nearly alone in her objections to plans for the new longhouse. By 1968 Howard Jim would succeed Henry as chief of the Wyam, but problems continued. The longhouse remained unfinished as the community prepared for its annual salmon ceremony in spring 1976.[10]

That progress on the rebuilding of the longhouse was so slow made visible the diminishment of Flora's influence in the community after her husband's death. Her day-to-day leadership in the community gave way to external requests to speak on behalf of

Celilo Village residents. In a long article published three months after Flora's passing, journalist George Lindsay wrote that after her husband's death Flora "grew into her role as the tribal matriarch."[11] Often called on to speak about Native issues, Flora grounded Indian rights in the Treaty of Middle Oregon she carried with her, and she signaled to her audiences her Indigeneity in dress and protocol.[12] When Secretary of the Interior Walter Hickel dedicated the Celilo Convertor Station in 1970, Flora presented him and members of his staff with beaded gifts and wore a buckskin dress.[13] She mildly chastised Warm Springs tribal chairman Henry Culpus for dressing "in a white man's suit," asking "how would anybody know who he was?"[14] Flora's influence grew from her experience and age rather than from the official capacity of a tribal council position. Though she was enrolled at Warm Springs and spent time on the reservation, she was also part of the network of River Indians who often challenged the authority of reservation governments.

The work Flora most proudly spoke of in oral history interviews conducted near the end of her life was the aid she provided in defense of Indian fishers at Cook's Landing in the spring of 1966. Fishers netted salmon under armed guard in what the *Oregonian* dubbed a "salmon war" to protest state regulations.[15] Flora recalled that Yakama fishers at Cook's Landing, which is on the Washington State side of the Columbia River, "came after Henry to go down and help him with problems. Chief Henry says 'I can not do anything about business affairs' but he did do a lot of work in feathers making outfits for war dances for the boys and the girls was about all he could do. But he was very poor in business so they came over to me and asked me to go down so I went down and we camped at The Dalles." Flora declared that a "grandmother's never afraid to face any case, especially in fishing."[16]

Flora and Linda joined dozens of others at Cook's Landing, where the press had gathered to document the protest. She brought "treaty papers along to prove where we are and so they asked me questions right and left. Mid-Oregon treaty, on Oregon side, and on the Washington side and I brought those treaty papers out and I had my husband's picture—this one he was along—and I brought that out."[17] A staff photographer captured her holding up the treaty in a photograph that was published in the *Oregonian*. The caption heralded Flora: "Note leathery, lined hands, proud face."[18] By bringing Linda and a photograph of her late husband, Flora connected herself to a multigenerational, familial struggle of Native fishing rights on the mid–Columbia River that began well before the development of dams and intensified after their completion. She illustrated her place in the struggle, which by the mid-1960s was developing into a regional movement, with the treaty and the photograph.[19] Although the fish wars of the Columbia River and Puget Sound are often cast as battles between male Indian fishers and law enforcement, women like Flora played critical roles in the ongoing struggle for Indigenous resource rights in the region.[20]

"A REALLY WONDERFUL OPPORTUNITY TO PUBLICIZE THE INDIANS' CAUSE"

In June 1959, David Sheer, the legislative chairman for the Anselm Forum, traveled from Chicago to visit Celilo Village, and in Oregon he stayed with Martha McKeown.[21] Sheer and the forum's director, Reuben Olson, who had visited a few years prior, exchanged letters with James that illuminate the evolving relationships between James, Martha, and Flora. Martha, Sheer reported to James, had "not quite gotten over Archie's death and is driving herself at a terrific pace to finish books his illness forced her to neglect."[22] After a long illness that necessitated the remodeling of their home, Archie's passing was still a shock, and she filled the time she had dedicated to nursing Archie with writing and other civic work. Tommy Thompson's death closely followed Archie's, and Martha deeply missed the person she described as "the wisest man she knew."[23] When David Sheer and his wife Bea arrived in the Hood River Valley, Martha was on crutches, recovering from a badly sprained ankle.[24] Nonetheless, Martha organized several meetings with River Indian families in Oregon and Washington for the Sheers, including a dinner at her home with Flora, her sister Effie, and Effie's husband.[25]

David Sheer returned to the Midwest inspired to continue the organization's efforts to assist those left at Celilo Village. He strategized two plans, one that was successful and one that was not. In the first, Sheer arranged for editor Harold Fey of the *Christian Century*, a nondenominational progressive Protestant magazine, to publish an article that Martha McKeown would write about the status of Celilo Village. Fey had an abiding interest in federal Indian policy and had written a series of articles about the topic in 1956, followed by a 1959 book coauthored with Salish-Kootenai intellectual and activist D'Arcy McNickle, *American Indians and Other Americans: Two Ways of Life Meet*.[26] Sheer wrote to James, "I am permitting Martha to do the article. She is closer to the problem than I am. It is a gratis job but should do the Wy-am cause some good."[27] The Anselm Forum printed one thousand copies of McKeown's "The Wy-am-pums of Celilo" for distribution.[28]

The second strategy was to present Martha McKeown with an award from the Anselm Forum. The award itself was less important than who could be called to give it. Sheer angled to secure Senator Richard Neuberger's participation, believing that doing so would provide an opportunity to publicize the ongoing problems at Celilo Village. "We prefer Celilo (for the presenting of the citation) so the Senator can see for himself the condition of the houses, the hazardous approach to the Columbia River Highway, the roadwork being done which will crowd the Celilo Indians against the cliff."[29] By early September, the forum's director was firming up the list of dignitaries to invite and contacting local TV stations about covering the event. Anselm Forum director Reuben Olson instructed James to draw up a guest list with McKeown to "make this a memorable occasion. . . . A really wonderful opportunity to publicize the Indians' cause and the labor of true friends."[30]

Unwilling to cooperate in this celebration of her work with Celilo families was Martha herself. By December the forum had secured Senator Neuberger's participation but had not been able to induce him to travel to Celilo Village for the event. Instead it was to be held in Portland, far from the problems at the Indian community. Furthermore, McKeown wrote to Neuberger that she could "not come to Portland and publically receive [the forum citation] from you because it implied that something had been accomplished for those people." McKeown was guided by her conscience—she saw no point in celebrating her efforts when there was still so much need in the community. Instead, McKeown invited Neuberger and his aides to meet her at Celilo Village to "see why men like Reuben Olson and David Sheer are deeply shocked by what has happened to the resident Indians."[31] It is unlikely that Senator Neuberger accepted McKeown's offer. Neuberger was privately suffering from a brain cancer that would take his life the following year.

Jimmie James began to share misgivings about Martha with Sheer and was especially concerned that she had garnered advantage from her Celilo children's books. When Sheer was in Oregon, James asked him to "see what you can find out about Martha—if she and Archie used the Indians up at Celilo Village to make money" with their books.[32] James blamed his concern on "conversation among the Indians in their general conversation," noting that if he was to speak to anyone directly about their concerns that "they would talk of something else."[33] At no point in his correspondence did James indicate who specifically complained about McKeown. On his return home, Sheer warned James to resist being taken up by "a tale that should best be ignored." He quoted from a letter Martha had written Sheer at the end of August: "Somehow, I sense in your letter that you are concerned because I don't see more, or write more, to Jimmie James." After providing specific examples of their closeness—visiting one another's homes where each had a pile of correspondence from the other, McKeown noted that "Jimmie and I won't get nearly so much done if we put in hours writing one to the other."[34] James worried that "this thing about Martha is sort of getting out of hand."[35] But it wouldn't be the last time that James articulated reservations about Martha McKeown and her relationship with River Indians.

MOUNTAINS AHEAD

The manuscripts Martha had been working so steadily included *Come to Our Salmon Feast*, released in 1959, and *Mountains Ahead*, which came out in February 1961. *Mountains Ahead* follows a wagon train as it travels across the Oregon Trail in the mid-1840s, placing at the center of the tale two protagonists, Gram Harrow, a gruff, capable woman near the end of her life, and Harmony, the young, middle-class, seemingly fragile woman Gram Harrow's grandson marries. The grudging respect that grows between the two women as Harmony repeatedly proves her worth mirrors the territorial advance at the heart of the plot. At the periphery sits the recognition that western land was not unoccupied, yet the novel is optimistic, and Martha depicted the advance of the United States across the continent as inevitable, as she covered what was well-worn ground in historical fiction by midcentury.[36] *Booklist* dismissed McKeown's sixth and final book, and her only novel, as one "for women readers."[37] Most reviews were lukewarm, remarking on the "stereotyped characters" and "overuse of dialect."[38] But they also praised the depth of McKeown's research and the novel's "emphasis on the woman's role" in westward expansion.[39]

It's hard not to read the novel as representative of Martha's move away from Indigenous politics on the Columbia River to the pioneer narratives of the Willamette Valley, as she physically left her home in the Hood River Valley for a home just outside Portland. But McKeown worked to maintain relationships with Native friends like Flora even as she left the midriver.[40] The move followed Martha's second marriage to a man she had known for decades. Martha met Marshall Dana as early as 1931 and it appears likely that he had struck up a friendship with Martha's mother, Almira.

Eight years Martha's senior, Dana had moved to Oregon from Ohio in 1908 with his first wife, Nora Valentine Dana. He was a reporter for the *Oregon Journal*, a statewide rival to the *Oregonian*. From 1938 to 1951, Dana was the paper's editorial editor. Dana immersed himself in the development and eventually the conservation of the region, playing important roles in the Portland Commission of Public Docks, the Oregon Reclamation Association, and the Inland Empire Waterways Association, leading one historian to christen Dana "the father of Oregon Reclamation."[41] In 1948 Richard Neuberger urged him to consider a run for the Democratic nomination for the gubernatorial race. Calling the support from the party "one of the most gratifying experiences of my

Marshall Dana with Charley Quintoken, Flora Thompson, and Tommy Thompson at Celilo Falls. CN018928, Oregon Historical Society

life," Dana nevertheless declined.[42] Republican Douglas McKay claimed victory over Democratic candidate Lew Wallace, propelling McKay to a position to advocate for what would eventually become the federal termination of Indian tribes. During the construction of The Dalles Dam, Dana and Martha sat on the board of the Oregon Historical Society and shared abiding interests in the state's history and the welfare of its Native residents.

Dana was well connected throughout the state. After his retirement from the *Oregon Journal*, he worked as the assistant to the president of the US National Bank and kept up a schedule filled with speaking engagements. When Martha married Dana she joined someone who publically aligned himself with the systematic development of the region's waterways and celebrations of the state's pioneering past. While Martha kept the dying Thompson company in 1959, Dana organized a three-city celebration of the state's one-hundred birthday, sponsored by the Sons and Daughters of Oregon Pioneers and the Portland Chamber of Commerce. With assistance from the state's Republican governor, Mark Hatfield, Dana arranged for Vice President Richard Nixon to speak at the festivities, which included "guides garbed in centennial buckskin and ruffles" to lead ticketed guests to their tables.[43] But Dana was not merely romantic about the region's first white settlers, he embraced and celebrated the progress their descendants brought to the midcentury, in terms of both industry and conservation of the state's natural resources and scenery. A longtime advocate of reclamation, Dana was one of the speakers at the dedication of The Dalles-Celilo Canal in 1915, the precursor to The Dalles Dam.[44]

The couple married on December 26, 1960, after Dana had been widowed. To facilitate her move to Dana's home, Martha transferred her half of the Hood River Valley orchard to her son David. The decision caused a rift between Martha and her only child, who "shed tears and said the place wasn't what he wanted."[45] David refused to attend the small wedding. But Martha was ecstatic and emphatically expressed her love for Marshall in letters she sent between their wedding day and the end of the school year, when she joined him at his home permanently. When she first envisioned her life with Dana, Martha excitedly imagined writing at adjacent desks in his spacious home. Instead she returned to the classroom, this time in Oregon City, and would not publish another book.

Jimmie James speculated that the marriage did not meet Martha's expectations. He wrote to Yakama Wilson Charley in June, just a few weeks after Martha would have arrived at her new home, that McKeown "has been calling Maude, and according to what she says she is far from happy and things are not going so good, and in so short of time, but two people and their personalities can either be good or not good."[46] A few months later he repeated his concerns to David Sheer when he reported that he had "talked with Martha the other day, and I believe she is not happy, something is wrong. As I know Mr. Dana, I can't see too much ahead for her, Maudie thinks the same, she has talked to her several times."[47] James didn't like Dana, believing that he had stepped in to stop Gertrude Jensen's work in opposition to The Dalles Dam several years earlier. His observations contradicted those of Dana's daughter, who wrote to the couple "whenever I think of you I always visualize that happy glow that seems to be ever present around you two."[48] Whether they were accurate or not, James's missives to mutual friends likely did not sit well with McKeown.

LINDA'S INDIAN HOME

Fractures within the ad-hoc group that formed to aid Celilo Village residents during and directly after the closing of The Dalles Dam became particularly visible in the events surrounding Flora's granddaughter, Linda Meanus. The conflict between James, Flora, and Martha over placing Linda in a home reverberates with the assimilationist pressures of Flora's youth and with postwar politics that venerated middle-class, nuclear families. Flora struggled with health issues after Tommy Thompson's death, spending time in and out of hospitals in The Dalles and Hood River and eventually having surgery to remove her gall bladder.[49] The problems required her to find more consistent care for her granddaughter. Flora placed Linda at the Christie School, a Catholic boarding school near Portland, before the inundation of Celilo Falls. Years later, Linda recalled that her grandmother did not want her to witness the flooding of the riverscape that shaped her early childhood.[50] Linda turned six years old just ten days after the inundation.

Apart from Flora and her extended family, a far-flung handful of people felt personally invested in Linda's welfare. Jimmie James called her "my special girl" and claimed that he and his wife would have raised her if not for his wife's poor health.[51] He asked Flora to secure permission from the school to have Linda visit him on weekends. David Sheer and Rueben Olson both met her when they visited Celilo Village and frequently asked James about her in their letters. David Sheer reported that he and his wife sent Linda a ten-dollar bill for each birthday. Martha also sent Linda gifts at Christmas and her birthdays and brought the little girl to her home for visits.[52] All four adults regularly wrote to Linda and she to them, and each occasionally spoke to Linda by phone. Given the distance between the school and the village, it was difficult for those at Celilo Village, including Flora, to look after Linda's welfare. But both Flora and Linda seemed satisfied with the arrangement.

That changed when Jimmie James claimed that the school's Mother Superior asked him to find Linda a permanent home. The school was undergoing a transition from a girls' residential boarding school to a residential treatment center for girls with "severe emotional problems," making it inappropriate for Linda.[53] James knew that Flora's one misgiving about the residential school was the difficulty in maintaining Linda's religious and ceremonial education when she was so far from the longhouse and the river's spiritual leaders. But he apparently rejected trying to return Linda to Flora's household. Instead he began to search for a suitable "family home" for her, one that reflected the values of middle-class, white, nuclear households. In a letter to David Sheer, James wrote, "I have to present it to Flora, someway, as the Catholic sisters asked me to do, and show Flora that Linda needs the close family contact all children need, and if she believes that way, I will find her a home, a real one."[54]

The assimilationist reform promoted by WNIA and other groups in the nineteenth and early twentieth century persisted in "common sense" reflected in James's assumptions about what was best for Linda. James was also certainly influenced by the more recent postwar valuing of nuclear family households that cast Indigenous extended intergenerational webs of kinship as an aberration. This is why he could consider the household of strangers a "family home" for Linda that was more appropriate than the homes of her grandmother or other relatives. In that, he wasn't alone. James merely reflected many contemporary beliefs that motivated the wholesale removal of Indian children from their biological and extended families to the homes of mostly white, Christian Americans. In letters regarding the adoption of Indian children, James praised the Mormon Indian Student Placement Program, which displaced as many as fifty thousand Native children into white homes for the school year between 1947 and 2000. He may have also been aware of the Indian Adoption Project (1959–67),[55] an experiment that brought together two government agencies, the Bureau of Indian Affairs and the Children's Bureau, with the private Child Welfare League of America to permanently place Indian children in the homes of non-Indian families. Concurrent to the removal of Native children was a widely publicized effort to place Korean children into American households;[56] the connections between the projects will become evident below. While fewer than four hundred children were displaced as part of the official Indian Adoption Project, it created "an efficient structure" for their removal. It also normalized the stigmatization of Indian child-rearing practices and the removal of

Indian children from their families into homes where well-meaning adults hoped to support the development of supposedly disadvantaged children and rectify what they saw as the injustices of the past.[57]

While these projects echoed the history of child removal from Indigenous homes for boarding schools in the nineteenth and early twentieth centuries, they revolutionized the practice of adoption. Until the late 1950s, racial "matching" of adoptees to their adoptive parents "was an overall practice in the field."[58] Many of the non-Native families who participated in such adoptions were deeply religious and concerned about racial conflicts within the United States. They saw transracial (as well as international) adoption as a way to bridge the divide between whites and other groups, as well as a means to help individual children mired in poverty. Historian Arissa Oh dubbed international, transracial adoptions of this period as "a new kind of missionary work."[59] Political supporters of such adoptions ensconced them within the rhetoric of Cold War nationalistic responsibility to disperse an apparently color-blind Christian democracy around the globe. Adoptees of Indian children were further motivated to ameliorate what they considered third-world settings in the nation itself. Historian Margaret Jacobs argues that the Indian Adoption Project "cultivated demand for Indian adoptees by exploiting liberal Americans' desires to reach across racial boundaries and undo legacies of colonial mistrust to form genuine relationships with American Indians."[60] To do so, though, required the dismantling of Indian homes and child-rearing practices. Tribal communities and American Indian organizations rallied against the trend and ultimately successfully lobbied for the passage of the Indian Child Welfare Act, meant to stop these adoptions, in 1978.

James assumed that cross-cultural adoptions could provide opportunities for nonwhite children and the means for deeper understanding between the races. In the early 1960s, James dabbled in placing needy Indian children in non-Native households, and littered throughout his correspondence during this time are references to families that adopted or were interested in adopting Indian children. Most of these placements were informal, arranged outside the auspices of state or county welfare agencies, although one family used James as a reference for an adoption arranged through the Boys and Girls Aid Society, Oregon's oldest child welfare and adoption agency.

In March 1961 and again in January 1962, Dawn Polson of Hood River contacted James inquiring as to whether he knew of any Indian children who needed a home. She explained her motivation to adopt a Native child to James:

> I feel this great country of ours is more—than the white
> people think—property of the Indians. I was brought up to
> know the Indians were first here and were a very honorable
> race. Where they have fought, it has been in self defense. So
> if I can help them in a small way by providing a home for
> one of the children and helping it to get a good education it
> will give me a lot of happiness and feeling of
> accomplishment.[61]

Paulson assured James that hers would be a suitable home for a child in need, telling him that she and her husband Vernon owned a fifteen-acre Hood River Valley farm, had a fifteen-year-old biological son in 1962, and had been married since 1946.[62] Vernon worked for the Hines Lumber Company, and they were members of the Valley Christian Church (Disciples of Christ).[63] An adoptee herself, Dawn Polson and her husband adopted two children from Seoul, Korea, in 1961, two-and-a-half year-old Sung Sang Moon (Joseph King Polson) and two-year-old Elnuny Lou Kim (Maridawn LaVern Polson).[64] Historian Arissa Oh describes the "profile of adoptive families" of Korean children: "predominately white middle-class Protestants who were very religious, fairly conservative, and living in small towns or rural areas."[65] The Polsons certainly fit the description, and in adopting Korean children they were part of a national wave of international adoptions that emanated from Oregon.

The children in the Polson household came from a fledgling international adoption agency in the Willamette Valley founded by Harry and Bertha Holt. When the Holts brought twelve Korean children to the United States in 1955, they "triggered what would eventually become a tidal wave of intercountry adoptions"[66] and "established the nation's first adoption agency specifically geared to Korean adoption."[67] Dawn Polson proudly recounted in her letters to James the special legislation that Congress had to pass to naturalize her adopted children. But the Polsons also believed "we should help our own citizens first—before we do the ones from other countries."[68] They were not alone in their convictions. Many couples who adopted Korean nationals also inquired about adopting Native children, so much so that David Fanshel, the social scientist for the Indian Adoption Project, thought that "good experiences of white couples with Korean adoptees, as the media highly publicized cases of good adaptation, motivated them to choose a Native child."[69] The Polsons hoped to permanently adopt an Indian child, and James thought he had just the right one for them—Linda.

But if the Polsons were intent on demonstrating their Christian charity by taking Linda into their home, Flora was just as intent on demonstrating her parental duties to her granddaughter. James's efforts culminated with the placement of Linda into the Polson household in early August 1962. She stayed for the academic year and then moved out, against Dawn Polson's wishes, to spend the summer with Flora in June 1963. James initiated the process by writing to the Christie School in June 1962, vouching for the Polsons. He wrote, "Somehow, and perhaps for no one reason, I believe the Polson's are dependable people, she has written me before, but no child was available at the time, perhaps this is a natural thing, in behalf of human beings, it could be so, and let's pray it is."[70] James then wrote to Polson, "the granddaughter of the Old Chief Tommy Thompson needs such a home as you describe in your letter," describing Linda as "my special girl, so to speak, I have seen her grow from a tiny baby and she is unspoiled, loveable and honest, she does need a home of her own, something to closely tie to like most all of us have had, she is talented and sincere, and I love her just like she was mine."[71] He recommended that Polson read *Linda's Indian Home*.

From his home in Portland, James arranged for Flora Thompson to meet Dawn Polson: "I sincerely hope this will be the means of you folks getting together on the friendliest terms."[72] Though the two would eventually connect, Linda's departure from the Christie School slowed when the school insisted that housing arrangements for Linda be made by Flora, her legal guardian. James concluded that Martha McKeown had intervened.[73] Polson wrote to McKeown to introduce herself, and on July 16, McKeown responded. Though pleasant ("Indeed I do remember you—your kindness to the Korean children . . ."), Martha was adamant that any placement of Linda would happen only through official channels. She wrote, "Linda loves the Christie School and wants to return there next year. The sisters care a great deal for her. The caseworker, who tells me he has written you, feels she might be better off in a family home. But the actual placing of Linda, if she is moved, will be by the Welfare Office."[74] When Polson told James about Martha's response, he prodded her to pressure Martha to set up a fund for "the children whose names she used in the books" and complained that the McKeowns charged him more for fruit than any other orchard in the Hood River Valley.[75] Their friendship would not survive this episode.

James pushed ahead, telling Polson that Flora was "alert and in command of her thoughts always" and could sign paperwork relinquishing care of Linda.[76] James's Portland-area lawyer drew up a one-page contract that Flora Thompson and Dawn Polson signed, permitting the Polsons to raise Linda "as though she were their own."[77] James sent two copies of the contract to Polson, but it's clear from their correspondence that she worried about its legality. James assured her, "I am sure that is legal." "I can see no reason why the welfare should cause trouble for either you or Linda or Flora," he wrote, "because Flora wanted Linda to go to your home and live as a part of your family, and you wanted her to come to your home as your own, and I believe that was the right thing to do as both you and Flora and Linda approved of it and so do I. . . . I do not believe you should worry too much."[78] But it is unclear if Flora actually agreed to the arrangement or realized that the Polsons understood it to be permanent.

The Polsons picked up nine-year-old Linda from Flora on Wednesday, August 8, 1962.[79] Dawn immediately began to make plans for the fall school year, writing to James that she intended "to have Linda registered in school under our name, even tho she isn't actually adopted." She also asked James about changing Linda's name. "There are so many Lindas in this neighborhood that I would like to have her take my first name and her middle name so it would be Dawn Marie Polson." Although she wanted to avoid the repetitious "Linda," the name Polson proposed was similar to her other adopted daughter's name, Maridawn. Polson explained that the new name would "make fewer questions for [Linda] to answer to other kids about why our name is Polson and hers is something else," but she had other reasons for the change too: "Mrs. McKeown's son and other relatives live near us and since they don't know the child by sight it might help to keep them minding their own business."[80] Polson also theorized that the name change would make it easier for Linda as she progressed to high school, as friends and neighbors would assume she was a legal member of the family. The name symbolized a larger transformation that Polson sought for Linda: transition into a permanent member of the household.

Polson and James were aligned in their thinking on this point. "I believe we have a choice," James declared in a letter to defend his placement of Linda in the Polson home the year after she left. "Not a radical one, but a moderate one." James argued that "we can still keep our culture, be proud of our race . . . we can put on our regalia and dance the history of our people while . . . standing alongside of another race taking part in a modern way of life."[81] James approved of and even encouraged Linda to maintain ties to her Native heritage as long as they did not interfere with her acquiescence to non-Native modern life and its obligations.

As fall gave way to winter, James wrote letters to Linda encouraging her to mind "Mother Polson," study hard, and spend her free time honing her artistic skills. He sent her colored pencils and other gifts.[82] To Polson, James wrote about two children—James identified them as Alex Saluskin's grandchildren—who needed a home, urging her to contact his lawyer who "is not in love with Welfare" about her possible adoption of them.[83] At Christmas, Flora took Linda to family celebrations at Warm Springs and Celilo Village, displeasing James, who believed that "for Linda's sake that she should spend her time with [Dawn], and to remember that [the Polson family] has never been in trouble, and that is mighty good for anyone," implicitly suggesting that Linda might be exposed to unsavory incidents or people if she spent time in the Native community.[84]

When the academic year ended, Flora approached the Polsons about taking Linda for the summer, at least in part to work in the valley's berry fields. Polson didn't want to let Linda leave, and James was alarmed at the prospect of young Linda living in camps of migrant workers. In a letter to Flora he again expressed his concerns for Linda's safety and signaled the permanency of her placement with the Polsons:

> Do you really believe it would be the best thing for Linda to go to the berry fields all summer, rather than remain in the home there and be a part of the family? Taking part in community affairs and family affairs, of course no one must forget the things a girl of her age may meet out in the fields—and I realize that is a thing all must meet, but, growing up in a home where she is wanted, cared for and appreciated, and having her education from grade school, and high school through college assured, and having a solid home background to make them secure, learning the things that makes them better men or women.[85]

If Flora immediately replied, James did not keep a record of it. She removed Linda from the Polson home. Flora sent James an update at the beginning of August. Linda was working in the berry fields in Gresham until the midmonth huckleberry feast. "She will not be adopted," she wrote James, and "she will hold her own name, Linda M. George."[86] Flora located a foster home for Linda in The Dalles but did not provide James with the address. James reported that Dawn Polson was distraught, "just like losing a real daughter," when Linda left. She and James continued to write one another while she searched for another Indian child to adopt permanently.[87]

The entire incident illustrates Flora's struggle to maintain her authority over her own grandchild even among friends. James thought that he knew what was best for Linda, making assumptions about Flora's ability to protect and raise Linda that reflected biases he held, privileging white, middle-class nuclear family environments and mainstream schooling over the kinship networks of the village and the ceremonial instruction she would have received there. James's biases mirrored those of nineteenth- and early-twentieth-century white reformers who promoted removing Indian children from their homes. In turn, Flora's actions reflect how Indigenous parents and grandparents attempted to bend assimilationist institutions to their own needs. To ensure that Linda would have the opportunity to attend school in The Dalles or Hood River, Flora temporarily placed her with local families in a pattern that echoed the workings of the boarding schools that Flora knew well from her own upbringing. Those placements were never intended to become permanent adoptions that would remove Linda from her grandmother's care or from the seasonal food and ceremonial education that she needed.

In his sincere attempts to help Flora, Linda, and the Polsons, James enacted the "logics of elimination" that Flora had fought against her entire life.[88] He critiqued Flora's ability to raise Linda, predicting danger in migrant camps, longhouse ceremonies, and village festivities. Alternatively, placement with a white family could provide relief from the poverty of Celilo Village, regular schooling, and a pathway into mainstream America. James wanted to "save" Linda, but to do so was to deny her an Indian home. In contrast, Flora wanted to ensure that Linda had access to good schools by temporarily placing her with white families in Hood River and The Dalles, but also ensure that she could attend the longhouse ceremonies, have time with relatives, and develop into a responsible young woman who contributed to the household. Flora especially wanted to expose Linda to the spiritual teachings that would anchor her resistance of the assimilationist assumptions of the often well-meaning whites who surrounded her. As her grandmother, Flora was responsible for maintaining an Indian home for Linda, a responsibility she had no intention of relinquishing.

STORIES OF PLIGHT, STORIES OF AGENCY

His experience with Linda and the Polsons destroyed James's confidence in his ability to help Indian families at Celilo. On the first day of 1964, he wrote a joint letter to Reuben Olson, David Sheer, and Flora Thompson to confront the conflict the events had exposed among them. "This whole thing seems to be out of hand, or there is a terrible misunderstanding," he complained. "From my point I have surely used a lot of time and a terribly lot of effort with only one thought—TRYING TO HELP, TRYING TO MAKE THAT HELP CONSTRUCTIVE, TRYING TO DO SOMETHING SO THIS HELP

WOULD BENEFIT. NOT JUST NOW, BUT FROM NOW ON, AND TRYING TO INFORM THE PUBLIC OF THE INDIANS PLIGHT, NEEDS AND THEIR BELIEFS AND DESIRES—HONESTLY, BELIVING THE INDIAN PEOPLE WERE SINCERE AND THAT THEY WOULD DO THEIR PART HONESTLY AND FRANKLY SO THERE WOULD BE NO CONFUSION OR MISREPRESENTA- TION OR MISUNDERSTANDING."[89] James pleaded for recognition of his good intent, but he also placed the blame for the fracture in relations on individuals at Celilo, perhaps most especially on Flora.

The fallout over the placement of Linda was part of a broader struggle James faced defining his role as helper and press agent after the dam's completion. Shortly after Tommy Thompson died and Henry Thompson was made chief of the Wyam, James asked whether Henry wanted James to represent Celilo Village as its press agent. Thompson accepted. But James quickly became unhappy in the role. In 1963, he wrote "never envy me being a press agent, there is absolutely no glamour in it." "I never hear about anything unless its troubles," he complained, and people expected "supernatural results" from him in tackling those troubles.[90]

The work was becoming increasingly unfulfilling. The lack of a central focus like opposition to The Dalles Dam likely played a role. Shifts in federal policy like termination were harder to track and oppose than the day-to-day problems faced at Celilo Village. James concentrated his efforts on the relocation of a road that threatened to shrink the village footprint yet again and spent much of his time collecting donations of clothes and household goods that could be distributed at the village. But that work seemed never-ending. The inundation of the falls left Celilo Village a community of elders and children, as McKeown wrote in the *Christian Century*. As elders died, their families gave away all their personal items and then asked James to replenish them. Despite years of connecting needy families to donated goods, the need never seemed to abate. James eventually began to blame some of the Celilo leadership and individual families for this.

James heard gossip that Flora, with whom he often left things to be distributed to others in the community, wasn't passing out items. Similar complaints were lodged against Ida Wynookie, Tommy Thompson's daughter. Churches and social clubs that made donations alerted him to their concerns that their efforts were benefitting only a few families. James chalked most of the gossip up to the grumbling of other community members, jealous of the ties that Flora had to a wider network of assistance. But he pleaded with her to assure him that the rumors weren't true.[91]

He also complained that community members were always grateful for a delivery of household items and would pick things up from his home, but when he arranged for Celilo residents to pick up furniture or appliances from other locations, they often sat for weeks and sometimes never were collected. In his sixties, James declared himself too old to deliver heavy items to Celilo Village. Moreover, his wife's illness kept him close to home, as he was her primary caregiver. But James also worried that his efforts would eventually be rebuked by whites, who would ultimately judge Celilo residents as unworthy of charity.[92]

James personally felt duped in an exchange with Henry Thompson in 1964. While visiting the James home in Portland, Henry struck a trade with the artist. James would give Henry his rifle and fifty dollars in exchange for an eagle feather headdress that needed some repair and a buckskin shirt. Instead, Henry brought James a headdress of turkey feathers, one of significantly less value than the eagle-feather headdress they had agreed on. "I told him to keep the gun and forget" the headdress, James wrote to Henry's sister, Ida. In a letter he hoped would remain confidential, James wrote that he would "not go along with anyone who talks crooked."[93]

The long litany of James's complaints suggests a man who felt estranged after years of writing letters and intervening in Indian lives. Yet James also embraced an identity rooted in self-sacrifice and shared racial experience. He oriented his efforts toward intimate forms of rescue of deserving individuals for whom he crafted "plight narratives" that justified benevolence directed toward them.[94] He constructed individual Indians as needy and then complained bitterly when they did not conform to standard of worthiness or rejected his rescue. James's plight narratives were directed at an audience of well-meaning whites, most of whom had little contact with actual Indian people. James worried that Native actions, such as not picking up items he told do-gooders they needed, would undermine his public judgment of Celilo Indian families. Maude's long illness and eventual death in 1965 likely compounded James's frustration.

When he complained about Henry Thompson taking advantage of him in a trade, he might have recalled the long history of Indians out-negotiating white traders (and probably chafed at being placed in the second group). James frequently alluded to his own Native background to suggest that his aid was not a form of cultural imperialism but one of empowerment, but doing so obscured his race and class privilege—which were clearly legible to others—only to himself. Moreover, James pivoted from a critique of federal policies that abrogated treaties to focus on charity directed at individuals to ameliorate but not challenge those policies. But charity uncoupled from justice creates the possibility of injustice, which the story of Linda's "adoption" illustrates. James's philosophical shift countered the efforts of Martha McKeown.

Christian Century editor Harold Fey opined, "Indians prefer justice to charity, just as we do" in one of a series of 1955 articles that indicted federal policies for the poverty of Indian people and spurred the interests of white allies such as those in the Anselm Forum.[95] Martha McKeown's activism on behalf of the families at Celilo Village seemed guided by this sentiment. In 1957 she wrote a similar statement in a letter to Jimmie James. Indian elders, she wrote, "shouldn't be objects of charity" and wouldn't need it if government policies didn't impoverish them.[96] Like James, McKeown directed her efforts toward Indian people she knew, publicizing how federal decisions affected their lives. Yet McKeown refuted "plight narratives" that painted Indian people as abject and in need of benevolence. Instead, her writings on Celilo families focused on the strength—grounded in tradition and resistance to assimilation—of individuals and the community itself. She confronted reader expectations of plight narratives by describing Flora as "a woman of rare distinction and intelligence."[97] When she called on DAR members to assist the Wyam in 1955, she recounted their participation in the Modoc War alongside white army soldiers. This philosophy and rhetorical strategy separated McKeown from James and may have accounted for some of the conflict between them.

McKeown's narratives of Indigenous agency also imagined a place populated by neighbors who shared regional history that obligated them to one another. Her narratives described a reciprocal compassion devoid of desires to reform the behaviors of Indian people, in which the children of pioneers and the children of tribal leaders owed one another neighborly generosity. Such imaginings obscured the possibilities for cultural appropriations embedded in McKeown's work with the Oregon Historical Society or nationalistic organizations like the DAR or in her writing. But they also acknowledged Indigenous agency and articulated the tribal sovereignty and cultural integrity that were the basis of Flora's leadership. Unlike James, whose focus on individuals consumed his time into the 1960s, Flora and Martha dedicated their narratives to empowering tribal groups—the Wyam, especially.

Flora inverted Martha's neighborly generosity to remind her listeners that charity was first shown by the Indigenous peoples who met fur-trading vessels, haggard missionaries, and exhausted wagon parties. She claimed Tommy Thompson could recall the arrival of settlers as a young boy. "Old dad was barefoot," she told an interviewer, laughing at the thought of her now deceased husband as a child. "The kids were all barefoot and they were all bouncing up and down in the sand, going down to greet the new settlers coming westward. They didn't know whether they were scared or whether they were glad to see newcomers. They sang this song, they were all singing this song, 'Now the children of the stars has come upon us.' They were greeting the newcomers. That was the first time they had seen different people, new settlers coming westward, so they called them 'children of the stars.'"[98] Flora's account of the arrival of settlers to what would become Oregon exposed the relative newness of the Americanized region and the vulnerability of settlers. Within her husband's lifetime, needy newcomers had arrived, only to transform the place and Indigenous relationships to it. In the transformation, Indians became impoverished, dependent on wage labor and charity, as settlers and their descendants fenced off and overharvested the resources that once were shared.

When Jimmie James died in 1967, the letters stopped, and information about Martha and Flora became more sporadic. Martha Ferguson McKeown Dana died in a Portland nursing home on August 11, 1974, from complications related to Parkinson's disease.[99] She was seventy years old. Marshall Dana preceded her in death, having passed away in 1966. McKeown died at a time when her beloved women's organizations were diminishing in influence and membership as women increasingly entered paid professional fields and focused on legally eradicating gender discrimination.[100] The *Oregonian* announced McKeown's passing, lauded her contributions to the region's literature, and noted her close relationships with Celilo Village families. Although she didn't publish another book after 1961, Martha indelibly shaped how Oregonians understood Celilo Village and the impact of The Dalles Dam. Her books remained in print, for sale in museum gift shops and area bookstores. They represent her most public contribution to bridging Native and settler communities on the mid–Columbia River. The assistance she extended to elderly Indian neighbors, her long relationship with Tommy and Flora Thompson and other Indians, and her activism on behalf of Celilo Village—while often covered by local media at the time—have been less visible. In 2014, historian Linda Tamura helped recover Martha's interventions at an event held to thank residents of Hood River who came to the aid of their Japanese neighbors after World War II.[101] Otherwise, her efforts to establish more equitable relationships between white settlers and their nonwhite neighbors have largely gone unheralded.

Less than four years after Martha's passing, Flora Thompson died in a fire that also claimed her home.[102] If disease kept Martha from being productive in the last years of her life, Flora pushed on.

In her last decade, Flora recorded two oral history interviews, her only surviving self-crafted historical narratives. Interviewers questioned Flora about Chief Thompson and used the recordings as the basis of a twenty-two-page booklet of verse, "Flora's Song: A Remembrance of Chief Tommy Kuni Thompson." Flora used the interviews to shape her deceased husband's legacy—he was, according to Flora, a generous and wise leader who conserved salmon runs and attended to the spiritual needs of his community. But Flora also offered listeners a lens into how she understood her own life. Non-Native settlement in her homelands constricted every aspect of her life, yet she was enriched by her faith, her extended family, and the traditions of those who had come before her. She would be remembered as Chief Tommy Thompson's wife most importantly, a figure of small stature but much vitality, standing next to her husband in dozens of photographs. It is probably the legacy she would have most wanted.

Central to life in the Pacific Northwest—and other settler colonies worldwide—is the ongoing fraught relationship between Indigenous people and the descendants of settlers. In the early 1980s, Warm Springs tribal chairman Delbert Frank recommended that the tribal government protect pioneer grave sites within the reservation. He said, "the graves deserved respect and protection because of our joint journey."[103] Recalling Frank's generosity toward the settlers who displaced his ancestors, poet Elizabeth Woody wrote that the Northwest was built "from many perspectives woven together through time."[104] These perspectives are not parallel but integrated; collectively they built the region. Historian Daniel Herman writes that when historians document tribal communities "they are writing about the making of other Americans, too. Or at least they should be." One story cannot be told without the other. To combine phrases from theorists Mary Louis Pratt and Scott Lauria Morgensen, the Northwest is asymmetrically "co-constitutive,"[105] created out of the experiences of settlers and Indians and shaped by the differences of power and authority between them.

The Dalles Dam posed a crisis to Native fisheries that prompted considerable collaboration between Indigenous and non-Native allies throughout the region. While ultimately not successful at stopping or relocating the dam, that collaboration left an important legacy: cross-cultural intellectual and social networks that mediated mid-twentieth century Pacific Northwest political practices, which persisted into the decades to come. Too often these networks built on irreconcilable notions of region; Native peoples and their white allies spoke past one another on issues of place, sovereignty, and entitlement. But to focus on their limitations would be to ignore their successes, the very attempt to face and interrupt the ongoing legacies of settlement.

Similarly, Flora Thompson and Martha McKeown countered federal policies that sought to transform the physical geography of the Columbia River Basin and the relationship between Indigenous and non-Indigenous residents of the region. Together they represent the many northwesterners concerned about the pace and process of the region's transformation at midcentury. Both women signaled to those outside and within the region how to comprehend the Northwest, its relationship to the nation, and Indian-white relations. Flora Thompson illustrates female Native leadership at the critical moment after World War II and before strategies of self-determination, when federal termination and politicized rhetorics of sovereignty battled for primacy. During this period, Indigenous leaders laid the foundation for the comanagement of resources and more comprehensive tribal autonomy of the future. Martha

McKeown, who recognized the distinctive legal status of Indian people and understood the complicated entanglements of federal Indian policy, and who respected the autonomy and wisdom of her Indian friends, exemplifies strategies employed by non-Native allies that are still potent today.

Settler claims to the region's physical spaces were and are created out of the ongoing displacements of the region's Indigenous peoples. Likewise, contemporary conflicts over access to resources such as salmon are manifestations of colonial systems that racialized rights (and often the resources themselves) and codified them in treaty agreements. Settler anxiety over their displacement of and violence directed at Indigenous people has historically led to a spectrum of responses from those who have most benefited from the resettlement of the West—from the development of moral reform movements that supported forced assimilation for the supposed good of Indian people, to the equally destructive romanticizing of Indigenous authenticity, to the support of sovereignty and resource rights and struggles to make white supremacy visible. Flora embodied the persistence of Indianness in the region, and her leadership was forged in resistance to colonial assimilation. Martha claimed a settler heritage in juxtaposition with her Native neighbors yet also offered assistance without demands for authenticity or assimilation. Nevertheless, she embodied the hierarchies of colonialism. In this way the two women represent the very essence of regional identity in the Pacific Northwest. For Indigenous and settler populations and their children, unequal co-constructed relationships bounded by a colonial past characterize what it means to be *of* the American Northwest.

NOTES

JJJP James J. James Papers, 1894–1967, Ax 553, Special Collections and
University Archives, University of Oregon Libraries, Eugene

1. HOMELANDS IN TRANSITION

1   See Erna Gunther, "An Analysis of the First Salmon Ceremony,"
American Anthropologist 28 (1926): 605–17; Erna Gunther, "A Further Analysis of the First Salmon Ceremony," *University of Washington Publications in Anthropology* 2 (1928): 129–73.

2   Herman, *Rim Country Exodus*, 13.

3   "Annual Salmon Festival of Tribesmen Draws Hundreds of Indians
to Ceclio [*sic*]," *Oregonian*, April 20, 1953.

4   Frank Brown (Bella Bella Heiltsuk) quoted in Andrew Gulliford,
Sacred Objects and Sacred Places: Preserving Tribal Traditions (Boulder: University of Colorado Press, 2000), 199.

5   Historian David Igler critiques characterizations of the Pacific
Northwest as a "colonial hinterland" or of the American West as a
"plundered province" (in Bernard DeVoto's words), arguing instead
for a reconceptualization of the nation's industrial past to recognize
divergent regional paths. Igler, "The Industrial Far West: Region and
Nation in the Late Nineteenth Century," *Pacific Historical Review* 69,
no. 2 (May 2000): 159–92.

6   Theorists and historians of settler colonialism that have informed
this work include Patrick Wolfe, Lorenzo Veracini, and James Belich.
Representative examples of their work include Patrick Wolfe, "Settler
Colonialism and the Elimination of the Native," *Journal of Genocide
Research* 8, no. 4 (December 2008): 387–409; Lorenzo Veracini,

Settler Colonialism: A Theoretical Overview (Hampshire, UK: Palgrave Macmillan, 2010); and James Belich, *Replenishing the Earth: The Settler Revolution and the Rise of the Anglo-World, 1783–1939* (Oxford: Oxford University Press, 2009).

7   Other histories of Celilo Village and Celilo Falls published since my first book in 2005 have also greatly influenced this project. See, for example, George Aguilar, *When the River Ran Wild! Indian Traditions on the Mid-Columbia and the Warm Springs Reservation* (Seattle: University of Washington Press, 2005); Joseph Dupris, Kathleen S. Hill, and William H. Rodgers Jr., *The Si'lailo Way: Indians, Salmon, and Law on the Columbia River* (Durham, NC: Carolina Academic Press, 2006); Andrew Fisher, *Shadow Tribe: The Making of Columbia River Identity* (Seattle: University of Washington Press, 2010); and John Dougherty, "Flooded by Progress: Law, Natural Resources, and Native Rights in the Postwar Pacific Northwest" (PhD Dissertation, University of California, Berkeley, 2014). David-Paul Hedberg, a graduate student under my supervision, wrote his thesis based on the correspondence between James James and Yakama fisher and activist Wilson Charley while I was working on this project. Our complementary projects exploited the James James collection and prompted months of conversations that enhanced our individual ventures. See David-Paul Hedberg, "'As Long as the Mighty Columbia River Flows': The Leadership and Legacy of Wilson Charley, a Yakama Indian Fisherman" (MA thesis, Portland State University, 2017).

8   Mary Dodds Schlick identifies Flora Cushinway by her Indian name in her book *Columbia River Basketry: Gift of the Ancestors, Gift of the Earth* (Seattle: University of Washington Press, 1994), 14.

9   *General Index to Pension Files, 1861–1934* (Washington, DC: National Archives and Records Administration), T288, 546 rolls.

10   BIA census rolls for 1930 indicate that Edgar was the son of Flora and Edgar Tewee, born in 1917. *Indian Census Rolls, 1885–1940* (National Archives Microfilm Publication), M595, 692 rolls; Records of the Bureau of Indian Affairs, Record Group 75; National Archives, Washington, DC.

11   Lillian Ackerman, "Nonunilinear Descent Groups in the Plateau Culture Area," *American Ethnologist* 21, no. 2 (May 1994): 286–309; Lillian Ackerman, "Kinship, Family, and Gender Roles," in *Handbook of North*

American Indians, vol. 12, edited by Deward Walker and William C. Sturtevant (Washington, DC: Smithsonian Institution: 1998): 515–24.

12 Flora Cushinway Thompson, interview, n.d., Oregon Historical Research Library, Portland.

13 Lillian Ackerman, *A Necessary Balance: Gender and Power among Indians of the Columbia Plateau* (Norman: University of Oklahoma Press, 2003), and Lillian Ackerman, "Plateau Women and Their Culture," in *A Song to the Creator: Traditional Arts of Native American Women of the Plateau*, edited by Lillian Ackerman, (Norman: University of Oklahoma Press): 5–15.

14 Taiaiake Alfred, *Wasáe: Indigenous Pathways of Action and Freedom* (Peterborough, ON: Broadview Press, 2005), 24.

15 The following biographical information about Martha McKeown comes from Katrine Barber, "Stories Worth Recording: Martha McKeown and the Documentation of Pacific Northwest Life," *Oregon Historical Quarterly* 110, no. 4 (Winter 2009): 546–69.

16 Martha Ferguson McKeown, "Historical Umatilla House at The Dalles," *Oregon Historical Quarterly* 31, no. 1 (March 1930): 37–41.

17 For more information about women regional writers, especially as they move between professional and amateur status, see Julie Des Jardins, *Women and the Historical Enterprise in America: Gender, Race, and the Politics of Memory, 1880–1945* (Chapel Hill: University of North Carolina Press, 2003). See also John Rhea, *A Field of Their Own: Women and American Indian History, 1830–1941* (Norman: University of Oklahoma Press, 2016), and Bonnie Smith, *The Gender of History: Men, Women, and Historical Practice* (Cambridge, MA: Harvard University Press, 2000).

18 Quoted in Louise Michele Newman, *White Women's Rights: The Racial Origins of Feminism in the United States* (New York: Oxford University Press, 1999): 117.

19 Newman, *White Women's Rights*, 119.

20 Lori Jacobson, "The WNIA and the Erotics of Reform," in *Women's National Indian Association: A History*, edited by Valerie Sherer Mathes (Albuquerque: University of New Mexico Press, 2015), 281.

21 Margaret Jacobs, *Engendered Encounters: Feminism and Pueblo Cultures, 1879–1934* (Lincoln: University of Nebraska Press, 1999). See also Karin J. Huebner, "An Unexpected Alliance: Stella Atwood, the

California Clubwomen, John Collier, and the Indians of the Southwest, 1917–1934," *Pacific Historical Review* 78, no. 3 (August 2009), 337–66; Lisa M. Tetzloff, "'Shall the Indian Remain Indian?' Native Americans and the Women's Club Movement, 1899–1954" (PhD dissertation, Purdue University, 2008).

22 "Oregon Women Back Plans to Aid Indians," *Oregonian*, May 15, 1933.

23 Lisa Tetzloff, "Elizabeth Bender Cloud: 'Working for and with Our Indian People,'" *Frontiers* 30, no. 3 (2009): 77–115.

24 Paige Raibmon and others have demonstrated how labels such as "primitive" and "traditional," even sympathetically employed, place Indigenous people into what anthropologist Michael Herzfeld calls "irremediable subordination." Michael Herzfeld, "Political Optics and the Occlusion of Intimate Knowledge," *American Anthropologist* 107, no. 3 (2005), 370. See Paige Raibmon, *Authentic Indians: Episodes of Encounter from the Late-Nineteenth-Century Northwest Coast* (Durham, NC: Duke University Press, 2005).

25 The Daughters of the American Revolution organized the American Indians Committee in 1941.

26 Roberta Ulrich, *American Indian Nations from Termination to Restoration, 1953- 2006* (Lincoln: University of Nebraska Press, 2010). Oregon was home to more terminated tribes than any other state.

27 Herzfeld, "Political Optics," 372; Kenneth R. Philip, "Termination: A Legacy of the Indian New Deal," *Western Historical Quarterly* 14, no. 2 (April 1983): 165–80, 180.

28 While most historians have characterized termination policy as harmful to Native people, not all tribal people rejected the policy out of hand. Historian Laurie Arnold artfully examines why some members of the Colville Indian Reservation in Eastern Washington advocated for federal termination of the tribe as a way to escape Bureau of Indian Affairs surveillance. Laurie Arnold, *Bartering with the Bones of Their Dead: The Colville Confederated Tribes and Termination* (Seattle: University of Washington Press, 2012).

2. MAINTAINING/MAKING HOME

1 "Quest Band Fails to Find Skeleton," *Oregonian*, October 3, 1930, 1.

2 "Youths Lost in Hood Snows," *Oregonian*, January 3, 1927, 1; "One Boy Found in Hood Search," *Oregonian*, January 4, 1927, 1–2; "Boy

Hunt Continues," *Oregonian*, August 9, 1927, 5; "Fate of Climbers in Past Recalled," *Oregonian*, September 9, 1933, 2.

3   "Many Seeking Work—Few Jobs Open," *Hood River News*, October 3, 1930.

4   "Hood Skeleton Unfound," *Oregonian*, October 4, 1930, 2.

5   "Mount Hood Deaths Since 1883," *Oregonian*/OregonLive, February 7, 2012, updated June 4, 2015. www.oregonlive.com/pacific-northwest -news/index.ssf/2012/02/mount_hood_climber_deaths.html

6   The McKeown wedding was written up in the *Oregonian*'s "Society" page. *Oregonian*, June 15, 1924, 43.

7   Ibid.

8   One male figure important to Martha at the time of her marriage was Tommy Thompson, who would eventually become Flora's husband. Martha introduced Archie to Chief Thompson once they were engaged, yet apparently Thompson did not attend the wedding.

9   Albert Hurtado, "Settler Women and Frontier Women: The Unsettling Past of Western Women's History," *Frontiers: A Journal of Women Studies* 22, no. 3 (2001), 3. Emphasis mine.

10 Mishuana Goeman, *Mark My Words: Native Women Mapping Our Nations* (Minneapolis: University of Minnesota Press, 2013), 87.

11 Evelyn Nakano Glen situates federal Indian policy into the broader context of settler colonialism in the United States in "Settler Colonialism as Structure: A Framework for Comparative Studies of U.S. Race and Gender Formation," *Sociology of Race and Ethnicity* 1, no. 1 (2015), 54–74. Her work updates and extends Dolores Janiewski, "Gendering, Racializing, and Classifying: Settler Colonization in the United States, 1590–1990," in *Unsettling Settler Societies: Articulations of Gender, Race, Ethnicity, and Class*, edited by Daiva Stasiulis and Nira Yuval-Davis, Sage Series on Race and Ethnic Relations, vol. 11 (Thousand Oaks, CA: Sage, 1995), 132–60.

12 Goeman, *Mark My Words*, 10.

13 Entry for Martha McKeown, national number 332261, *Oregon state roster of ancestors [sic], Daughters of the American Revolution, 1963* (Tillamook: Oregon Society, D.A.R., 1963), 227.

14 "Albert W. Ferguson," *Portrait and Biographical Record of Western Oregon: Containing Original Sketches of Many Well Known Citizens of the Past and Present* (Chicago: Chapman, 1904), 838–39.

15   Cathleen Cahill, *Federal Fathers and Mothers: A Social History of the United States Indian Service, 1869–1933* (Chapel Hill: University of North Carolina Press, 2011), 35.

16   Richard H. Chused, "The Oregon Donation Act of 1850 and Nineteenth Century Federal Married Women's Property Law," *Law and History Review* 2, no.1 (Spring 1984), 55.

17   James Belich, *Replenishing the Earth: The Rise of the Anglo-World, 1783–1939* (Oxford: Oxford University Press, 2009).

18   John C. Weaver, *The Great Land Rush and the Making of the Modern World, 1650–1900* (Montreal: McGill-Queen's University Press, 2003). See also Marilyn Lake and Henry Reynolds, *Drawing the Global Colour Line: White Men's Countries and the International Challenge of Racial Equality* (Cambridge: Cambridge University Press, 2008).

19   Ferguson was in the California goldfields in October 1850, where a census taker recorded his occupation as "miner of gold." A biographical sketch indicates that he was in Astoria by the end of the year. Records of the Bureau of the Census, 1850. Seventh Census of the United States (National Archives Microfilm Publication M432, 1009 rolls); Record Group 29; National Archives, Washington, DC. Roll: M432–34; Page: 273B; Image: 52; "Albert W. Ferguson," *Portrait and Biographical Record.*

20   "Albert W. Ferguson," *Portrait and Biographical Record.*

21   The Oregon Territorial Legislature appointed Ferguson to a three-person committee to determine "selection of places for location and erection of public buildings of the Territory of Oregon" on January 21, 1853. *Journal of the Council of the Territory of Oregon Legislative Assembly during the fourth regular session of the legislative assembly, December 6, 1952* (Oregon: Asehal Bush, public printer, 1853), 102. Information regarding Ferguson's contributions to Oregon's infrastructure from 1853 to 1864 can be traced through *Territorial and Provisional Government Papers Index,* Oregon, Biographical and Other Cards, Oregon Historical Society, Portland.

22   Wasco County was 130,000 square miles when originally designated in 1854. Though reduced in size by the 1860s, the county was still a formidable territory to police when Ferguson was county sheriff.

23   "Albert W. Ferguson," *Portrait and Biographical Record*; and United States Department of the Interior, National Park Service, 1984,

National Register of Historic Places Inventory, Nomination Form, Albert W. Ferguson house.

24 Three Astoria homes on the National Historic Register were designed and built by the Fergusons: the Captain J. H. D. Gray or Harvey house (built 1880); the Albert W. Ferguson house (built 1886), designed by Albert Ferguson, who was bedridden at the time of its construction, and built by his son, James; the John N. Griffin house (built 1892), designed and built by James Ferguson. United States Department of the Interior, National Park Service, 1984. National Register of Historic Places Inventory, Nomination Form, Captain J. H. D. Gray house; United States Department of the Interior, National Park Service, 1984. National Register of Historic Places Inventory, Nomination Form, Albert W. Ferguson house; United States Department of the Interior, National Park Service, 1984. National Register of Historic Places Inventory, Nomination Form, John N. Griffin house.

25 Richard Engeman, *The Oregon Companion: An Historical Gazetteer of the Useful, the Curious, and the Arcane* (Portland, OR: Timber Press, 2009), 369.

26 Oscar Osburn Winther, *The Old Oregon Country: A History of Frontier Trade, Transportation, and Travel* (Lincoln: University of Nebraska Press, 1950); G. Thomas Edwards, "The Oregon Trail in the Columbia Gorge: The Final Ordeal," *Oregon Historical Quarterly* 97, no. 2 (Summer 1996): 134–75.

27 Ward Tonsfeldt and Paul G. Claeyssens, "Treaty with the Tribes of Middle Oregon" (Oregon History Project, 2004, updated and revised by OHP staff, 2014), in "Central Oregon: Adaptation and Compromise in an Arid Landscape," www.oregonhistoryproject.org/narratives /central-oregon-adaptation-and-compromise-in-an-arid-landscape /finding-central-oregon/treaty-with-the-tribes-of-middle-oregon/# .VabE_kjgeyQ; Les McConnell, "The Treaty Rights of the Confederated Tribes of Warm Springs," *Pacific Northwest Quarterly* 97, no. 4 (Fall 2006), 190.

28 Les McConnell, "The Treaty Rights," 191.

29 Department of the Interior, Office of Indian Affairs, *Annual Report of the Commissioner of Indian Affairs, for the Year 1900*, "Report of Supervisor in Charge of Warm Springs Agency" by A. O. Wright, August 6, 1900, Part I (Washington, DC: Government Printing Office, 1900), 367, http://digital.library.wisc.edu/1711.dl/History.AnnRep1900p1.

30 This is only part of Albert Kuckup's description of the reservation boundaries. *The Warm Springs Tribes of Indians of Oregon v. The United States*, Transcript of Testimony Taken at Warm Springs Agency, August 12, 1931, MS 2582, Oregon Historical Society Research Library, Portland, page 8.

31 George Aguilar, *When the River Ran Wild! Indian Traditions on the Mid-Columbia and the Warm Springs Reservation* (Portland: Oregon Historical Society Press, 2005), 15.

32 Portion of interview with Jeff Van Pelt by Donna Sinclair conducted in 1999, edited for publication in Clark Hansen, "Indian Views of the Stevens-Palmer Treaties Today," *Oregon Historical Quarterly* 106, no. 3 (Fall 2005), 478.

33 For a thorough examination of the Huntington Treaty as well as early calls for federal protection of river village sites like Celilo Village, see Les McConnell, "The Treaty Rights," 190–201.

34 Andrew Fisher, *Shadow Tribes: The Making of Columbia River Indian Identity* (Seattle: University of Washington Press, 2010).

35 National Archives and Records Administration, *U.S., Civil War Pension Index: General Index to Pension Files, 1861–1934*, Jim Cushinway, *Curry, Michael–Dabney, Clark*, T288, roll 108.

36 Boyd Cothran, *Remembering the Modoc War: Redemptive Violence and the Making of American Innocence* (Chapel Hill: University of North Carolina Press), 59–64; Thomas Dunlay, *Wolves for the Blue Soldiers: Indian Scouts and Auxiliaries with the U.S. Army, 1869–1890* (Lincoln: University of Nebraska Press, 1987). See also Ron Field, *Elite 91: U.S. Army Frontier Scouts, 1840–1921* (Oxford: Osprey, 2003), 14–15.

37 "Our Indian Allies," *San Francisco Bulletin*, June 17, 1873, 1.

38 Boyd Cothran addresses the problems Native American veterans and their widows faced in securing benefits, including the requirement to provide written documentation of marriages, deaths, and service. Cothran, *Remembering the Modoc War*, 152–60.

39 Department of the Interior, Bureau of Indian Affairs Records, RG 75, Records of the Warm Springs Indian Agency, Warm Springs, Oregon, 1861–1972, WS 10: Old Decimal Files, 1908–1952, ARC # 566736, Box 45, Field Matron Records, 1920–1922, 11.

40 Flora Cushinway Thompson, interviewer unknown, n.d., SR 9586, transcript. Oregon Historical Research Library, Portland, 2–3.

41   Quoted in Valerie Sherer Mathes, "Nineteenth Century Women and Reform: The Women's National Indian Association." *American Indian Quarterly* 14, no. 1 (1990), 5.

42   My analysis of the Dawes Allotment Act and the Oregon Donation Land Act have been greatly enhanced by Tonia M. Compton, "Proper Women / Propertied Women: Federal Land Laws and Gender Order(s) in the Nineteenth Century Imperial American West" (PhD diss., University of Nebraska, 2009). See also Delores Janiewski, "Learning to Live 'Just Like White Folks': Gender, Ethnicity, and the State in the Inland Northwest," in *Gendered Domains: Rethinking Public and Private in Women's History*, edited by Dorothy Helly and Susan Reveby (Ithaca, NY: Cornell University Press, 1992).

43   Melinda Jette, *At the Hearth of the Crossed Races: A French-Indian Community in Nineteenth Century Oregon, 1812–1859* (Corvallis: Oregon State University Press, 2015), 195.

44   Amy Kaplan, "Manifest Domesticity," *American Literature* 70, no. 3 (September 1998), 581–606.

45   Bethany Ruth Berger, "After Pocahontas: Indian Women and the Law, 1830 to 1934," *American Indian Law Review* 21, no.1 (1997), 61.

46   Quoted in Tonia M. Compton, "Proper Women / Propertied Women," 118. See also Nicole Tonkovich, *The Allotment Plot: Alice C. Fletcher, E. Jane Gay, and Nez Perce Survivance* (Lincoln: University of Nebraska Press, 2012), and Louise Michele Newman, *White Women's Rights: The Racial Origins of Feminism in the United States* (New York: Oxford University Press, 1999), especially chapter 5.

47   Chused, "The Oregon Donation Act," 73.

48   Quoted in Chused, "The Oregon Donation Act," 73.

49   "Indians Scout Here for Berry Season," *Hood River News*, May 10, 1940.

3. GROWING UP

1   "Odell Folk to Hear Noted Indian Story," *Hood River Glacier News*, September 14, 1922.

2   F. H. Balch, *The Bridge of the Gods: A Romance of Indian Oregon*, 23rd ed. (Chicago: A. C. McClurg and Co., 1921), 44.

3   Ibid., 54.

4   Ibid., 183–84.

5   Ibid., 184.

6   Ibid., 152.

7   Ibid., 233.

8   Oregon Cultural Heritage Commission, 2003, "Frederic Homer Balch—A Troubled Christian Writer's Brief Life" by Walt Curtis, www.ochcom.org/pdf/Frederic-Balch.pdf, 1.

9   Thomas Willing Balch, *Balch Genealogica* (Philadelphia: Allen, Lane and Scott, 1907), 92–93; *Publishers Weekly*, no. 1594 (August 16, 1902), 242.

10 Almira Ferguson became friends with Balch's sister, Gertrude Ingalls, who helped cement her brother's legacy by becoming a writer herself. In 1900, she wrote a two-page treatment of her brother's work and his literary influence, casting him as a tragic figure who poured all his energy into his writing only to die at twenty-nine, leaving behind the notes and outlines for six books that he never got to write. Gertrude Balch Ingalls, "Frederic Homer Balch. Author of 'The Bridge of the Gods,'" *Pacific Monthly: A Magazine of Education and Progress* 4 (May–October 1900), 85–86.

    In 1932, the Oregon Society of the Daughters of the American Revolution commemorated the author and his mother, who was a descendent of an American Revolutionary veteran and therefore eligible for membership, when they placed a marker at the first school Balch attended. "Monument to Memory of Noted Oregon Author to Be Dedicated Today at Tallman," *Oregonian*, June 12, 1932.

11 "Women Preserve 'The Bridge of the Gods,'" *Oregonian*, October 15, 1911, 4. The quotations come from Richard Etulain, "Frederic Homer Balch (1861–1891): Romancer and Historian," *Oregon Historical Quarterly* 117, no. 4 (Winter 2016), 629. Etulain has produced the most comprehensive examination of Balch's writings to date.

12 David Glassberg, "Public Ritual and Cultural Hierarchy: Philadelphia's Civic Celebrations and the Turn of the Twentieth Century," *Pennsylvania Magazine of History and Biography* 107, no. 3 (July 1993), 431. See also David Glassberg, *American Historical Pageantry: The Uses of Tradition in the Early Twentieth Century* (Chapel Hill: University of North Carolina Press, 1990).

13 "Indian Legends of Great Stone Arch to Be Told with Panoramic Pictures," *Oregonian*, June 2, 1912, 22. Indians hired on to perform in such nationalistic displays for many reasons, including for wages and the opportunity to travel. See, for example, Paige Raibmon,

Authentic Indians: Episodes of Encounter from the Late Nineteenth-Century Pacific Coast (Durham, NC: Duke University Press, 2006), and Dan Moos, *Outside America: Race, Ethnicity, and the Role of the American West in National Belonging* (Durham, NC: Duke University Press, 2006). Earlier in the decade, Indians from around the region performed as part of the Lewis and Clark Centennial Exposition's amusement strip, the "Trail." See Emily Trafford, "Hitting the Trail: Live Displays of Native American, Filipino, and Japanese People at the Portland World's Fair," *Oregon Historical Quarterly* 116, no. 2 (Summer 2015), 158–95.

14   "More Seats Necessary," *Oregonian*, June 7, 1912, 9.

15   "Indians Rehearse Play," *Oregonian*, July 3, 1912, 14.

16   Scott Lauria Morgensen describes the dialectical construction of "Native" and "settler" as "co-constitutive," in which "settlers are intrinsically *relational* subjects, defined by a perpetual process of indigenous replacement." Morgensen, "Theorizing Gender, Sexuality and Settler Colonialism: An Introduction," *Settler Colonial Studies* 2, no. 2 (2012), 12.

17   Indigenous persistence created and re-created what political scientist Kevin Bruyneel calls "the third space of sovereignty," as Indians demanded "rights and resources from the liberal democratic settler-state while also challenging the imposition of colonial rule on their lives." Bruyneel, *The Third Space of Sovereignty: The Postcolonial Politics of U.S.-Indigenous Relations* (Minneapolis: University of Minnesota Press, 2007), xvii.

18   James and Almira Ferguson's children were Edward (b. 1884), Alma (b. 1893), Almont (b. 1894), and Martha (b. 1903).

19   "Mrs. Hawthorne's Funeral Yesterday," *Hood River Glacier*, August 25, 1921.

20   Martha Hawthorne's husband was Samuel (b. 1835), their son Mont (b. 1866), and daughters Almira (b. 1874), Sarah (b. 1864), and Julia (b. 1861).

21   "Mrs. Hawthorne's Funeral Yesterday."

22   Martha Ferguson McKeown, *Them Was the Days: An American Saga of the '70s* (Lincoln: University of Nebraska Press, 1961), 181.

23   Ibid.

24   Ibid., 234–35.

25   Ibid., 181, 236.

26 "Mrs. Harford Re-elected President of W.C.T.U.," *Morning Astorian*, October 11, 1901.

27 Almira Ferguson was well known in the local temperance and religious community for oration and spoke regularly before audiences of the local chapter of the Epworth League, an association for young adult Methodists. *Morning Astorian*, November 17, 1900; "Epworth League Reception," *Morning Astorian*, March 22, 1901; "Mrs. Harford Re-elected President of W.C.T.U."

28 *Morning Astorian*, June 12, 1900.

29 For an examination of the evangelical foundations of the WCTU and WNIA, see Helen Bannan, "The WNIA in the Context of Women's History," in *Women's National Indian Association: A History*, edited by Valerie Sherer Mathes (Albuquerque: University of New Mexico Press, 2015).

30 Anne M. Boylan, *Sunday School: The Formation of an American Institution, 1790–1880* (New Haven, CT: Yale University Press, 1990), 121. See also Anne M. Boylan, "Evangelical Womanhood in the Nineteenth Century: The Role of Women in Sunday Schools," *Feminist Studies* 4, no. 3 (October 1978): 62–80.

31 Gerald Gamm and Robert D. Putnam, "The Growth of Voluntary Associations in America, 1840–1940," *Journal of Interdisciplinary History* 29, no. 4 (Spring 1999), 511–57. Gamm and Putnam identified the most robust growth of voluntary organizations as occurring in the West and Midwest and in small towns and cities rather than in large northeastern cities. Historians have often viewed women's voluntary club work as part of the broadening of women's professional options. See Alice Kessler-Harris's classic study *Out to Work: A History of Wage-Earning Women in the United States* (New York: Oxford University Press, 1982).

32 Anne Firor Scott, *Natural Allies: Women's Associations in American History* (Urbana: University of Illinois Press, 1991), 178.

33 Helen Laville, *Organized White Women and the Challenge of Racial Integration, 1945–1965* (Basingstoke, UK: Palgrave Macmillan, 2017), 2. Laville argues that the postwar membership bump can be attributed to the overwhelming societal push of white middle-class women into private domesticity during the Cold War. Voluntary associations were an attractive alternative to domestic life for women who watched their professional options otherwise narrow.

34 The *Hood River Glacier* helpfully chronicled various visitors to the valley, including the seven visits Martha Ferguson made between 1906 and 1911.

35 "Blanket of Snow Wraps Northwest," *Oregonian*, January 8, 1912, 1.

36 Works Project Administration, *Inventory of the County Archives of Oregon*, vol. 14: *Hood River County* (Portland: Oregon Historical Records Survey Project, 1939), 11.

37 For a fascinating history of Mount Hood National Forest that addresses the site's changing designations, see Taylor Rose, "Seeing the Forest for the Roads: Auto-tourism and Wilderness Preservation in Mount Hood National Forest, 1913–64" (MA thesis, Portland State University, 2016).

38 Sydney G. Babson, "Hood River Valley Wild Night," *Oregon Historical Quarterly* 70, no. 1 (Spring 1969), 51.

39 Oregon Agricultural College Extension Service, *Report of the Hood River County Agricultural Economic Conference, Hood River Oregon, December 4, 5 and 20, 1924*. Oregon State Library Online Catalog.

40 William G. Loy, Stuart Allan, Aileen R. Buckley, and James E. Meacham, *Atlas of Oregon*, 2nd ed. (Eugene: University of Oregon Press, 2001). Average farm size in Hood River County was smaller than in any other Oregon county (in 1997, the average farm in the county was just fifty-three acres).

41 Loy et al., *Atlas of Oregon*, 26–27.

42 Babson, "Hood River Valley Wild Night," 52.

43 "Hood River Knows How to Enjoy Life as Well as Raise Apples," *Oregonian*, September 1, 1912, 3.

44 Joseph Ellison, "The Beginnings of the Apple Industry in Oregon," *Agricultural History* 11, no. 4 (October 1937), 329.

45 "Hood River Knows How to Enjoy Life."

46 Joseph Ellison, "The Cooperative Movement in the Oregon Apple Industry, 1910–1929," *Agricultural History* 13, no. 2 (April 1939), 77.

47 "Hood River Apple Is Known All Over the World," *Oregonian*, February 4, 1911, 24.

48 Ellison, "The Beginnings of the Apple Industry in Oregon," 339.

49 Ibid., 82.

50 Ibid.

51 Ibid.

52 John Goodenberger, "Astoria's Historic Resources and Heritage" (City of Astoria, August 2006), 11.

53 *Hood River News*, September 25, 1912.

54 "Odell," *Hood River Glacier*, November 16, 1911, and April 11, 1912.

55 "Ferguson Class," *Hood River Glacier*, May 1, 1913.

56 Ibid.

57 "Mrs. Hawthorne's Funeral Yesterday."

58 *Hood River Glacier*, February 27, 1919.

59 "Miss Ferguson Gives Recital," *Hood River Glacier*, July 5, 1917.

60 "Mrs. Gould Shepard Gives Bible Prizes," *New York Times*, April 4, 1915.

61 "Hood River Girl Determined to Win Bible," *Oregon Daily Journal*, February 24, 1919, and "Miss Ferguson Honored," *Hood River Glacier*, September 18, 1919.

62 "Odell Graduates Have Records," *Hood River Glacier*, June 5, 1919.

63 "Hood River Knows How to Enjoy Life."

64 "Hood River Apple."

65 "Beautiful Homes of Orchardists Dot Hills in Hood River Region," *Oregonian*, November 19, 1911, 6; Frederick Jackson Turner, *The Significance of the Frontier in American History* (Madison: State Historical Society of Wisconsin, 1894).

66 "Beautiful Homes of Orchardists."

67 National Society, United States Daughters of 1812, 1892–1939, *News-Letter* 14, no. 1 (July 1939), 41–43.

68 *Hood River Glacier*, November 12, 1908.

69 Hood River County Historical Society, *History of Hood River County, Oregon, 1852–1982*, vol. 1 (Hood River, OR: Hood River County Historical Society, 1982), 254. This overview is gleaned from eleven family histories published in this volume, including the family history of author Linda Tamura, whose work I've relied on, and the history of the Yasui family, the subject of Lauren Kessler's wonderful book, *Stubborn Twig: Three Generations in the Life of a Japanese American Family* (New York: Random House, 1993).

70 Marjorie Stearns, "The Settlement of the Japanese in Oregon," *Oregon Historical Quarterly* 39, no. 3 (September 1938), 264–65.

71 Linda Tamura, "Railroads, Stumps, and Sawmills: Japanese Settler of the Hood River Valley," *Oregon Historical Quarterly* 94, no. 4 (Winter 1993/1994), 377.

72 Oregon state representative L. N. Blowers quoted in Linda Tamura, *Nisei Soldiers Break Their Silence: Coming Home to Hood River* (Seattle: University of Washington Press, 2012), 26.

73 Eiichiro Azuma, "A History of Oregon's Issei, 1880–1952," *Oregon Historical Quarterly* 94, no. 4 (Winter 1993/1994), 335–38.

74 *History of Hood River County, Oregon,* 444.

75 Katherine Story French, "Culture Segments and Variation in Contemporary Social Ceremonialism on the Warm Springs Reservation, Oregon" (PhD dissertation, Columbia University, 1955), 55.

76 Descriptions of Plateau birth practices are drawn from Caroline James, *Nez Perce Women in Transition, 1877–1990* (Moscow: University of Idaho Press, 1996).

77 French, "Culture Segments and Variation," page 1 of abstract and page 1 of preface.

78 A. O. Wright, "Report of Supervisor in Charge of Warm Springs Agency," August 6, 1900, United States, Office of Indian Affairs, *Annual Report of the Commissioner of Indian Affairs, for the Year 1900,* Part 1 (Washington, DC: G.P.O., [1900]), http://digital.library.wisc.edu/1711.dl/History.AnnRep1900p1, 367.

79 Wright, "Report of Supervisor," 368.

80 French, "Culture Segments and Variation," 33.

81 RG 75, Bureau of Indian Affairs, Portland Area Office, Land Transaction Case Files, 1946–65, 310 Umatilla, Warm Springs, Box 156, Folder WS 310, NARA, Seattle, Washington.

82 French, "Culture Segments and Variation," 24.

83 Ibid., 13.

84 The United States Court of Claims, Transcript of Testimony Taken at Warm Springs Agency, 12 August 1931, *The Warm Springs Tribes of Indians of Oregon vs. The United States,* No. M-112, 4.

85 Mary C. Wright, "The Woman's Lodge: Constructing Gender on the Nineteenth-Century Pacific Northwest Plateau," *Frontiers: A Journal of Women Studies* 24, No. 1 (2003), 1.

86 Ibid., 6.

87 Ibid., 2.

88 Allotment accelerated the transformation of Indigenous naming practices to conform to an individual first name followed by a family surname. BIA commissioner T. J. Morgan instructed reservation agents to impose last names on their wards: "under the allotment act, the

inheritance of property will be governed by the laws of the respective States, and it will cause needless confusion and, doubtless, considerable, ultimate loss to the Indians if no attempt is made to have the different members of a family known by the same family name on the records and by general reputation." Morgan recommended that agents use Indigenous names for Indian families, perhaps Americanizing, shortening, or otherwise making them easier for non-Natives to pronounce, if necessary. H. Ex. Doc., 2d sess., 51st Cong., vol. XII, cxlvi–clii, clx. See Aguilar, *When the River Ran Wild!*, for information about Plateau Indigenous naming practices and their connections to history keeping. See James C. Scott, *Seeing Like a State: How Certain Schemes to Improve the Human Condition Have Failed* (New Haven: Yale University Press, 1999) for information about how states demanded that Indigenous naming practices change to conform to the needs of government documentation.

89 Aguilar, *When the River Ran Wild!*, 60–61.

90 Ibid., 61.

91 James, *Nez Perce Women in Transition*, 2.

92 Kim Anderson, *A Recognition of Being: Reconstructing Native Womanhood* (Toronto, ON: Sumach Press, 2000), 120.

93 The reservation had two boarding schools during this period, one near the agency and one at Simnasho. By the time Flora enrolled, the schools had been consolidated into a single boarding school. See Janice White Clemmer, "The Confederated Tribes of Warm Springs, Oregon: Nineteenth Century Indian Education History" (PhD Dissertation, University of Utah, 1980).

94 In describing traditional Nez Perce marriage, Caroline James noted that "spouses of siblings could be sexual partners, and the approval of sexual intimacy between these potential mates (anticipatory levirate and sororate) illustrates the way the complete family—not just one couple—is united" through marriage. Though Effie's relationship to William was different, her marriage to him could have had the same unifying effect between families because she was the second sibling to marry a Sookoit. James, *Nez Perce Women in Transition*, 84.

95 Clemmer, "The Confederated Tribes of Warm Springs," 166.

96 John Smith to T. B. Odeneal, September 1, 1872, 42nd Cong., 3rd sess., vol. I, H. Ex. Doc. 1, pt. 5, vol. III, pt. 1, 749–51.

97 Department of the Interior, Bureau of Indian Affairs Records, RG 75, Records of the Warm Springs Indian Agency, Warm Springs, Oregon, 1861–1972, Box 154, Indian Agency Ed Program Records, 1891–1923, Daily Record of Warm Springs Boarding School, 236–37.

98 Janice Clemmer's dissertation documents the complaints of superintendents regarding school absenteeism over several decades in the nineteenth century. Those complaints persisted well into the twentieth century as well. Additionally, records do not accurately reflect attendance because "school population totals were often erroneously given based on an initial enrollment of children. While a child may have his or her name listed, such action did not guarantee continued attendance." Clemmer, "The Confederated Tribes of Warm Springs," 201.

99 Ibid.

100 Ibid., 237.

101 Department of the Interior, Bureau of Indian Affairs Records, RG 75, Records of the Warm Springs Indian Agency, Warm Springs, Oregon, 1861–1972, Box 154, Indian Agency Ed Program Records, 1891–1923, Daily Record of Warm Springs Boarding School, 268–69.

102 Clemmer, "The Confederated Tribes of Warm Springs," 242.

103 *Indian Census Rolls, 1885–1940*; Year: 1918; Roll: M595, roll 636; Line 14; Agency: Warm Springs (National Archives Microfilm Publication M595, 692 rolls); Records of the Bureau of Indian Affairs, Record Group 75; National Archives, Washington, DC.

104 Ackerman, *A Necessary Balance*, 54.

105 *Indian Census Rolls, 1885–1940*; Year: 1930; Roll: M595, roll 638; Line 1; Agency: Warm Springs (National Archives Microfilm Publication M595, 692 rolls); Records of the Bureau of Indian Affairs, Record Group 75; National Archives, Washington, DC.

106 Department of the Interior, Bureau of Indian Affairs Records, RG 75, Records of the Warm Springs Indian Agency, Warm Springs, Oregon, 1861–1972, Subject Files, 1908–25, Box 28, Tribal Herds—ED, Law and Order, Misc.

107 Johnnie Tewee and Mabel Henning Tewee divorced sometime between 1928 and 1932. See *Indian Census Rolls, 1885–1940* (National Archives Microfilm Publication M595), 692 rolls; Records of the Bureau of Indian Affairs, Record Group 75; National Archives, Washington, DC.

108 Department of the Interior, Bureau of Indian Affairs Records, RG 75, Records of the Warm Springs Indian Agency, Warm Springs, Oregon, 1861–1972, WS 10: Old Decimal Files, 1908-1952, ARC # 566736, Box 45, Field Matron Records, 1920-1922, 202.

109 See Lisa E. Emmerich, "Promoting Homemaking on the Reservations: WNIA Field Matrons," in *Women's National Indian Association: A History*, edited by Valerie Sherer Mathes (Albuquerque: University of New Mexico Press, 2015), and Lisa E. Emmerich, "'Right in the Midst of My Own People': Native American Women and the Field Matron Program," *American Indian Quarterly* 15, no. 2 (1991): 201–16. See also Cathleen D. Cahill, *Federal Fathers and Mothers: A Social History of the United States Indian Service, 1869-1933* (Chapel Hill: University of North Carolina Press, 2011).

110 Complete field matron records for the Warm Springs Reservation do not exist, but Minnie Holcomb's records for the years 1920-22 do survive. Department of the Interior, Bureau of Indian Affairs Records, RG 75, Records of the Warm Springs Indian Agency, Warm Springs, Oregon, 1861–1972, WS 10: Old Decimal Files, 1908-1952, ARC # 566736, Box 45, Field Matron Records, 1920-1922.

111 Department of the Interior, Bureau of Indian Affairs Records, RG 75, Records of the Warm Springs Indian Agency, Warm Springs, Oregon, 1861–1972, WS 10: Old Decimal Files, 1908-1952, ARC # 566736, Box 45, Field Matron Records, 1920-1922, 200.

112 Ibid., 10.

113 Ibid., 223.

114 Ibid., 163.

115 Bruce Howard Wendt, "An Administrative History of the Warm Springs, Oregon, Indian Reservation, 1855-1955" (PhD Dissertation, Washington State University, 1989), 158.

116 Sarah Carter, *Capturing Women: The Manipulation of Cultural Imagery in Canada's Prairie West* (Montreal: McGill-Queen's University Press, 1997), 162.

117 Anderson, *A Recognition of Being*, 100.

118 This child was a very young infant when he passed. Flora and Boise also lost a young daughter, whose death she describes in her oral history. See chapter 4.

119 Aguilar, *When the River Ran Wild!*, 13.

120 Flora Cushinway Thompson, interviewer unknown, n.d., SR 9586, transcript, Oregon Historical Research Library, Portland, Oregon.

121 "Young Boise," Ancestry.com, *Washington, Select Death Certificates, 1907–1960* [database online] (Provo, UT: Ancestry.com Operations, Inc., 2014).

122 Lucy Miller was a Warm Springs Indian whose maiden name was Papaluit. Like Flora Cushinway, she was born in 1898.

123 David H. and Katherine S. French Papers, Box 16, Folder 7, Special Collections, University of Washington Libraries, Seattle.

124 Flora Cushinway Thompson, interviewer unknown, n.d., SR 9586, transcript, Oregon Historical Research Library, Portland, Oregon.

125 "Gone Are Old Days; Indians Vainly Seek Food Store of Yore," *Oregon Daily Journal*, August 1, 1920.

126 The local press reported on the arrest of Indian hunters for poaching with some frequency, though rarely did they identify the arrested men by name. For example, in 1932 the *Hood River News* reported that three Indians from the Warm Springs Reservation were arrested with fourteen deer, including bucks and does. "Indians Nabbed with Many Deer," *Hood River News*, March 25, 1932.

127 The United States Court of Claims, Transcript of Testimony Taken at Warm Springs Agency, August 12, 1931, *The Warm Springs Tribes of Indians of Oregon vs. The United States*, No. M-112, 57.

128 Ibid., 61.

129 *History of Hood River County*, 367.

4. CONVERGING PATHS OF LEADERSHIP

1 Freda Mowrey, "Wife of Celilo Indian Chief Tells Efforts of Tribal Women to Improve People's Lot," *Oregonian*, October 16, 1949, 49.

2 "Oregon Women Back Plans to Aid Indians," *Oregonian*, May 15, 1933.

3 "Winema Chapter, D.A.R., Observes Annual Guest Day at Stiles Home," *Corvallis Gazette-Times*, October 15, 1949.

4 Martha Ferguson McKeown, "Certain Aspects of Thoreau's Emphasis on Self" (MA thesis, University of Oregon, 1938).

5 It is unclear why McKeown left her position at Multnomah College after three years. Limited records for Multnomah College are held at the University of Portland Archives.

6   "Dream Come True," *(Salem) Statesman Journal*, January 23, 1949.

7   F. E. Perkins, December 31, 1931, "Welfare and Social Conditions; Family Conditions," Narrative Section, Annual Report, 1932, Warm Springs Agency, Warm Springs, Oregon, WS 10: Old Decimal Files, 1908–1952, Box 42, RG 75, National Archives—Pacific Northwest Region.

8   F. E. Perkins, December 31, 1931, "Industrial Development; Off the reservation—employment," Narrative Section, Annual Report, 1932, Warm Springs Agency, Warm Springs, Oregon, WS 10: Old Decimal Files, 1908–1952, Box 42, RG 75, National Archives—Pacific Northwest Region.

9   F. E. Perkins, December 31, 1931, "Agricultural Development; On the reservation," Narrative Section, Annual Report, 1932, Warm Springs Agency, Warm Springs, Oregon, WS 10: Old Decimal Files, 1908–1952, Box 42, RG 75, National Archives—Pacific Northwest Region. Virginia Beavert writes about the twentieth-century use of horses on the Yakama Reservation in "Wántwint Inmí Tiináwit: A Reflection of What I Have Learned" (PhD dissertation, University of Oregon, 2012).

10 F. E. Perkins, December 31, 1931, "Welfare and Social Conditions; Family Conditions," Narrative Section, Annual Report, 1932, Warm Springs Agency, Warm Springs, Oregon, WS 10: Old Decimal Files, 1908–1952, Box 42, RG 75, National Archives—Pacific Northwest Region.

11 Chad Hamill, *Songs of Power and Prayer in the Columbia Plateau: The Jesuit, the Medicine Man, and the Indian Hymn Singer* (Corvallis: Oregon State University Press, 2012), 1.

12 Hattie Boise died April 8, 1933, and Martha Cushinway died April 14, 1933. Oregon State Library; *Oregon Death Index 1931–1941*; Reel Title: *Oregon Death Index M–Z*; Year Range: *1931–1941*, Ancestry.com. *Oregon, Death Index, 1898–2008* [database online] (Provo, UT: Ancestry.com Operations Inc., 2000).

13 Flora Cushinway Thompson, interviewer unknown, n.d., SR 9586, transcript, Oregon Historical Research Library, Portland.

14 See Aguilar, *When the River Ran Wild!*, 161–166; Hamill, *Songs of Power and Prayer*, 111–125; and Beavert, "Wántwint Inmí Tiináwit," 71–93.

15 Flora Cushinway Thompson, interviewer unknown, n.d., SR 9586, transcript, Oregon Historical Research Library, Portland.

16 Ibid.

17 Hamill, *Songs of Power and Prayer*, 17.

18 Ibid., 13.

19 Ibid., 41.

20 Flora Cushinway Thompson, interviewer unknown, n.d., SR 9586, transcript, Oregon Historical Research Library, Portland.

21 Ibid.

22 Andrew Fisher addresses Babcock's regulation of Shaker ceremonies on the Warm Springs Reservations in *Shadow Tribe: The Making of Columbia River Indian Identity* (Seattle: University of Washington Press, 2010), 130–32. Babcock objected to healing ceremonies in particular, arguing that they were in violation of federal restrictions on traditional Indian healing practices, put into place in 1907. To protect their standing, the Indian Shaker Church incorporated in Oregon in 1907, followed by incorporation in Washington (1910) and California (1932). Church member responses to Babcock's suppression can be found in the folder "Law and Order, Religious Organizations," Department of the Interior, Bureau of Indian Affairs Records, RG 75, Records of the Warm Springs Indian Agency, Warm Springs, Oregon, 1861–1972, Subject Files, 1908–25, Box 29, ED: Law and Order, Education. Superintendent Babcock.

23 "Indians Have Peculiar Religion," *Hood River Glacier*, August 19, 1912.

24 Washington, *Select Death Certificates, 1907–1960* [database online] (Provo, UT: ancestry.com).

25 United States of America, Bureau of the Census, *Sixteenth Census of the United States, 1940* (Washington, DC: National Archives and Records Administration, 1940), T627, 4,643 rolls. Place: Toppenish Rural, Yakima, Washington. Roll: T627, roll 4372, page 1B.

26 Timothy George and Flora Boice [*sic*], *Washington, Marriage Records, 1865–2004* [database online] (Provo, UT: Ancestry.com Operations, Inc., 2012).

27 United States of America, Bureau of the Census, *Fifteenth Census of the United States, 1930* (Washington, DC: National Archives and Records Administration, 1930), T626, 2,667 rolls. Place: Odell, Hood River, Oregon. Roll: 1942, page 7A.

28 Historians Joel Perlmann and Robert A. Margo point out that the teaching profession offered women "opportunities to acquire managerial skills [and use them] that were scarcely available to women

elsewhere in the economy at the time." Perlmann and Margo, *Women's Work? American Schoolteachers, 1650–1920* (Chicago: University of Chicago Press, 2001), 130. See also Geraldine Clifford, "'Daughters into Teachers': Educational and Demographic Influences on the Transformation of Teaching into 'Women's Work' in America," in *Women Who Taught: Perspectives on the History of Women and Teaching*, edited by Alison Prentice and Marjorie Theobald (Toronto: University of Toronto Press, 1991). Interestingly, Clifford's book, *Those Good Gertrudes: A Social History of Women Teachers in America* (Baltimore: Johns Hopkins University Press, 2014), 150, 167, 300, draws from Martha McKeown's *Them Was the Days* to describe frontier teachers through Mont Hawthorne's recollection of them.

29   Perlmann and Margo, *Women's Work?*, 90, dates the dominance of women in the American teaching profession to the Civil War. By 1870, in all regions save the South, women were in the majority as teachers. By 1915, 82 percent of teachers in the West were women.

30   Lynn Weiner, *From Working Girl to Working Mother: The Female Labor Force in the United States, 1820–1980* (Chapel Hill: University of North Carolina Press, 1985), 89.

31   Lynn Weiner delineates the various controversies surrounding married working women from 1820 to 1980. Between 1920 and 1940, feminists valued the independence and intellectual stimulation that paid work could bring middle-class women, but others argued that employment threated women's health, the stability of their families, and the economy as a whole. Weiner, *From Working Girl to Working Mother*, 100–110. Weiner argues that women entered the workforce in increasing numbers in the twentieth century as a result of changing perceptions of the American standard of living.

32   "Dream Come True," *(Salem) Statesman Journal*, January 23, 1949.

33   Martha Ferguson McKeown, "What Shall I Tell Him in this Crisis?," guest editorial, *Oregon Daily Journal*, October 22, 1940.

34   Oral History Interview of Russ Beaton, Katy Barber, Portland, Oregon, October 9, 2014.

35   Jessie Scott, from a blurb printed in "The Grapevine," a regular local gossip column, *Oregonian*, May 2, 1954. *Tyee* is the Chinook wawa word for headman.

36 Philip J. Deloria, *Playing Indian* (New Haven, CT: Yale University Press, 1998), 115.

37 Jennifer Helgren, "Native American and White Camp Fire Girls Enact Modern Girlhood," *American Quarterly* 66, no. 2 (June 2014), 341.

38 "Oregon Older Girls' Conference Session Scheduled for Next Week End in Portland," news clipping in scrapbook, undated (likely 1948 in either late February or early March), Oregon Older Girls' Conference, vol. 3 of 5, Mss 2790, Oregon Historical Society, Research Library, Portland.

39 Ibid.

40 Program for Silver Jubilee, Oregon Older Girls' Conference, Westminster Presbyterian Church, Portland, Oregon, March 5–7, 1937, Mss 2790, Oregon Historical Society, Research Library, Portland.

41 Program, 21st Oregon Older Girls' Conference, Corvallis, Oregon, April 1–2, 1933. Oregon Older Girls' Conference, vol. 3 of 5, Mss 2790, Oregon Historical Society, Research Library, Portland. With a birth year of 1907, Ruth Nomura was one of the first children born to Japanese parents in Oregon. Nomura graduated from Oregon State College in 1930 with a BS in home economics. Her talk addressed a 1926 trip to Japan, which she took shortly after graduating from Jefferson High School in Portland. During World War II, she and her husband relocated to Minneapolis, Minnesota, where she remained until her death in 2008. See "Ruth Nomura," posted on October 12, 2009, Oregon State University, Special Collections and Archives Research Center Blog, "Speaking of History."

42 David A. Holliger, "After Cloven Tongues of Fire: Ecumenical Protestantism and the Modern Encounter with Diversity," *Journal of American History* 98, no. 1 (June 2011), 21.

43 Ibid., 23.

44 Simon Wendt, "Defenders of Patriotism or Mothers of Fascism? The Daughters of the American Revolution, Antiradicalism, and Un-Americans in the Interwar Period," *Journal of American Studies* 47, Special Issue 04 (November 2013): 943–69.

45 This story is recounted in many places, including Allida Black, "Championing a Champion: Eleanor Roosevelt and the Marian Anderson 'Freedom Concert,'" *Presidential Studies Quarterly* (Fall 1990): 719–36, and National Archives and Records Administration,

Rediscovering Black History, "Marian Anderson and the Easter Sunday Concert, April 9, 1939," rediscovering-black-history.blogs.archives.gov/2014/05/20/marian-anderson-and-the-easter-sunday-concert-april-9-1939/.

46 "Local DAR Mum on Riff," *Oregonian*, October 13, 1945.

47 "Race Issue Stirs D.A.R. State Meet," *Oregonian*, April 2, 1947, 1 and 7.

48 "Multnomah" (Portland, est. 1896) referenced a Chinook headman and a tribal peoples; "Chemketa" (Salem, est. 1915) was a Kalapuyan word meaning "home" or "council ground." "Quenett" (The Dalles, est. 1917), the chapter closest to Celilo Village, took its name from the journals of Lewis and Clark, where the Native word for the mouth of present-day Mill Creek was recorded. "Umpqua" (est. 1918), "Winema" (est. 1920), "Yamhill" (est. 1920), Eulalona (est. 1922), and Wauna (est. 1928) all reflected symbolic connections to the state's first peoples. See Mrs. Clyde E. Lewis, *History of Oregon Society, Daughters of American Revolution, Incorporated* (Portland, OR: Columbian Press, 1930).

49 "McNary Defends Chemawa," *Oregonian*, May 20, 1933, 9; "False Economy" (editorial), *Oregonian*, May 25, 1933, 8; "Indians' Rights Assured," *Oregonian*, May 27, 1933, 3; "School Closing Fought," *Oregonian*, May 29, 1933, 8; "Hope Held for School," *Oregonian*, June 2, 1933, 9; "The Victory of Chemawa School" (editorial), *Oregonian*, June 28, 1933, 6.

50 For more about the interwar "history wars" and the role of patriotic societies, see Jonathan Zimmerman, "'Each "Race" Could Have Its Heroes Sung': Ethnicity and the History Wars in the 1920s," *Journal of American History* 87, no. 1 (June 2000): 92–111.

51 "D.A.R. to Hold State Meet at Hood River," *Hood River News*, March 15, 1940, 1 and 8.

52 "DAR to Meet in Portland Soon," *Hood River News*, February 21, 1941.

53 As an English teacher, it is likely that Martha McKeown avoided the controversies regarding how American history was taught in public schools that engulfed many patriotic organizations. For a description of these controversies in the interwar years, see Zimmerman, "'Each "Race" Could Have Its Heroes Sung.'"

54 "Education Is D.A.R. Feature," *Hood River News*, March 29, 1940, 6.

55 *Advancing the Status of Women Worldwide: A History of Zonta International, 1919–1999* (Paducah, KY: Turner, 2000).

56   Linda Tamura, *Nisei Soldiers Break Their Silence: Coming Home to Hood River* (Seattle: University of Washington Press, 2012), xvii.

57   Cherstin Lyon, *Prisons and Patriots: Japanese American Wartime Citizenship, Civil Disobedience, and Historical Memory* (Philadelphia: Temple University Press, 2011), 52–53, 121.

58   Archie White McKeown's grave at the Idlewilde Cemetery in Hood River is decorated with a bronze American Legion marker. See www.findagrave.com.

59   Kirby Neumann-Rea, "Kaleidoscope: What Would You Do?," *Hood River News*, January 15, 2014. Dale Soden places the efforts of Methodists to combat discriminatory actions directed at returning Japanese and Japanese Americans in Hood River Valley into a broader history of religious activism in the region in *Outsiders in a Promised Land: Religious Activists in Pacific Northwest History* (Corvallis: Oregon State University Press, 2015).

60   Martha McKeown, "Frank Hachiya: He Was American at Birth—and at Death," *Oregonian*, May 20, 1945, 49.

61   Ibid.

62   The description of the memorial service and the quote from Ray Yasui are found in William Robbins, "'The kind of person who makes this America strong': Monroe Sweetland and Japanese Americans," *Oregon Historical Quarterly* 113, no. 2 (Summer 2012), 198–229. Quote on page 199.

63   Anne Blankenship, "Religion and the Japanese American Incarceration," *Religion Compass* 8, no. 10 (October 2014), 320.

64   See, for example, Cherstin Lyon, *Prisons and Patriots: Japanese American Wartime Citizenship, Civil Disobedience, and Historical Memory* (Philadelphia: Temple University Press, 2011).

65   Willard Hughes Rollings, "Citizenship and Suffrage: The Native American Struggle for Civil Rights in the American West, 1830–1965," *Nevada Law Journal* 5, no. 126 (Fall 2004): 126–40.

66   Kenneth William Townsend, *World War II and the American Indian* (Albuquerque: University of New Mexico Press, 2000).

67   William Minthorne, May 8, 1951, U.S. Congress, House Committee on Appropriations, *Civil Functions, Department of the Army, Appropriations for 1952 Hearings*, 82nd Cong., 1st and 2nd sess., 1951, 374.

68 In the 1940s, Tommy Thompson's adoption of James Dyer became a point of contention in Celilo Fish Committee meetings, where Yakama representatives argued that he should not be allowed to fish at Celilo Falls. BIA field agent C. G. Davis also argued that Thompson should not be able to include non-Native men in the fishery. Thompson appealed to Oregon representative Walter Pierce to uphold the adoption. The issue remained unresolved, however. In 1950, Dyer was arrested for fishing without a license; Dyer argued that he was legally fishing in accord with treaty fishing rights. Minutes, Meeting Celilo Fish Committee, September 1, 1949, Box 1545, "Celilo Fish Committee, Minutes and Resolutions, 1953–54, 004, File 1 of 2," page 13, RG 75, PAO 58, National Archives—Pacific Northwest Region; Tommy Thompson and John Whiz to To Whom It May Concern, October 31, 1941, Box 22, Folder 14, Walter M. Pierce Papers, Coll. 068, Special Collections and University Archives, University of Oregon Libraries, Eugene; "Adopted Indian Defends Self Against Illegal Fishing Charges," *The Dalles Chronicle*, May 2, 1950.

69 Flora Cushinway Thompson, interviewer unknown, n.d., SR 9586, transcript, Oregon Historical Research Library, Portland.

70 Correspondence between Joseph Murphy (Toppenish lawyer), C. G. Davis, and Flora Boise in May 1948, BIA Portland Area Office, Field Agent, The Dalles, Oregon, General Subject Correspondence, 1939–53, Folder "Thompson, Tommy (Otis, Ellen Andrew; Wilbur Kunehi)," PAO 71, RG 75, National Archives—Pacific Northwest Region.

71 Flora Cushinway Thompson, interviewer unknown, n.d., SR 9586, transcript, Oregon Historical Research Library, Portland.

72 Gladys M. Struck, "A Visit to the Home of Chief Tommy Thompson," February 4, 1949, in possession of the author.

73 Flora Cushinway Thompson, interviewer unknown, n.d., SR 9586, transcript, Oregon Historical Research Library, Portland.

74 Ibid.

75 "Leading Ladies Meet," *Oregonian*, October 8, 1956.

76 Katrine Barber, *Death of Celilo Falls* (Seattle: University of Washington Press, 2005), 138–47.

77 Freda Mowrey, "Wife of Celilo Indian Chief Tells Efforts of Tribal Women to Improve People's Lot," *Oregonian*, October, 16, 1949, 49.

78 The DAR's Eulalona chapter out of Klamath Falls put out a call for deer hides after hearing Flora Thompson's presentation to the state

society. "DAR Seeks Deer Hides for Indians," *Herald and News* (Klamath Falls, OR), October 7, 1950.

5. PROTECTING HOME

1   Hedberg, "'As Long as the Mighty Columbia River Flows.'"

2   Flora Cushinway Thompson, interviewer unknown, n.d., SR 9586, transcript, Oregon Historical Research Library, Portland.

3   "Celilo Chief Pleads for Tribal Rights; Wins Pledge of Support From Chamber," *Oregonian*, October 18, 1949, 10.

4   Ibid.

5   C. G. Davis's typed notes, Conference at Celilo, November 28, 1949, Box 155U-155, "Minutes, 1939–49," RG 75, PAO, Field Agent—The Dalles, OR, General Subject Correspondence, 1939–1953, National Archives—Pacific Northwest Region.

6   Ibid.

7   Martha F. McKeown, "Celilo Indians: Fishing Their Way of Life," *Oregonian*, October 6, 1949, 59.

8   Ibid.

9   Ibid.

10 "Oregon Voices: Barbara MacKenzie," *Oregon Historical Quarterly* 108, no. 4 (Winter 2007), 686–87.

11 McKeown, "Celilo Indians."

12 Ibid.

13 Ibid.

14 Amanda Zink, "Fictions of American Domesticity: Indigenous Women, White Women, and the Nation, 1850–1950" (PhD dissertation, University of Illinois at Urbana-Champaign, 2013).

15 McKeown, "Celilo Indians."

16 Ibid.

17 Ibid.

18 Thomas Borstelmann, *The Cold War and the Color Line: American Race Relations in the Global Arena* (Cambridge: Harvard University Press, 2001), 268. I first saw this quote in Paul C. Rosier, "'They Are Ancestral Homelands': Race, Place, and Politics in Cold War Native America, 1945–1961," *Journal of American History* 92, no. 4 (March 2006), 1300.

19 Rosier, "'They Are Ancestral Homelands,'" 1309.

20 Arnold, *Bartering with the Bones.*

21 Rosier, "'They Are Ancestral Homelands,'" 1310.

22 United States of America, Bureau of the Census, *Sixteenth Census of the United States, 1940* (Washington, DC: National Archives and Records Administration, 1940), T627, 4,643 rolls. Place: Portland, Multnomah, Oregon; Roll: T627_3388; Page: 61A.

23 "Charcoal Technique of Portland Artist Inspired by Primitive Indian Drawings," *Oregonian*, April 13, 1950, 16.

24 Jimmie James to Alex Saluskin, January 1, 1954, JJJP, Box 1, Folder 58: "You appointed me press agent for the Yakimas, which was an honor, perhaps the most wonderful that I have known in my lifetime."

25 Jimmie James to Wayne Morse, March 12, 1953, JJJP, Box 1, Folder 56.

26 James claimed to be part Native on his mother's side, but he never indicated which tribe(s) his family may have come from. In a statement he probably wrote in 1955, James suggested more colorful motives for his connections to the region's Native people than what he described to Senator Wayne Morse: "When I was 17 years old, I took off my clothes and walked into the desert to live as man had thousands of years ago, I took in nothing with me but a notebook and a pencil, nothing else, because the men who drove me out there in a wagon returned with all I possessed, so starting from scratch, with nothing but my bare hands and a knowledge gotten from old records of the first Indians, and the stories told me during youth and came out with primitive clothes and good health, and with a better understanding of simplicity and a knowledge of what it means to live from Mother Earth." James James, "Why I have fought for the Yakima's Rights!," with April 1955 letters, JJJP, Box 1, Folder 60.

27 Jimmie James to Martha McKeown, January 21, 1953, JJJP, Box 1, Folder 56.

28 Jimmie James to Martha McKeown, March 21, 1953, JJJP, Box 1, Folder 56.

29 Jimmie James to Mrs. Vera T. Peterson, President of the Women's Forum, March 23, 1953, JJJP, Box 1, Folder 56.

30 Jimmie James to Robert Sawyer, February 19, 1953, JJJP, Box 1, Folder 56.

31 Ibid.

32 Leona M. Weatherford to Jimmie James, June 20, 1952, JJJP, Box 1, Folder 51.

33 Freda Mowery, "DAR Member, Ardent Nature Lover, Widens Field to Include Family Trees," *Oregonian*, April 11, 1954, 77.

34 "Forum Buying View Point as Part of Gorge Project," *Oregonian*, March 3, 1956, 83.

35 Jimmie James to Wilson Charley, January 28, 1953, JJJP, Box 1, Folder 56.

36 "McKay to Get Gorge Issue," *Oregonian*, May 4, 1952.

37 A eulogy written by Roy Craft, editor emeritus of the *Skamania County Pioneer*, and delivered at Gertrude Jensen's memorial service, March 13, 1987, Portland, provided relevant biographical information used here. Oregon senator Mark Hatfield entered the eulogy into the *Congressional Record* 134, no. 25 (March 4, 1988).

38 Gertrude Glutsch Jensen, interviewed by Roberta Watts, April 24, 1978, SR 9429, transcript, Oregon Historical Research Library, Portland. James in a letter to McKeown describes the meeting as anything but accidental, writing that he had contacted Alex Saluskin and "directed him so he will meet Mrs. Jensen there, she so wanted it that way because I believe she will take them with her in the fight to save Celilo Falls." Jimmie James to Martha McKeown, January 21, 1953, JJJP, Box 1, Folder 56.

39 Gertrude Glutsch Jensen, interviewed by Roberta Watts, April 24, 1978, SR 9429, transcript, Oregon Historical Research Library, Portland.

40 Gertrude Jensen to Jimmie James, February 2, 1953, JJJP, Box 1, Folder 49.

41 Horace Marden Albright to Jimmie James, January 2, 1953, JJJP, Box 1, Folder 49.

42 Jimmie James to Alex Saluskin, February 9, 1953, JJJP, Box 1, Folder 56.

43 Jimmie James to Richard Neuberger, March 1, 1953, JJJP, Box 1, Folder 56.

44 Eve Vogel, "Defining One Pacific Northwest among Many Possibilities: The Political Construction of a Region and Its River During the New Deal," *Western Historical Quarterly* 42, no. 1 (2011), 28–53. doi:10.2307/westhistquar.42.1.0028. Page 37.

45 Marshall N. Dana, "The Celilo Canal—Its Origin—Its Building and Meaning," *Quarterly of the Oregon Historical Society* 16, no. 2 (1915), 109–24. www.jstor.org.proxy.lib.pdx.edu/stable/20609995. Page 111.

46 Chief Rising Sun to To Whom It May Concern, July 3, 1950, JJJP, Box 1, Folder 32.

47 Jimmie James to Alex Saluskin, February 12, 1953, JJJP, Box 1, Folder 56.

48 Jimmie James to Chief Rising Sun, February 23, 1953, JJJP, Box 1, Folder 56.

49 Jimmie James to Alex Saluskin, March 31, 1953, JJJP, Box 1, Folder 56.

50 Jimmie James to Wayne Morse, March 12, 1953, JJJP, Box 1, Folder 56.

51 "Picture of the Week," *Life*, June 1, 1953, 27.

52 Wallace Turner, "Picture of 'Chief' in Magazine Spread Recalls 'Healer's' Career in Portland," *Oregonian*, June 7, 1953, 47.

53 Chief Rising Sun to Jimmie James, June 3, 1953, JJJP, Box 1, Folder 32.

54 Turner, "Picture of 'Chief.'"

55 John Higham, *Strangers in the Land: Patterns of American Nativism, 1860–1925* (New Brunswick, NJ: Rutgers University Press, 2002), 277.

56 "Fine Feathers Fool Senators Hearing Plea Against Dam by Yakima Indians, Pearson Says," Drew Pearson, July 22, 1953, *Oneonta (NY) Star.*

57 Jimmie James to Wilson Charley, October 20, 1954, JJJP, Box 1, Folder 59. Apparently, Chief Rising Sun rented a room at Portland's Heathman Hotel for a lecture that was attended by "only 6 people," two of whom "were policemen, 2 were reporters and I don't know who the others were." Jimmie James to Wilson Charley, November 22, 1954, JJJP, Box 1, Folder 59.

58 Wallace Turner, "Dates Conflict on Records Involved in Indian Deal," *Oregonian*, February 2, 1952, 16.

59 A year later, Martha McKeown complained to Jimmie James, "the Oregonian used photostats and pictures we took on the Slim Jim case, in fact Wallace Turner, who did the stories used my notes, he hasn't met Slim Jim. But I didn't make a dent down there when I tried to get them interested in Celilo housing or displaced persons from the Bonneville Dam." Martha McKeown to Jimmie James, February 1, 1953, JJJP, Box 1, Folder 18.

60 "Fraud Charges Link Trio to Indian Timber Profits," *Oregonian*, February 13, 1952, 9.

61 Ibid.

62 Wallace Turner, "Suit to Cancel Sale of Indian's Timber Dropped after out-of-Court Settlement," *Oregonian*, February 12, 1952, 9.

63   Wallace Turner, "Timber Sale Set Tuesday," *Oregonian*, July 31, 1952, page 13; "Slim Jim Gets His Wampum" (editorial), *Oregonian*, August 7, 1952, 14.

64   Martha McKeown to Jimmie James, March 7, 1957, JJJP, Box 1, Folder 18.

65   *Oregonian*, January 19, 1953.

66   It is likely that McKeown collected these documents when she was in Washington, DC, for the DAR annual meeting in 1949. C. G. Davis's typed notes, Conference at Celilo, November 28 1949, Box 155U-155, "Minutes, 1939–49," RG 75, PAO, Field Agent—The Dalles, OR, General Subject Correspondence, 1939–1953, National Archives—Pacific Northwest Region.

67   Martha McKeown to Jimmie James, March 7, 1957, JJJP, Box 1, Folder 18.

68   Martha McKeown to Jimmie James, March 7, 1957, JJJP, Box 1, Folder 18.

69   Martha McKeown to Jimmie James, February 1, 1953, JJJP, Box 1, Folder 18.

70   Martha McKeown to Jimmie James, February 10, 1953, JJJP, Box 1, Folder 18.

71   "Indians Hold Fish Festival," *Oregonian*, April 16, 1951, 7. For protests by Celilo residents to their relocation as a result of highway expansion, see C. G. Davis's typed notes, Conference at Celilo, November 28, 1949, Box 155U-155, "Minutes, 1939–49," RG 75, PAO, Field Agent—The Dalles, OR, General Subject Correspondence, 1939–1953, National Archives—Pacific Northwest Region. Martha McKeown attended this meeting and spoke on behalf of Tommy Thompson.

72   James Stuart, "Indian Chinook Salmon Feast at Celilo Punctuated by Blasting Operations for Proposed The Dalles Dam," *Oregonian*, April 21, 1952, 12.

73   "Annual Salmon Festival of Tribesmen Draws Hundreds of Indians to Cecilo [*sic*]," *Oregonian*, April 20, 1953, 12.

74   Jimmie James to Alex Saluskin, April 15, 1953, JJJP, Box 1, Folder 56.

75   Special Meeting of the Celilo Fish Committee, The Dalles, April 25, 1945, Box 155U-155, "Minutes, 1939–49," RG 75, PAO, Field Agent—The Dalles, OR, General Subject Correspondence, 1939–1953, National Archives—Pacific Northwest Region.

76　"The Yakima Tribe instituted an action in the United States District Court, for the Eastern District of Washington, against the Guy F. Atkinson Company, in the year 1948, to enjoin the contractor from proceeding with the Construction of the dam." "Statement of The Yakima Indians in Defense of Their Vested Fishing and Property Rights at Celilo Falls in the Columbia River that will Be Destroyed by the Construction of The Dalles Lock and Dam," in James James Collection, Subject File—Celilo, Box 2, Folder 16, page 4. The Guy F. Atkinson Company also won the contract for powerhouse excavation at The Dalles Dam in 1951. "Before the Senate Appropriations Committee, 82nd Congress, 2nd Session, Statement of the Yakima Tribe of Indians of the State of Washington in Opposition to the Construction of the Dalles Lock and Dam," in James James Collection, Subject File—Celilo, Box 2, Folder 16, page 2. The same company was involved in other Columbia River dams, notably, Grand Coulee Dam.

77　The Affiliated Tribes of Northwest Indians had its birth in 1949 when tribes from the four northwestern states signed an intertribal agreement, the first in modern history, according to newspaper accounts. Saluskin was at the initial meetings that devised the agreement in Yakima, Washington, but deferred signing it on behalf of the Yakama Nation until the tribal council could review it. The ATNI was officially founded in 1953 in Spokane, Washington. "Northwest Indians Sign Historical Pledge of Peace," *Oregonian*, June 23, 1949, 16; "History," The Affiliated Tribes of Northwest Indians, www.atnitribes.org/history.

78　"In 1948, tribes began receiving mandates, issued by the Internal Revenue Service, who sought to collect back income tax on profits generated by crops—sighting [sic] the 16th Amendment to the U.S. Constitution, which had been ratified in 1913. It allowed Congress to tax 'incomes, from whatever source derived, without apportionment among the several States, and without regard to any census or enumeration.' Although the law had never been applied to tribes, they were now being ordered to pay, but refused, based on land trust agreements." "History," The Affiliated Tribes of Northwest Indians, www.atnitribes.org/history.

6. NEW NARRATIVES IN AN ANCIENT LAND

1　For more about this process, see Barber, *Death of Celilo Falls*, and Dupris, Hill, and Rodgers, *The Si'lailo Way*.

2   Max Boise to Jimmie James, December 6, 1955, JJJP, Box 1, Folder 49.

3   Jimmie James reported his progress to Max Boise, December 8, 1955; James to Eisenhower, December 8, 1955; James to Neuberger, December 8, 1955, JJJP, Box 1, Folder 61, "Letters Sent, Aug–Dec 1955."

4   Jimmie James to Rueben Olson, Director of the Anselm Forum, December 8, 1955, JJJP, Box 1, Folder 61, "Letters Sent, Aug–Dec 1955."

5   James kept copies: "Letters Sent, Aug–Dec 1955," JJJP, Box 1, Folder 61.

6   Clarence O. Adams to Jimmie James, December 19, 1955, JJJP, Box 1, Folder 1, "Incoming Correspondence."

7   Martha McKeown to Jimmie James, January 28, 1956, JJJP, Box 1, Folder 18.

8   "Chief Tommy Marks 100th With Salmon, Gift Cake," *Oregonian*, December 16, 1954, 17.

9   Click Relander to Jimmie James, November 6, 1954, JJJP, Box 1, Folder 31.

10 Click Relander to Jimmie James, February 27, 1954, JJJP, Box 1, Folder 31.

11 Rosier, " 'They Are Ancestral Homelands,' " 1305.

12 Rollings, "Citizenship and Suffrage," 132. See *McKay v. Campbell* 2 Sawy. 118;15 Am. Law T. Rep. U. S. Cts. 407.

13 *Elk v. Wilkins,* 112 U.S. 94, 99 (1884).

14 Michael L. Tate, "From Scout to Doughboy: The National Debate over Integrating American Indians into the Military, 1891–1918," *Western Historical Quarterly* 17, no. 4 (October 1986), 429.

15 Jeanette Wolfley, "Jim Crow, Indian Style: The Disenfranchisement of Native Americans," *American Indian Law Review* 16, no. 1 (1991), 178.

16 Washington passed an Alien Land Law in 1921, while Oregon passed a similar bill through its legislature in 1923. These laws were part of a wave of legislation passed in several mostly western states that prevented immigrants who could not be nationalized from owning property. However, both states had restricted landownership among Asian immigrants in the nineteenth century as well.

17 Wolfley, "Jim Crow, Indian Style," 175–76.

18 Rollings, "Citizenship and Suffrage," 126.

19 Washington State Constitution, Section 1, Amendment 63, 1974 Senate Joint Resolution No. 143, p. 807. Approved November 5, 1974.

20   "State of Washington Twenty-third Biennial Report of the Attorney General, George W. Hamilton, 1935–1936" (Olympia: State Printing Office, 1936), 127.

21   Rollings, "Citizenship and Suffrage," 135.

22   Alexander Keyssar, *The Right to Vote: The Contested History of Democracy in the United States* (New York: Basic Books), 227.

23   Jere Franco, "Empowering the World War II Native American Veteran: Postwar Civil Rights," *Wicazo Sa Review* 9, no. 1 (Spring, 1993), 32–37.

24   In an article that urges Indigenous leaders in Australia, Canada, and New Zealand to use electoral politics as part of a multipronged strategy to protect self-governance, Michael Murphy summarizes the historical reasons why they have been reluctant to do so. Murphy, "Representing Indigenous Self-Determination," *University of Toronto Law Journal* 58, no. 2 (Spring 2008), 185–216.

25   See, for example, Albert Furtwangler, *Bringing Indians to the Book* (Seattle: University of Washington Press), 2005; Sally Zanjani, *Sarah Winnemucca* (Lincoln: University of Nebraska Press), 2001; Cothran, *Remembering the Modoc War*; and Elliott West, *The Last Indian War: The Nez Perce Story* (New York: Oxford University Press), 2011.

26   Helen L. Paterson, "American Indian Political Participation," *Annals of the American Academy of Political and Social Science,* vol. 311, *American Indians and American Life* (May 1957), 124–25.

27   Martha McKeown to Jimmie James, March 7, 1955, JJJP, Box 1, Folder 18.

28   "Could Be Home on the Range?," *Oregonian*, December 19, 1954, 30.

29   Martha McKeown to Jimmie James, March 7, 1955, JJJP, Box 1, Folder 18.

30   Resolution, Oregon State Society of the National Society, Daughters of the American Revolution, March 1,1955, among the records kept by the Celilo Community Club, in possession of the author.

31   Martha McKeown was an Oregon Historical Society board member for a four-year term (1955–1959). *Oregon Historical Quarterly* 57, no. 4 (December 1956), 378.

32   Martha McKeown to Jimmie James, January 28, 1956, JJJP, Box 1, Folder 18.

33   Ibid.

34 Apparently records for this committee are not available within the institutional records of the Oregon Historical Society. Personal communication with Scott Daniels, reference service coordinator, Oregon Historical Society, October 11, 2014.

35 Records in the author's possession.

36 Martha McKeown to Jimmie James, undated letter that James stamped received 16 May 1956, JJJP, Box 1, Folder 18.

37 *Oregonian*, April 23, 1956, 18. For more information about the library program see *Oregonian*, April 22, 1956, 72, and April 29, 1956, 45.

38 Martha McKeown to Jimmie James, undated letter that James stamped received 16 May 1956, JJJP, Box 1, Folder 18.

39 *Christian Century* 66, no. 147 (February 2, 1949).

40 Verne Bright, Review of *Them Was the Days*, *Oregon Historical Quarterly* 51 (1950), 135.

41 "McKeown Book Selling Rapidly," *Oregonian*, December 17, 1948, 40.

42 Richard Neuberger, "Martha McKeown Writes New Volume Picturing Period Between 1870 and '83," *Oregonian*, May 7, 1950, 12.

43 "The Library Corner," *Arlington (Illinois) Heights Herald*, June 16, 1950, and "Library to Hold Open House In Fairbanks Sunday," *Fairbanks (Alaska) Daily News-Miner*, February 9, 1951.

44 Advertisement for Meier and Frank Department store, *Oregonian*, April 21, 1952, 16.

45 "Uncle Mont's Saga," *Oregonian*, July 12, 1952, 6.

46 Martha McKeown to Jimmie James, February 1, 1953, JJJP, Box 1, Folder 18.

47 Martha McKeown to Jimmie James, May 19, 1956, JJJP, Box 1, Folder 18.

48 Martha McKeown to Jimmie James, undated letter that James stamped received 16 May 1956, JJJP, Box 1, Folder 18.

49 Ibid.

50 In some handwritten notes Martha McKeown described how she collected her uncle's stories: "It is only in the winter when his Hood River orchard is asleep that my eighty-two year old uncle, Mont Hawthorne, takes time to sit by the fire and weave word histories of the early days up north." Handwritten notes, Box 2, Folder 18, "Miscellaneous Materials of Dana's Second Wife," Marshall Newport Dana papers, MSS 1798, Oregon Historical Society (OHS) Research Library, Portland.

51 There are too many regional books of this genre to name them all, but it's likely that Martha McKeown would have been familiar with many of them. Perhaps the best-known settler observer—and according to anthropologist Leland Donald author of the first ethnographic study of the area—was James Swan, who wrote about his time at Shoalwater Bay in Washington Territory in *The Northwest Coast: Or Three Years Residence in Washington Territory* (1857); Donald, *Aboriginal Slavery on the Northwest Coast of North America* (Berkeley: University of California Press, 1997). Lucullus Virgil McWhorter wrote about and advocated for Plateau Indians, publishing *Yellow Wolf: His Own Story* (Caldwell, ID: Caxton Press, 1940) and *Hear Me, My Chiefs: Nez Perce Legends and History* (Caldwell, ID: Caxton Press, 1952), while Click Relander—who knew Martha, corresponded with James James, and shared many Native acquaintances with each—wrote *Drummer and Dreamers: The Story of Smowhala to Prophet and His Nephew Puck Hyah Toot, the Last Prophet of the . . . Wanapums* (Caldwell, ID: Caxton Press, 1956). For more information about how white women dominated the development of Native American historiography, see John Rhea, *A Field of Their Own: Women and American Indian History, 1830–1941* (Norman: University of Oklahoma Press, 2016).

52 Archie McKeown with a fawn. Unknown photographer, date unknown. Binford and Mort Papers, Box 1, Folder 8, Reed College Library, Portland, Oregon.

53 Martha McKeown to Jimmie James, February 1, 1953, JJJP, Box 1, Folder 18.

54 Carol J. Williams, *Framing the West: Race, Gender, and the Photographic Frontier in the Pacific Northwest* (New York: Oxford University Press, 2003), 8.

55 Sarah Potter's *Everybody Else: Adoption and the Politics of Diversity in Postwar America* (Athens: University of Georgia Press, 2014), which addresses adoption practices in Chicago, illustrates the intense value placed on nuclear families and domesticity after the upheavals of the Great Depression and World War II.

56 Hubka and Kenny describe the "emergence of a national housing culture" between 1900 and 1930, in which the house plan described above became ubiquitous. Thomas C. Hubka and Judith T. Kenny, "Examining the American Dream: Housing Standards and the

Emergence of a National Housing Culture, 1900–1930," *Perspectives in Vernacular Architecture* 13, no. 1 (2006), 49.

57 See, for example, Elaine Tyler May, *Homeward Bound: American Families in the Cold War* (New York: Basic Books, 1988), as well as *Not June Cleaver: Women and Gender in Post War America, 1945–1960*, edited by Joan Meyerowitz (Philadelphia: Temple University Press, 1994).

58 Lori Jacobson points out that reformer concerns about single-room homes and homes that did not include separate bedrooms were rooted in anxiety about the sexual practices of Indigenous people. In Victorian America and later, sex was to be relegated to the private marriage bedroom, but in households without designated bedrooms, sexual activity threatened to spill out into shared spaces. Lori Jacobson, "'Environed by Civilization': WNIA Homebuilding and Loan Department," in *Women's National Indian Association: A History*, edited by Valerie Sherer Mathes (Albuquerque: University of New Mexico Press, 2015).

59 Jane E. Simonsen, *Making Home Work: Domesticity and Native American Assimilation in the American West, 1860–1919* (Chapel Hill: University of North Carolina Press, 2006), 8.

60 K. Tsianina Lomawaima, "Domesticity in the Federal Indian Schools: The Power of Authority over Mind and Body," *American Ethnologist* 20, no. 2 (May 1993), 227–40.

61 As Jane Simonsen points out, "Model homes and domestic training were part of reform efforts directed at the working class," immigrants, and African Americans as well as at Indians. Simonsen, *Making Home Work*, 98.

62 Martha McKeown, *Come to Our Salmon Feast* (Portland: Binford and Mort, 1959), 56.

63 Ackerman, *A Necessary Balance*, 3.

64 Ackerman, *A Necessary Balance*, 193.

65 McKeown, *Come to Our Salmon Feast,* 42.

66 Ibid., 40.

67 Ibid., 14.

68 Ibid., 68.

69 Ibid., 74.

70 Ibid.

71 Contemporary theorists have argued that decolonial cultural revitalization among Indian communities rests on gendered balance and

activism rooted in traditional gender roles. For example, Michelle Jacob points to the division between male and female spaces in Columbia River Plateau longhouses as representative of a "complementary gender balance of power and organization among [Yakama] people" that supports a contemporary Yakama decolonizing practice. In other words, recent activists could draw from Flora Thompson's enactment of traditional gender roles at such events as the annual salmon ceremony, which modeled gender balance. Michelle Jacob, *Yakama Rising: Indigenous Cultural Revitalization, Activism, and Healing* (Tucson: University of Arizona Press, 2013), 110.

72 David French, "Old Days at Celilo Falls," review of *Come to Our Salmon Feast* by Martha Ferguson McKeown, *Pacific Northwest Quarterly* 50 (1950), 161.

73 Ibid.

74 *Oregon Historical Quarterly* 59 (1958), 173, and *Oregon Historical Quarterly* 62 (1961), 102.

75 "Celilo Falls Pictured," *Oregon Journal*, June 10, 1956, 8.

76 Martha McKeown to Jimmie James, March 7, 1955, JJJP, Box 1, Folder 18.

77 Martha McKeown to Jimmie James, undated letter, JJJP, Box 1, Folder 18.

78 *Oregonian*, May 7, 1956.

79 Martha McKeown to Jimmie James and Rueben Olson, June 9, 1956, JJJP, Box 1, Folder 18.

80 Martha McKeown to Jimmie James, June 9, 1956, JJJP, Box 1, Folder 18.

81 Martha McKeown to Jimmie James, October 9, 1956, JJJP, Box 1, Folder 18.

82 Ibid.

83 Ibid.

84 Ibid.

85 Martha McKeown to Jimmie James, January 1, 1957, JJJP, Box 1, Folder 18.

86 Ibid.

87 Ibid.

88 Ibid.

89 Jimmie James to Martha McKeown, March 12, 1957, JJJP, Box 2, Folder 1, "Letters Sent, Jan–July 1957."

90 Jimmie James to Flora Thompson, May 9, 1957, JJJP, Box 2, Folder 1.

91 Martha McKeown to Jimmie James, May 5, 1957, and September 7, 1957, JJJP, Box 1, Folder 18.

92 Martha McKeown to Jimmie James, October 28, 1957, JJJP, Box 1, Folder 18.

93 Ann Sullivan, "Indian Drums, Voices Pay Homage to Chief Tommy Thompson," *Oregonian*, April 15 1959.

94 Jimmie James to Dwight Eisenhower, April 12, 1959, JJJP, Box 2, Folder 4.

95 Jimmie James to Dwight Eisenhower, May 11, 1959, JJJP, Box 2, Folder 5.

96 Sullivan, "Indian Drums, Voices."

97 Ibid.

98 Linton and Eva Winishut, February 2, 1952, Katherine French fieldnotes, Folder 7, Sahaptin Fieldnotes, 1952–55, David H. and Katherine S. French Papers, Manuscript Collection 5496, Special Collections, University of Washington.

99 Ibid.

100 Jimmie James to Secretary, U.S. Engineers, May 11, 1959, JJJP, Box 2, Folder 5. Oregon senator Wayne Morse introduced a bill into Congress in February 1955 to provide compensation for unenrolled Indians who lived at Celilo Village, which included Tommy Thompson. Carol Craig, "Relocation and the Community at Celilo Village," *Oregon Historical Society* 108, no. 4 (Winter 2007), 701.

101 Jimmie James to Richard Neuberger, May 3, 1959, JJJP, Box 2, Folder 5.

7. AFTERMATH

1 *Farewell to Celilo* was a thirty-minute documentary aired on April 20, 1959, on KGW-TV. Tom McCall, who was a news analyst for the television station and their radio affiliate, narrated the special. Recording in possession of the author.

2 Flora Thompson oral history interview, interviewer unknown, no date. In possession of the author.

3 Davinne McKeown-Ellis, "McKeown Takes Up Quest for Wy'am Rights, *Dalles Chronicle*, March 11, 2007.

4 *Washington, Select Death Certificates, 1907–1960* [database online] (Provo, UT: Ancestry.com Operations, Inc., 2014).

5   George Lindsay, "Indians Push Drive for Longhouse," *Oregonian*, February 6, 1966.

6   Ann Sullivan, "New Celilo Longhouse Has Location Problems," *Oregonian*, October 15, 1967.

7   Ibid.

8   Jimmie James to David Sheer, August 31, 1959, JJJP, Box 1, Folder 6.

9   Jimmie James to Flora Thompson, September 20, 1961, JJJP, Box 2, Folder 9.

10   "Tribes Plan Housing Talks, *Oregonian*, March 15, 1976.

11   Lindsay also, incidentally, credited Martha McKeown with helping him gain access to Flora and other residents at Celilo Village. George Lindsay, "Celilo Indians: The Vanishing Wyams," *Oregonian*, June 25, 1978.

12   For example, Flora Thompson was invited to the dedication of Celilo Park in 1961 and to speak to the Portland Women's Forum on "Problems of My Tribal Peoples" in 1975. "Engineers Turn Over Celilo Park; Chief Unveils Commemorative Plaque," *Oregonian*, April 27, 1960, and "Problems Explored," *Oregonian*, March 2, 1975.

13   "Hickel Asserts Hope for Survival Keyed to Utilization of Resources," *Oregonian*, August 26, 1970; Flora Cushinway Thompson, interviewer unknown, n.d., SR 9586, transcript. Oregon Historical Research Library, Portland.

14   Flora Cushinway Thompson, interviewer unknown, n.d., SR 9586, transcript. Oregon Historical Research Library, Portland.

15   Leverett Richards, "Armed Indians End 'Own Season' with Fete," *Oregonian* April 30, 1966.

16   Flora Cushinway Thompson, interviewer unknown, n.d., SR 9586, transcript. Oregon Historical Research Library, Portland.

17   Ibid.

18   Blaine Schultz, "Root of 'Salmon War' Found in Indian Treaty," *Oregonian*, May 8, 1966.

19   Andrew Fisher notes that Flora Thompson's prominent display of the treaties at the Cook's Landing incident may have undermined the protestors' argument that they did not have to abide by tribal fishing restrictions any more than they were beholden to state regulations. To some degree the treaties came to symbolize the federal favoring of tribal governments over autonomous River Indian families and villages, and Flora certainly understood that tension when she counseled Chief Thompson to distinguish his hereditary authority from

the tribally authorized Celilo Fish Committee. However, while federal agencies viewed the treaties as agreements between tribal entities and the United States, Flora understood them to recognize the rights of the region's Native people broadly. Andrew Fisher, *Shadow Tribe: The Making of Columbia River Indian Identity* (Seattle: University of Washington Press, 2010), 217.

20 In discussing the fish battles on the Puget Sound, Donna Hightower Langston writes, "women were key public figures in the fish-in movement." Langston, "American Indian Women's Activism in the 1960s and 1970s," *Hypatia* 18, no. 2 (Spring 2003), 123.

21 Reuben Olson, director of the Anselm Forum, visited Martha McKeown and Jimmie James when he was in Oregon in May 1956. David Sheer's visit was a follow-up trip also under the official auspices of the forum. Reuben Olson to Jimmy James, 13 March 1956 and Reuben Olson to Peter Binford 22 May 1956.

22 David Sheer to Jimmie James, July 22, 1959, JJJP, Box 1, Folder 33.

23 David Sheer to Jimmie James, May 21, 1959, JJJP, Box 1, Folder 33.

24 Martha McKeown to Jimmie James, August 26, 1959, JJJP, Box 1, Folder 33.

25 David Sheer to Jimmie James, July 22, 1959, JJJP, Box 1, Folder 18.

26 Margaret Jacobs, *A Generation Removed: The Fostering and Adoption of Indigenous Children in a Postwar World* (Lincoln: University of Nebraska Press, 2014), 42. For more information about the *Christian Century* magazine, see Elesha Coffman, *The* Christian Century *and the Rise of the Protestant Mainline* (Oxford: Oxford University Press, 2013).

27 David Sheer to Jimmie James, December 12, 1959, JJJP, Box 1, Folder 33.

28 David Sheer to Jimmie James, January 10, 1959, JJJP, Box 1, Folder 33.

29 David Sheer to Jimmie James, August 29, 1959, JJJP, Box 1, Folder 33.

30 Reuben Olson to Jimmie James, September 6, 1959, JJJP, Box 1, Folder 1.

31 Martha McKeown to Senator Richard Neuberger, December 26, 1959, cc'ed to Reuben Olson and Jimmie James, JJJP, Box 1, Folder 18.

32 James quotes from an earlier letter in this missive to David Sheer, September 22, 1959, JJJP, Box 2, Folder 5.

33 Ibid.

34 David Sheer to Jimmie James, September 15, 1959, JJJP, Box 1, Folder 33.

35 Jimmie James to David Sheer, September 22, 1959, JJJP, Box 2, Folder 5.

36 See, for example, Richard Etulain, *Telling Western Stories: From Buffalo Bill to Larry McMurtry* (Albuquerque: New Mexico University

Press, 1999), and Donna Campbell, "'Written with a Hard and Ruthless Purpose': Rose Wilder Lane, Edna Ferber, and Middlebrow Regional Fiction," in *Middlebrow Moderns: Popular American Women Writers of the 1920s*, edited by Lisa Botshon and Meredith Goldsmith (Boston: Northeastern University Press, 2003), 26–43.

37   *Booklist*, April 16, 1961, 519.

38   Ibid.

39   *New York Herald Tribune*, February 12, 1961.

40   "I talked to Mrs. Dana, (Martha) and she said she was trying to help Ida's daughter get her money and I talked to those they suggested and they said they would do all they could to help." Jimmie James to Flora Thompson, October 19, 1961, JJJP, Box 2, Folder 9.

41   Lancaster Pollard, "Dedication of Dam Recalls Opening of Celilo Canal," *Oregonian*, October 18, 1959.

42   Undated letter from Dana to Drain, Marshall Newport Dana Papers, 1869–1969, Mss 1798, Box 4, Folder 14, Oregon Historical Research Library, Portland.

43   "Staging a Banquet in Bank Proves Complex Problem," *Oregonian*, February 2, 1959. See also "Vice-President to Speak at State Birthday Dinner," *Oregonian*, January 1, 1959, and "Gourmet Menus Posed in Three Cities Celebrating Oregon Statehood," *Oregonian*, February 13, 1959.

44   Pollard, "Dedication of Dam."

45   Marshall Newport Dana Papers, 1869–1969, Mss 1798, Box 3A, Folder 16, Oregon Historical Research Library, Portland.

46   Jimmie James to Wilson Charley, July 26, 1961, JJJP, Box 2, Folder 9.

47   Jimmie James to David Sheer, September 20, 1961, JJJP, Box 2, Folder 8.

48   Margie Dana to Marshall and Martha Dana, April 26, 1961, Mss 1798, Box 5, Folder 15, Oregon Historical Research Library, Portland.

49   Letters from Jimmie James to Flora Thompson, August 26, 1961, and August 31, 1961, JJJP, Box 2, Folder 9.

50   Email correspondence with Linda Meanus, August 9, 2016.

51   Jimmie James to Dawn Polson, June 4, 1962, JJJP, Box 2, Folder 11.

52   Jimmie James to Flora Thompson, February 15, 1962, JJJP, Box 2, Folder 10.

53   "Christie's Face Has Changed: Its Values Remain the Same," *Ventures* 12, no. 1 (Fall 2015), 2.

54 Jimmie James to David Sheer, February 14, 1962, JJJP, Box 2, Folder 10.

55 Jacobs, *A Generation Removed*, 87.

56 "Americans came to adopt more than 4,000 orphaned Korean children between 1955 and 1961." Arissa Oh, "A New Kind of Missionary Work: Christians, Christian Americanists, and the Adoption of Korean GI Babies, 1955–1961," *Women's Studies Quarterly* 33, no. 3/4 (2005), 161.

57 Claire Palmiste, "From the Indian Adoption Project to the Indian Child Welfare Act: The Resistance of Native American Communities," *Indigenous Policy Journal* 22, no. 1 (Summer 2011), 5. Both Palmiste and Margaret Jacobs illustrate the successful public relations campaign that accompanied the Indian Adoption Project.

58 Palmiste, "From the Indian Adoption Project," 1.

59 See Oh, "A New Kind of Missionary Work"; and Arissa Oh, *To Save the Children of Korea: The Cold War Origins of International Adoption* (Stanford: Stanford University Press, 2015).

60 Jacobs, *A Generation Removed*, 48.

61 Dawn Polson to Jimmie James, January 25, 1962, JJJP, Box 1, Folder 8.

62 Dawn Polson to Jimmie James, December 4, 1962, JJJP, Box 1, Folder 29.

63 Ibid.

64 US Government Printing Office Idaho, Oregon, and Washington Petitions for Naturalization, 1932–1991. Records of the District Courts of the United States, RG 21. The National Archives at Seattle, Seattle, Washington. 75 STAT. 908—An Act for the Relief of Mary Dawn Polson (Emmy Lou Kim) and Joseph King Polson (Sung Sang Moon). 87th Congress, 1st Session, 1961, Volume 75, p. 908. In a 1982 publication of Hood River County history, Maridawn Polson wrote short biographical sketches for herself and her brother Joe King. She wrote that they "loved our new family" and that she was "glad Joe and I were brought to this wonderful town where we have had so many golden opportunities." Hood River County Historical Society, *History of Hood River County, Oregon, 1852–1982*, Vol. 1 (Hood River, OR: Hood River County Historical Society, 1982), 324.

65 Oh, "A New Kind of Missionary Work," 167.

66 Ibid., 162.

67 Ibid., 164.

68 Dawn Polson to Jimmie James, March 29, 1961, JJJP, Box 1, Folder 29.

69 Palmiste, "From the Indian Adoption Project," 2.

70 Jimmie James to the Christie School, June 4, 1962, JJJP, Box 2, Folder 11.

71 Jimmie James to Dawn Polson, June 4, 1962, JJJP, Box 2, Folder 11.

72 Jimmie James to Dawn Polson, June 27, 1962, JJJP, Box 2, Folder 11.

73 Jimmie James to Dawn Polson, July 5, 1962, JJJP, Box 2, Folder 11.

74 Martha Dana to Dawn Polson, July 16, 1962, JJJP, Box 1, Folder 18.

75 Jimmie James to Dawn Polson, July 28, 1962, JJJP, Box 2, Folder 11.

76 Jimmie James to Dawn Polson, July 17, 1962, and July 25, 1962, JJJP, Box 2, Folder 11.

77 Althea Adams (a Toppenish District elementary school teacher), Alice Casebeer (a Portland high school teacher), Leo Honner (an acquaintance of James's), and Jimmie James all acted as witnesses. JJJP, Box 1, Folder 34.

78 Jimmie James to Dawn Polson, September 10, 1962, JJJP, Box 2, Folder 11.

79 Dawn Polson to Jimmie James, August 2, 1962, JJJP, Box 1, Folder 29.

80 Ibid.

81 Jimmie James to Rueben Olson, David Sheer, and Flora Thompson, January 1, 1964, JJJP, Box 2, Folder 13.

82 Jimmie James to Linda George, November 20, 1962, JJJP, Box 2, Folder 11.

83 Jimmie James to Dawn Polson, December 27, 1962, JJJP, Box 2, Folder 11.

84 Ibid.

85 Jimmie James to Flora Thompson, June 7, 1963, JJJP, Box 2, Folder 12.

86 Flora Thompson to Jimmie James, August 2, 1962, JJJP, Box 1, Folder 34.

87 Jimmie James to Rueben Olson, David Sheer, and Flora Thompson, January 1, 1964, JJJP, Box 2, Folder 13.

88 This term is from Patrick Wolfe, "Settler Colonialism and the Elimination of the Native," *Journal of Genocide Research* 8, no. 4 (December 2008): 387–409.

89 Jimmie James to Rueben Olson, David Sheer, and Flora Thompson, January 1, 1964, JJJP, Box 2, Folder 13.

90 Jimmie James to Mrs. Del Val, December 29, 1963, JJJP, Box 2, Folder 12.

91 Jimmie James to Rueben Olson, David Sheer, and Flora Thompson, January 1, 1964, JJJP, Box 2, Folder 13.

92   Jimmie James to Rueben Olson, David Sheer, and Flora Thompson, January 1, 1964, JJJP, Box 2, Folder 12.

93   Jimmie James to Ida Wynookie, April 28, 1964, and Jimmie James to Rueben Olson, David Sheer, and Flora Thompson, January 1, 1964, JJJP, Box 2, Folder 13.

94   I've borrowed the term "plight narratives" from Jacobs, *A Generation Removed*.

95   Harold Fey, "Our Neighbor the Indian," *Christian Century* 72 (March 23, 1955), 361. When Martha McKeown sent her manuscript to David Sheer, he hand-delivered it to Fey at his home.

96   Martha McKeown to Jimmie James, March 7, 1957, JJJP, Box 1, Folder 18.

97   McKeown, "Celilo Indians."

98   Flora Thompson interview, interviewer unknown, no date. In possession of the author.

99   "Martha Dana, Indian Historian, Educator, Dies," *Oregonian*, August 13, 1974.

100 Laville, *Organized White Women*, 8.

101 Kirby Neumann-Rea, "Kaleidoscope: What Would You Do?," *Hood River News*, January 15, 2014.

102 "Chieftain's Widow Dies in House Fire," *Oregonian*, March 4, 1978.

103 I was unable to find the newspaper coverage of this. It must have occurred between 1980 and 1983, the years when Delbert Frank was the tribal chair. Elizabeth Woody discusses it in her essay "Voice of the Land: Giving the Good Word," in *Speaking for the Generations: Native Writers on Writing*, edited by Simon J. Ortiz (Tucson: University of Arizona Press, 1998), 148–73.

104 Woody, "Voice of the Land," 149.

105 Morgensen, "Theorizing Gender."

BIBLIOGRAPHY

BOOKS BY MARTHA MCKEOWN

The Trail Led North, Mont Hawthorne's Story. New York: Macmillan, 1948.
Them Was the Days, Another Mont Hawthorne Story. New York: Macmillan, 1950.
Alaska Silver, Another Mont Hawthorne Story. New York: Macmillan, 1951.
Linda's Indian Home. Portland, Oregon: Binford and Mort, 1956.
Come to Our Salmon Feast. Portland, Oregon: Binford and Mort, 1959.
Mountains Ahead: A Novel. New York: Putnam, 1961.

ARCHIVAL RECORDS

Binford and Mort Papers. Special Collections and Archives, Reed College. Portland, Oregon.
Celilo Community Club Records. In possession of the author.
Dana, Marshall. Marshall Newport Dana Papers. Oregon Historical Society Research Library. Portland, Oregon.
French, David and Katherine. David H. and Katherine S. French Papers. Special Collections, University of Washington Libraries, Seattle.
James, James. James J. James Papers. Special Collections and University Archives, University of Oregon Libraries, Eugene.
Jensen, Gertrude. Gertrude Glutsch Jensen Papers. Special Collections & University Archives. University of Oregon Libraries, Eugene.
Oregon Older Girls' Conference. Oregon Historical Society, Research Library. Portland, Oregon.
Pierce, Walter. Walter M. Pierce Papers. Special Collections & University Archives, University of Oregon Libraries, Eugene.

Struck, Gladys. Gladys M. Struck Papers. In possession of the author.

Territorial and Provisional Government Papers Index. *Oregon, Biographical and Other Cards.* Oregon State Library. Salem.

The Warm Springs Tribes of Indians of Oregon v. The United States. Transcript of Testimony Taken at Warm Springs Agency, August 12, 1931. Oregon Historical Society Research Library, Portland.

US Bureau of Indian Affairs. Portland Area Office. Subject Files of the Area Director, 1946–1957. Desk Files of the Realty Division, 1947–1965. Jurisdiction Files of the Realty Branch and Predecessors, 1935–1961. Desk Files of the Tribal Operations Branch, 1934–1951. Desk Files of the Tribal Operations Branch, 1953–1967. Tribal Council Minutes and Resolutions, 1946–1965. Subject Files of the Field Agent at The Dalles Oregon, 1939–1950. Celilo Fish Committee, Minutes and Resolutions, 1953–54. Land Transaction Case Files, 1946–65. All in Record Group (RG) 75, National Archives—Pacific Northwest Region, Seattle, Washington.

———. Records of the Warm Springs Indian Agency. Letters Received from the Commissioner of Indian Affairs, 1898–1908. Letters Sent to the Commissioner of Indian Affairs, 1869–1914. Subject Files, 1908–1925. Old Decimal Files, 1908–1952. New Decimal Files, 1933–1959. Education Program Records, ca. 1891–ca. 1923. Tribal Council Records, 1934–1951. Field Matron Record Books, 1916–1922. All in Record Group (RG) 75, National Archives—Pacific Northwest Region, Seattle, Washington.

GOVERNMENT REPORTS AND DOCUMENTS

Hamilton, George W. "State of Washington Twenty-third Biennial Report of the Attorney General, George W. Hamilton, 1935–1936." Olympia, WA: State Printing Office.

Oregon Agricultural College Extension Service. Report of the Hood River County Agricultural Economic Conference, Hood River Oregon, December 4, 5 and 20, 1924. Oregon State Library Online Catalog. Accessed January 4, 2015.

US Bureau of the Census. Census information for 1900, 1910, 1920, 1930, 1940. All in Record Group 29, National Archives, Washington, D.C. National Archives Microfilm Publication.

US Bureau of Indian Affairs. *Annual Report of the Commissioner of Indian Affairs, for the Year 1900,* by A. O. Wright, August 6, 1900, Part I. Washington, DC: Government Printing Office, 1900. Accessed January 3, 2015. http://digital.library.wisc.edu/1711.dl/History.AnnRep1900p1.

———. *Indian Census Rolls, 1885–1940*. Record Group 75, National Archives, Washington, DC. National Archives Microfilm Publication.

US Congress. House. House Committee on Appropriations. *Civil Functions, Department of the Army, Appropriations for 1952 Hearings, Part 2*, 82nd Cong., 1st and 2nd sess., 1951.

US National Archives and Records Administration. *General Index to Pension Files, 1861–1934*. Washington, DC.

———. *U.S., Civil War Pension Index: General Index to Pension Files, 1861–1934*. Accessed January 4, 2015. ancestry.com.

US National Park Service. National Register of Historic Places Inventory, Nomination Forms for the Albert W. Ferguson house, Captain J. H. D. Gray house, John N. Griffin house, Marshall Dana house.

Washington, Marriage Records, 1865–2004. Accessed May 18, 2016. ancestry.com.

Washington, Select Death Certificates, 1907–1960. Accessed on May 16, 2016. ancestry.com.

NEWSPAPERS AND MAGAZINES

Arlington Heights (Illinois) Herald
Booklist
Eugene Register-Guard
Fairbanks Daily News-Miner
Hood River Glacier
Hood River News
Life magazine
New York Herald Tribune
Oneonta (NY) Star
Oregon Daily Journal
Oregonian
San Francisco Bulletin
Skamania County Pioneer
The Dalles Chronicle

ORAL HISTORIES

Beaton, Russ. 2012. Interview by Katrine Barber. In the author's possession.

Jensen, Gertrude. 1978. Interview by Roberta Watts. Oregon Historical Society Research Library, Oregon.

McKenzie, Barbara. Oregon Voices, "Barbara McKenzie." *Oregon Historical Quarterly* 108, no. 4 (2007), 686–87.

Thompson, Flora. Oral History Interview, nd. Oregon Historical Society Research Library, Portland.

Thompson, Flora. Oral History Interview, nd. In the author's possession.

FILMS AND TELEVISION PROGRAMS

Farewell to Celilo. Special Report, aired April 20, 1959 by KGW-TV, Portland, Oregon. Recording in possession of the author.

Oregon Historical Society. *The Last Salmon Feast.* Directed by Thomas Vaughn, 1956. Accessed July 15, 2015. https://youtu.be/UY_GOokgYkE.

DISSERTATIONS

Clemmer, Janice White. "The Confederated Tribes of Warm Springs, Oregon: Nineteenth Century Indian Education History." PhD dissertation, University of Utah, 1980.

Compton, Tonia M. "Proper Women / Propertied Women: Federal Land Laws and Gender Order(s) in the Nineteenth Century Imperial American West." PhD dissertation, University of Nebraska, 2009.

French, Katherine Story. "Culture Segments and Variation in Contemporary Social Ceremonialism on the Warm Springs Reservation, Oregon." PhD dissertation, Columbia University, 1955.

Morgan, Francesca Constance. "'Home and Country': Women, Nation, and the Daughters of the American Revolution, 1890–1939." PhD dissertation, Columbia University, 1998.

Tetzloff, Lisa M. "'Shall the Indian Remain Indian?': Native Americans and the Women's Club Movement, 1899–1954." PhD dissertation, Purdue University, 2008.

Truesdell, Barbara. "God, Home, and Country: Folklore, Patriotism, and the Politics of Culture in the Daughters of the American Revolution." PhD dissertation, Indiana University, 1996.

BOOKS AND ARTICLES

Ackerman, Lillian. "Kinship, Family and Gender Roles." In *Handbook of North American Indians*, vol. 12, edited by Deward Walker and William C. Sturtevant, 515–24. Washington, DC: Smithsonian Institution.

———. *A Necessary Balance: Gender and Power among Indians of the Columbia Plateau.* Norman: University of Oklahoma Press, 2003.

———. "Nonunilinear Descent Groups in the Plateau Culture Area." *American Ethnologist* 21, no. 2 (May 1994): 286–309.

———, editor. *A Song to the Creator; Traditional Arts of Native American Women of the Plateau.* Norman: University of Oklahoma Press.

Aguilar, George. *When the River Ran Wild! Indian Traditions on the Mid-Columbia and the Warm Springs Reservation.* Portland: Oregon Historical Society Press, 2005.

Anderson, Kim. *A Recognition of Being: Reconstructing Native Womanhood.* Toronto, ON: Sumach Press, 2000.

Arnold, Laurie. *Bartering with the Bones of Their Dead: The Colville Confederated Tribes and Termination.* Seattle: University of Washington Press, 2012.

Azuma, Eiichiro. "A History of Oregon's Issei, 1880–1952." *Oregon Historical Quarterly* 94, No. 4 (Winter 1993/94): 315–67.

Babson, Sydney G. "Hood River Valley Wild Night." *Oregon Historical Quarterly* 70, no. 1 (Spring 1969): 50–55.

Balch, F. H. *The Bridge of the Gods, A Romance of Indian Oregon.* 23rd ed. Chicago: A. C. McClurg and Co., 1921.

Balch, Thomas Willing. *Balch Genealogica.* Philadelphia: Allen, Lane and Scott, 1907.

Barber, Katrine. *Death of Celilo Falls.* Seattle: University of Washington Press, 2005.

———. "Stories Worth Recording: Martha McKeown and the Documentation of Pacific Northwest Life." *Oregon Historical Quarterly* 110, no. 4 (Winter 2009): 546–69.

Barker, Joanne, editor. *Sovereignty Matters: Locations of Contestation and Possibility in Indigenous Struggles for Self-Determination.* Lincoln: University of Nebraska Press, 2005.

Basso, Keith. *Wisdom Sits in Places: Landscape and Language among the Western Apache.* Albuquerque: New Mexico University Press, 1996.

Belich, James. *Replenishing the Earth: The Settler Revolution and the Rise of the Anglo-World, 1783–1939.* Oxford: Oxford University Press, 2009.

Berger, Bethany Ruth. "After Pocahontas: Indian Women and the Law, 1830 to 1934." *American Indian Law Review* 21, no.1 (1997): 1–62.

Biolsi, Tom. "Imagined Geographies: Sovereignty, Indigenous Space, and American Indian Struggle." *American Ethnologist* 32, no.2 (2005): 239–59.

Borstelmann, Thomas. *The Cold War and the Color Line: American Race Relations in the Global Arena.* Cambridge, MA: Harvard University Press, 2001.

Bruyneel, Kevin. *The Third Space of Sovereignty: The Postcolonial Politics of U.S.-Indigenous Relations*. Minneapolis: University of Minnesota Press, 2007.

Cahill, Cathleen. *Federal Fathers and Mothers: A Social History of the United States Indian Service, 1869–1933*. Chapel Hill: University of North Carolina Press, 2011.

Carter, Sarah. *Capturing Women: The Manipulation of Cultural Imagery in Canada's Prairie West*. Montreal: McGill-Queen's University Press, 1997.

Chused, Richard H. "The Oregon Donation Act of 1850 and Nineteenth Century Federal Married Women's Property Law." *Law and History Review* 2, no.1 (Spring 1984): 44–78.

Cothran, Boyd. *Remembering the Modoc War: Redemptive Violence and the Making of American Innocence*. Chapel Hill: University of North Carolina Press, 2014.

Curtis, Walt. "Frederic Homer Balch—A Troubled Christian Writer's Brief Life." Oregon Cultural Heritage Commission, 2003. Accessed December 28, 2015. www.ochcom.org/pdf/Frederic-Balch.pdf.

Dana, Marshall N. "The Celilo Canal—Its Origin—Its Building and Meaning." *Quarterly of the Oregon Historical Society* 16, no. 2 (1915): 109–24.

Davies, Wallace. *Patriotism on Parade: The Story of Veterans' and Hereditary Organizations in America, 1783–1900*. Cambridge, MA: Harvard University Press, 1955.

Deloria, Philip J. *Playing Indian*. New Haven, CT: Yale University Press, 1998.

Dunlay, Thomas. *Wolves for the Blue Soldiers: Indian Scouts and Auxiliaries with the U.S. Army, 1869–1890*. Lincoln: University of Nebraska Press, 1987.

Edwards, G. Thomas. "The Oregon Trail in the Columbia Gorge: The Final Ordeal." *Oregon Historical Quarterly* 97, no. 2 (Summer 1996): 134–75.

Ellison, Joseph. "The Beginnings of the Apple Industry in Oregon." *Agricultural History* 11, no. 4 (October 1937): 328–43.

———. "The Cooperative Movement in the Oregon Apple Industry, 1910–1929." *Agricultural History* 13, no. 2 (April 1939): 77–96.

Emmerich, Lisa E. "'Right in the Midst of My Own People': Native American Women and the Field Matron Program." *American Indian Quarterly* 15, no. 2 (1991): 201–16.

Engeman, Richard. *The Oregon Companion: An Historical Gazetteer of the Useful, the Curious, and the Arcane*. Portland, OR: Timber Press, 2009.

Fellows, Mary Louise, and Sherene Razack. "The Race to Innocence: Confronting Hierarchical Relations Among Women." *Journal of Gender, Race and Justice* 1, no. 2 (1998): 335–52.

Fey, Harold. "Our Neighbor the Indian." *Christian Century* 72 (March 23, 1955): 361–64.

Field, Ron. *Elite 91: U.S. Army Frontier Scouts, 1840–1921*. Oxford, UK: Osprey Publishing, 2003.

Fisher, Andrew. *Shadow Tribes: The Making of Columbia River Indian Identity*. Seattle: University of Washington Press, 2010.

Fixico, Donald. *Termination and Relocation: Federal Indian Policy, 1945–1960*. Albuquerque: University of New Mexico Press, 1990.

Franco, Jere. "Empowering the World War II Native American Veteran: Postwar Civil Rights." *Wicazo Sa Review* 9, no. 1 (Spring 1993): 32–37.

Furtwangler, Albert. *Bringing Indians to the Book*. Seattle: University of Washington Press, 2005.

Glassberg, David. *American Historical Pageantry: The Uses of Tradition in the Early Twentieth Century*. Chapel Hill: University of North Carolina Press, 1990.

———. "Public Ritual and Cultural Hierarchy: Philadelphia's Civic Celebrations and the Turn of the Twentieth Century." *Pennsylvania Magazine of History and Biography* 107, no. 3 (July 1993): 421–48.

Glen, Evelyn Nakano. "Settler Colonialism as Structure: A Framework for Comparative Studies of U.S. Race and Gender Formation." *Sociology of Race and Ethnicity* 1 no. 1 (2015): 54–74.

Goeman, Mishuana. *Mark My Words: Native Women Mapping Our Nations*. Minneapolis: University of Minnesota Press, 2013.

Gulliford, Andrew. *Sacred Objects and Sacred Places: Preserving Tribal Traditions*. Boulder: University of Colorado Press, 2000.

Gunther, Erna. "An Analysis of the First Salmon Ceremony." *American Anthropologist*, 28 (1926): 605–17.

———. "A Further Analysis of the First Salmon Ceremony." *University of Washington Publications in Anthropology*, 2 (1928): 129–73.

Hansen, Clark. "Indian Views of the Stevens-Palmer Treaties Today." *Oregon Historical Quarterly* 106, no. 3 (Fall 2005): 475–89.

Herzfeld, Michael. "Political Optics and the Occlusion of Intimate Knowledge." *American Anthropologist* 107, no. 3 (September 2005): 369–76.

Higham, John. *Strangers in the Land: Patterns of American Nativism, 1860–1925*. New Brunswick, NJ: Rutgers University Press.

Hubka, Thomas C., and Judith T. Kenny, "Examining the American Dream: Housing Standards and the Emergence of a National Housing Culture, 1900–1930." *Perspectives in Vernacular Architecture* 13, no. 1 (2006): 49–69.

Huebner, Karin J. "An Unexpected Alliance: Stella Atwood, the California Clubwomen, John Collier, and the Indians of the Southwest, 1917–1934." *Pacific Historical Review* 78, no. 3 (August 2009): 337–66.

Hunn, Eugene. *Nch'i-Wána, "The Big River": Mid-Columbia Indians and Their Land*. Seattle: University of Washington Press, 1991.

Hurtado, Albert. "Settler Women and Frontier Women: The Unsettling Past of Western Women's History." *Frontiers: A Journal of Women Studies* 22, no. 3 (2001): 1–5.

Igler, David. "The Industrial Far West: Region and Nation in the Late Nineteenth Century." *Pacific Historical Review* 69, no. 2 (May 2000): 159–92.

Ingalls, Gertrude Balch. "Frederic Homer Balch, Author of 'The Bridge of the Gods." *Pacific Monthly: A Magazine of Education and Progress* 4 (May–October 1900): 85–86.

Jacobs, Margaret. *Engendered Encounter: Feminism and Pueblo Cultures, 1879–1934*. Lincoln: University of Nebraska Press, 1999.

———. *A Generation Removed: The Fostering and Adoption of Indigenous Children in the Postwar World*. Lincoln: University of Nebraska Press, 2014.

James, Caroline. *Nez Perce Women in Transition, 1877–1990*. Moscow: University of Idaho Press, 1996.

Jette, Melinda. *At the Hearth of the Crossed Races: A French-Indian Community in Nineteenth Century Oregon, 1812–1859*. Corvallis: Oregon State University Press, 2015.

Johnson, Jay T., and Soren C. Larsen, editors. *A Deeper Sense of Place: Stories and Journeys of Collaboration in Indigenous Research*. Corvallis: Oregon State University Press, 2013.

Kaplan, Amy. "Manifest Domesticity." *American Literature* 70, no. 3 (September 1998): 581–606.

Keyssar, Alexander. *The Right to Vote: The Contested History of Democracy in the United States*. New York: Basic Books, 2000.

Lake, Marilyn, and Henry Reynolds. *Drawing the Global Colour Line: White Men's Countries and the International Challenge of Racial Equality*. Cambridge, UK: Cambridge University Press, 2008.

Langston, Donna Hightower. "American Indian Women's Activism in the 1960s and 1970s." *Hypatia* 18, no. 2 (Spring 2003): 114–32.

Lawrence, Bonita. "Gender, Race, and the Regulation of Native Identity in Canada and the United States: An Overview." *Hypatia* 18, no. 2 (Spring 2003): 3–31.

Lewis, Clyde E. *History of Oregon Society, Daughters of American Revolution, Incorporated.* Portland, OR: Columbian Press, 1930.

Lomawaima, K. Tsianina. "Domesticity in the Federal Indian Schools: The Power of Authority over Mind and Body." *American Ethnologist* 20, no. 2 (May 1993): 227–40.

Loy, William G., Stuart Allan, Aileen R. Buckley, and James E. Meacham. *Atlas of Oregon,* 2nd ed. Eugene: University of Oregon Press, 2001.

Lyon, Cherstin. *Prisons and Patriots: Japanese American Wartime Citizenship, Civil Disobedience, and Historical Memory.* Philadelphia: Temple University Press, 2011.

MacMurray, J. W. "The 'Dreamers' of the Columbia River Valley, in Washington Territory." *Transactions of the Albany Institute,* Vol. 11 (1887): 241–48.

McConnell, Les. "The Treaty Rights of the Confederated Tribes of Warm Springs." *Pacific Northwest Quarterly* 97, no. 4 (Fall 2006): 190–201.

McLerran, Jennifer. "Clubwomen, Curators: Early- to Mid-Twentieth Century Navajo Weaving Improvement Projects." *American Indian Art Magazine* (Autumn 2011): 54–63.

Moos, Dan. *Outside America: Race, Ethnicity, and the Role of the American West in National Belonging.* Durham, NC: Duke University Press, 2006.

Morgensen, Scott Lauria. "Theorizing Gender, Sexuality and Settler Colonialism: An Introduction." *Settler Colonial Studies* 2, no. 2 (2012): 2–22.

Murphy, Michael. "Representing Indigenous Self-Determination." *University of Toronto Law Journal* 58, no. 2 (Spring 2008): 185–216.

National Society, United States Daughters of 1812. *1892–1939 News-Letter* 14, no. 1 (July 1939).

Oh, Arissa. "A New Kind of Missionary Work: Christians, Christian Americanists, and The Adoption of Korean GI Babies, 1955–1961." *Women's Studies Quarterly* 33, no. 3/4 (2005): 161–88.

———. *To Save the Children of Korea: The Cold War Origins of International Adoption.* Stanford: Stanford University Press, 2015.

Oregon Society, Daughters of the American Revolution. *Oregon State Roster of Ancestors [sic], Daughters of the American Revolution, 1963.* Tillamook: Oregon Society, D.A.R., 1963.

Palmiste, Claire. "From the Indian Adoption Project to the Indian Child Welfare Act: The Resistance of Native American Communities." *Indigenous Policy Journal* 22, no. 1 (Summer 2011): 1–10.

Paterson, Helen L. "American Indian Political Participation." *Annals of the American Academy of Political and Social Science,* Vol. 311, *American Indians and American Life* (May 1957), 116–26.

Philip, Kenneth R. "Termination: A Legacy of the Indian New Deal." *Western Historical Quarterly* 14, no. 2 (April 1983): 165–80.

Pitzer, Paul. *Grand Coulee: Harnessing a Dream.* Pullman: Washington State University Press, 1994.

Porter, Theodore. *Trust in Numbers: The Pursuit of Objectivity in Science and Public Life.* Princeton: Princeton University Press, 1995.

Portrait and Biographical Record of Western Oregon: Containing Original Sketches of Many Well Known Citizens of the Past and Present. Chicago: Chapman, 1904.

Pratt, Mary Louise. "Arts of the Contact Zone." *Profession* (1991): 33–40.

Raibmon, Paige. *Authentic Indians: Episodes of Encounter from the Late-Nineteenth-Century Northwest Coast.* Durham, NC: Duke University Press, 2005.

Robbins, William. "The Kind of Person Who Makes This America Strong': Monroe Sweetland and Japanese Americans." *Oregon Historical Quarterly* 113, no. 2 (Summer 2012): 198–229.

Rollings, Willard Hughes. "Citizenship and Suffrage: The Native American Struggle for Civil Rights in the American West, 1830–1965." *Nevada Law Journal* 5, no. 126 (Fall 2004): 126–40.

Roiser, Paul C. " 'They Are Ancestral Homelands': Race, Place, and Politics in Cold War Native America, 1945–1961." *Journal of American History* 92, no. 4 (March 2006), 1300–1326.

Schlick, Mary Dodds. *Columbia River Basketry: Gift of the Ancestors, Gift of the Earth.* Seattle: University of Washington Press, 1994.

Schulten, Susan. "How to See Colorado: The Federal Writers' Project, American Regionalism, and the 'Old New Western History.'" *Western Historical Quarterly* 36, no. 1 (Spring 2005), 49–70.

Scott, James C. *Seeing Like a State: How Certain Schemes to Improve the Human Condition Have Failed.* New Haven, CT: Yale University Press, 1998.

Simonsen, Jane E. *Making Home Work: Domesticity and Native American Assimilation in the American West, 1860–1919.* Chapel Hill: University of North Carolina Press, 2006.

Soden, Dale E. *Outsiders in a Promised Land: Religious Activists in Pacific Northwest History.* Corvallis: Oregon State University Press, 2015.

Stasiulis, Daiva, and Nira Yuval-Davis, editors. *Unsettling Settler Societies: Articulations of Gender, Race, Ethnicity and Class.* Sage Series on Race and Ethnic Relations, vol. 11. Thousand Oaks, CA: Sage Publications, 1995.

Stearns, Marjorie. "The Settlement of the Japanese in Oregon." *Oregon Historical Quarterly,* Vol. 39, No. 3 (September 1938): 262–269.

Steiner, Michael. "Regionalism in the Great Depression." *Geographic Review* 73, no. 4 (October 1983): 430–46.

Tamura, Linda. *Nisei Soldiers Break Their Silence: Coming Home to Hood River.* Seattle: University of Washington Press, 2012.

Tamura, Linda. "Railroads, Stumps, and Sawmills: Japanese Settler of the Hood River Valley." *Oregon Historical Quarterly* 94, no. 4 (Winter 1993/1994): 368–98.

Tate, Michael L. "From Scout to Doughboy: The National Debate over Integrating American Indians into the Military, 1891–1918." *Western Historical Quarterly* 17, no. 4 (October 1986): 417–37.

Tetzloff, Lisa. "Elizabeth Bender Cloud: 'Working for and with Our Indian People.'" *Frontiers: A Journal of Women Studies* 30, no. 3, Women's Clubs at Home and in the World (2009): 77–115.

Tonsfeldt, Ward, and Paul G. Claeyssens. "Treaty with the Tribes of Middle Oregon." Oregon History Project, 2004. Updated and revised by OHP staff, 2014. Accessed July 15, 2015. www.oregonhistoryproject.org /narratives/central-oregon-adaptation-and-compromise-in-an-arid -landscape/finding-central-oregon/treaty-with-the-tribes-of-middle -oregon/#.VabE_kjgeyQ.

Trafford, Emily. "Hitting the Trail: Live Displays of Native American, Filipino, and Japanese People at the Portland World's Fair." *Oregon Historical Quarterly* 116, no. 2 (Summer 2015): 158–95.

Ulrich, Roberta. *American Indian Nations from Termination to Restoration, 1953–2006.* Lincoln: University of Nebraska Press, 2010.

Veracini, Lorenzo. *Settler Colonialism: A Theoretical Overview.* Hampshire, UK: Palgrave Macmillan, 2010.

Vogel, Eve. "Defining One Pacific Northwest among Many Possibilities: The Political Construction of a Region and Its River during the New Deal." *Western Historical Quarterly* 42, no. 1 (Spring 2011): 28–53.

Wendt, Simon. "Defenders of Patriotism or Mothers of Fascism? The Daughters of the American Revolution, Antiradicalism, and Un-Americans in the Interwar Period." *Journal of American Studies* 47, Special Issue 04 (November 2013): 943–69.

West, Elliott. *The Last Indian War: The Nez Perce Story.* New York: Oxford University Press, 2011.

Williams, Carol J. *Framing the West: Race Gender and the Photographic Frontier in the Pacific Northwest.* New York: Oxford University Press, 2003.

Winther, Oscar Osburn. *The Old Oregon Country: A History of Frontier Trade, Transportation, and Travel.* Lincoln: University of Nebraska Press, 1950.

Wolfe, Patrick. "Settler Colonialism and the Elimination of the Native." *Journal of Genocide Research* 8, no. 4 (December 2008): 387–409.

Wolfley, Jeanette. "Jim Crow, Indian Style: The Disenfranchisement of Native Americans." *American Indian Law Review* 16, no. 1 (1991): 167–202.

Woody, Elizabeth. "Voice of the Land: Giving the Good Word." In *Speaking for the Generations: Native Writers on Writing*, edited by Simon J. Ortiz, 148–73. Tucson: University of Arizona Press, 1998.

Wright, Mary C. "The Woman's Lodge: Constructing Gender on the Nineteenth-Century Pacific Northwest Plateau." *Frontiers: A Journal of Women Studies* 24, no. 1 (2003): 1–18.

Zanjani, Sally. *Sarah Winnemucca.* Lincoln: University of Nebraska Press, 2001.

INDEX

A

Adams, Clarence, 163
adoption: of Korean children into
 white homes, 209, 212–13; of
 Native children to white homes,
 23, 209–19, 222; of non-Natives
 into tribes, 12, 115–16, 123,
 254n68
Affiliated Tribes of Northwest
 Indians (ATNI), 158–59, 260n77
African Americans, 35, 104, 105, 148
Aguilar, George, 38, 76
Alien Land Law, 69, 261n16
allotments, 9, 16, 29–30, 45, 72–73,
 81, 182, 243n88; fraudulent,
 152–54; for women, 43, 45, 47.
 See also Dawes Allotment Act
American Indian Committee, 172
Angell, Homer D., 144
Anselm Forum, 195, 200–202, 222
Apples Growers' Union, 62, 68
Army Corps of Engineers, 20, 137,
 158, 161, 191
Arnest, Mary, 142
assimilation, 41, 50, 75, 182, 207, 227;
 in boarding schools, 17, 76, 81;
 and citizenship, 44, 89, 114,
 165–66; and clubwomen efforts,
 13–17, 53, 58, 89–90, 106, 136,
 209; and domesticity, 44–45, 70,
 81–83, 135, 180–82; federal
 policies, 20–21, 39–40, 43–44, 72,
 138, 159, 181; resistance to, 10–11,
 14–18, 23, 54, 70, 104, 186,
 217–18, 222
Astoria, Ore., 11, 31, 34, 46, 53,
 55–56, 59–60, 235n24

B

Babcock, Omar, 82, 98, 249n22
Balch, Frederic Homer, 238n10;
 Bridge of the Gods, 18, 50–54, 87,
 134–35
Binford and Mort, 176
Black Braids, 135*fig.*
boarding schools, 17, 77–81, 106–7,
 170, 182, 210, 217, 244n93
Boise, Max, 91, 93, 99–100, 135*fig.*,
 162, 188, 192
Boise, Nancy Brown, 94–97
Boise, Steve, 136
Boise, Young, 9, 25–26, 28, 80–81,
 83–84, 91, 93–94, 97, 99; arrest
 for poaching, 85–86
Bonneville Dam, 19, 137, 154,
 158, 161

Bureau of Indians Affairs, 80, 93, 106, 115, 120, 197; assimilation policies, 14, 16–17, 98, 138, 181, 209; Celilo relocation efforts, 129, 131–33, 156, 169, 181; fraud in, 128, 151–54, 156; termination (policy), 20

Burgoyne, Sherman, 111

C

Celilo Canal, 145, 206

Celilo Converter Station, 199

Celilo Falls, 7*fig.*, 85, 192; inundation of, 20, 115, 124–26, 161, 173, 190; protection campaigns for, 115, 124, 126, 128, 139–50, 157–59, 164, 168, 173; as trading site, 36, 38

Celilo Fish Committee, 130, 132, 154, 157, 168

Celilo Village, 10, 23, 40–41, 72, 87, 100; advocacy and support efforts for, 13, 16–22, 89, 106–8, 122–24, 128, 170–72, 201–2, 207, 218–24; ceremonies, 3–6, 22, 97, 162–63, 172, 184–86; governance of, 115–16, 120, 130–33, 138, 154; inundation of, 6, 16–17, 124–26, 162, 190; literary depictions of, 12, 18, 125–26, 133–35, 173–74, 176–80, 183–87, 201, 224; longhouse, 194–97; relocations of, 30, 90, 128–33, 156, 162, 172, 181–82, 189–90, 202

Charley, Alice Slim Jim, 154–55

Charley, Wilson, xi, 127, 144, 164, 173, 206

Chemawa Indian School, 104, 106–7, 170

"Chief Rising Sun," 128, 146–50, 149*fig.*, 151, 153

Christie School, 207, 213–14

citizenship, 22, 127; and kinship, 114–15, 123; restrictions on, 42, 67–69, 110, 112–14, 138, 148, 165, 167; through assimilation, 44, 89, 114, 165–66; tribal, 114–15, 123, 139, 141

Cloud, Elizabeth Bender, 15

Cloud, Henry Roe, 15

clubwomen, 66, 91, 123–24, 168, 195, 240nn31,33; Columbia River Gorge support, 21, 127, 143; Native assimilation efforts, 13–17, 53, 58, 89–90, 106, 136–209. *See also names of clubs*

Columbia Plateau, 10, 71, 97, 184

Columbia River: damming of, 6, 16, 19, 46, 115, 124, 137, 158, 161, 163; Native fisheries, 19, 21–23, 38–40, 47, 85, 92, 138, 142, 194, 199–200; navigation of, 34, 59, 137. *See also* Celilo Falls; The Dalles Dam

Columbia River Gorge, 128, 142–45, 173

Columbia River Indians, 12, 153, 201; foodways, 40, 85; governance, 129–30, 195, 199. *See also names of tribes*

Confederated Tribes of the Umatilla Indian Reservation, 8, 15, 20, 35, 39, 120, 130, 161

Confederated Tribes of the Warm Springs Reservation, 6, 8, 20, 53, 60, 74*fig.*, 81–83, 123, 170, 192, 199, 225; allotment policy, 16, 72–73; assimilation policies, 70–80, 98; built structures, 73–75; economy of, 71–72, 78, 92–93; family structure on, 70–73, 76–78; federal monitoring of, 71, 81–86, 93, 98; formation of, 9–10,

29, 35–39, 46–47; gender roles on, 74–75, 77–78, 80; land fraud, 150–53; off-reservation rights, 39–41, 85–86
Cook's Landing, 199–200
Culpus, Henry, 199
Cushinway, Catherine, 184
Cushinway, Effie, 4, 77–78, 82–83, 99, 121, 201, 244n94
Cushinway, James, 73, 77–78, 80, 83
Cushinway (Cushny), Jim, 8, 41–42, 73, 75
Cushinway, Martha, 8, 42, 69–70, 72–73, 75, 78, 81, 182; death of, 94–95

D

Dana, Marshall, 143, 145–46, 172–73, 205*fig.*, 224; marriage to Martha, 204–7
Daughters of the Revolution (DAR), Oregon, 31, 66, 109, 121, 238n10; membership rules, 123–24; racism in, 102, 104–5, 108; support of Chemawa, 106–8, 170; support of Celilo, 17–18, 89, 106, 121–22, 129, 169–74, 222
Dawes General Allotment Act (Severalty Act), 14, 31, 43–45, 166
Davies, Ralph, 69
Dee, Ore., 60, 67
domesticity: gendering of, 10, 134–36, 183–86; government monitoring of, 16, 42, 81–83, 135, 182; in land policy, 43–47; as resistance, 110, 133–37, 180; as a tool of assimilation, 13, 16, 42, 44–47, 81–83, 135, 180–82, 208–19, 265n58
Dyer, James, 132, 254n68

E

Eisenhower, Pres. Dwight, 20, 138, 147, 157, 162, 191
Elliott, Jasper, 153
Eneas, Dave, 144

F

Fanshel, David
Fey, Harold, 201, 222
Ferguson, Albert, 11, 31, 33–35, 234nn19,21
Ferguson, Almira E. Hawthorne, 11, 50, 55–59, 63–64, 66, 204, 238n10
Ferguson, James Ernest, 11, 34, 56, 63, 67
Ferguson, Margaret Wetzel, 33
field matrons, 16, 42, 81–83, 135, 182
fishing: for ceremonial purposes, 4–6; commercial, 56; federal monitoring of, 40, 85, 120, 125–26, 199–200; methods of, 7*fig.*, 56, 133, 136; Native management of, 10, 115–16, 120, 130, 132, 154, 157, 162, 168; subsistence, 26, 28, 40, 67, 71–73, 79, 86, 92, 180; threats to, 6, 18–20, 38–39, 47, 115, 124, 126, 137, 142–44, 161–62, 170, 187, 190, 226; treaty rights to, xi, 8, 20–22, 39, 120, 126–27, 137–38, 157–59, 162, 170, 173, 194, 199–200; women's labor, 135–36, 184–86
Fletcher, Alice, 45
Flinn, Clyde, 152–53, 156
foodways, 71, 85. *See also* fishing; hunting; seasonal rounds
French, David, 186–87
fruit industry, 27, 29, 59–62, 66, 66*fig.*; Japanese growers, 67–69; labor, 47, 66–67, 86–87, 173; marketing of, 63

G

gender roles, 6, 10, 14, 110; ceremonial, 5, 70, 75–77, 80, 183–84; dress, 4, 185; labor, 3, 47, 58, 72, 92, 101–2, 122, 134–36, 180–81, 184–86, 224, 250n31; as performance, 102. *See also* clubwomen; domesticity

George, Timothy, 9, 99, 116, 118

Governors Interstate Council on Indian Affairs, 138

H

Hachiya, Frank, 110–12, 113*fig.*

Hanby Nursing Home, 155, 188–90

Hawthorne, Mont, 11, 56–57, 59, 174–77, 263n50

Hickel, Walter,

Highway 30, 18, 90, 120, 126, 129, 131, 137, 156, 162, 169, 181

Holcomb, Minnie, 16, 81–83

"home," 31, 44, 51, 73, 180. *See also* domesticity

Hood, Mount, 25, 28, 31, 60, 65, 66*fig.*, 69; food gathering on, 69, 83, 92

Hood River Anti-Alien Association, 68–69

Hood River Chapter of the American Legion, 111

Hood River Valley, vii, 66*fig.*, 118, 128, 151; fruit industry in, 61–68, 71, 91, 122; Japanese settlement in, 66–69, 104, 110–13; resettlement of, 17, 59–65

horses, 38–39, 71–72, 76, 93

huckleberries, 25, 29, 71, 78, 83, 92, 179–80, 185, 217

hunting, 84–85, 122, 159; restrictions to, 38–40, 85–86, 247n126; subsistence, 26, 28, 37–40, 67, 71, 73, 79

Huntington, J. W. Perit, 39–40, 86

Huntington Treaty, 40, 86

I

Indian Adoption Project, 209–12

Indian Appropriations Act, 33

Indian Child Welfare Act, 210

Indian Citizenship Act, 114, 141, 166–67

Indian Reorganization Act, 44

Indian Shaker Church, 71, 94, 97–98, 99*fig.*, 249n22

Issei, 67–69, 104, 111, 114

J

Jack, Sowallus, 78

James, James (Jimmie), viii, 8, 141*fig.*, 162–63, 191–92, 195, 200–202, 224, 256n26; aid efforts, 151, 170, 196–98, 219–22; campaign against The Dalles Dam, 19, 21–22, 124, 125–28, 139–50, 156–59, 164, 167–68, 173, 190; conflict with Martha, 202–3, 206–7; Linda Meanus adoption, 22–23, 207–19

James, Maude, 127

Japanese and Japanese Americans, 67, 103; citizenship, 114–15, 166; discrimination against, 68–69, 104, 109–14, 166; incarceration of, 69, 110, 114; military service of, 110–13

Japanese Methodist Church, 68

Jensen, Gertrude, 21, 124, 127–28, 142–47, 149–50, 173, 207

Jim, Howard, 197–98

Jim, Kiutus, 159

Jim, Maggie, 197

Johnlee, Minnie Charlie, 135*fig.*

K

kinship: and citizenship, 114–16; Indigenous connections, 30, 115, 123, 134, 136, 209, 217; nonbiological, 123; of settler colonialism, 30–31, 123
Kiyokawa, Riichi, 67–68
Koreans, 209, 212–13
Kuckup, Albert, 37–38, 73

L

League of Liberty and Justice, 111
longhouse, 132, 135*fig.*, 162; ceremonial role of, 3, 5, 94–96, 172, 177, 183–85, 191–92, 208, 218; gender divisions in, 183–85; rebuilding of, 195–98
Long Narrows, 20, 187

M

Mackenzie, Barbara, 134
marriage: and as colonizing ritual, 27, 30–31, 80, 93; kinship connections in, 9, 77–78, 84, 244n93; status of women in, 10, 91, 119–20, 186, 250n31
Maxwell, Chrystalee, 104
McKay, Donald, 41–42, 43*fig.*
McKay, Douglas, 20, 119, 138, 172, 205
McKay, Maude, 119, 119*fig.*
McKay, William, 165
McKeown, Archie, 26, 29, 90–91, 100–101, 111, 127, 178*fig.*; illness and death, 188, 190–91, 200–201; photography, 4, 5*fig.*, 12, 103*fig.*, 109, 152*fig.*, 163, 174*fig.*, 177, 179–80
McKeown, Martha Ferguson, vii, 4, 6–8, 103*fig.*, 130*fig.*, 135*fig.*, 174*fig.*, 194*fig.*, 226; advocacy of Indian rights, 12, 18, 69, 90, 102–5, 107–8, 129–37, 169, 151–54, 200–202, 222–27; advocacy of Japanese and Japanese American rights, 68–69, 109–13; *Alaska Silver*, 12, 175; as author, 11–12, 18, 21, 91, 101, 109–10, 125–26, 173–87, 200–201, 203–4, 224, 263n50; "Celilo Indians: Fishing Their Way of Life," 126, 133–37; clubwoman activities of, 13–14, 16–19, 21, 90–91, 100, 102–4, 107–9, 129, 130*fig.*, 170–73, 223; *Come to Our Salmon Feast*, 12, 177, 183–87, 203; correspondence with Jimmie James, 22, 125–26, 140, 143, 146, 150, 190, 202–3, 206–7; death, 224; early life, 11, 17, 55–60, 63–65; friendship with the Thompsons, 12–13, 18, 87, 90, 92, 101, 103*fig.*, 115–16, 121, 123–24, 125–26, 128, 133–37, 155–56, 162–63, 173, 188–89, 193–95, 213–15, 233n8; and land fraud case, 128, 151–54, 258n59; *Linda's Indian Home*, ix, 12, 23, 163, 173–74, 177, 179–83; marriages, 26–29, 31, 194–95, 204–7; *Mountains Ahead*, 12, 203; religious practices, 14, 17, 64, 104, 108; The Dalles Dam protest, 13, 16–19, 21, 128, 140; settler past, 17, 27–31, 33–35, 47, 50, 101–2, 227; support of Celilo Village, 12–13, 18, 90, 125, 128–37, 155, 129–37, 169, 188–90, 201, 219, 222, 224; teaching career, 91, 100–102; *Them Was the Days*, 11–12, 175; *The Trail Led North*, 12, 91, 174–75
McNary, Charles, 106
McNary Dam, 158, 161
McNickle, D'Arcy, 201

Meacham, Alfred B., 40–41
Meanus, Josepha, 99
Meanus, Linda George, 99, 163, 188, 200; adoption of, 23, 190, 195, 207–19, 222; children's book portrayal, ix, 12, 23, 163, 173, 179–83
Methodist churches, 57, 63–64, 68, 103–4, 111–12
Middle Oregon Treaties, 8–10, 35–40, 138, 165, 199–200
military service, 42–43, 110–12, 114–15, 122, 138–39
Miller, Lucy, 84
Minthorne, William, 115
Modoc War, 41, 53, 122, 139, 222
Moore, Arline, 151, 152*fig.*, 153
Mormon Church, 97, 189, 209
Morse, Wayne, 127, 148, 151, 170
Multnomah College, 91, 100, 102

N
Neuberger, Richard, 127, 163, 175, 192, 201–2, 204
Nez Perce, 8, 20, 35, 76, 244n94
Nisei, 68, 110, 113
Nomura, Ruth, 104, 251n41

O
Odell, Ore., 61, 63, 100–111
off-reservation, 92, 182; activism, 21, 133, 167; as colonial binary/transgression, 29, 31, 85–86; food gathering, 78, 85, 138; rights, 39–40, 138, 164
Olson, Reuben, 200, 202, 208
Oregon Columbia River Gorge Commission, 173
Oregon Donation Land Act, 28, 31, 35, 43; and women's property rights, 33, 44–46

Oregon Federation of Women's Clubs, 15, 142
Oregon Historical Society, 172, 187, 205, 223
Oregon Older Girls Association, 91, 102–4, 108–9
Oregon Trails Women's Club, 15

P
Pacific Northwest Regional Planning Commission, 145
Paiutes, 70–71
Parkdale, Ore., 60, 86
Pe las kow yai, 70, 76
Peplon, Irma, 170
Perkins, F. E., 92–93
placemaking, 25, 30
place-naming, 38–39
Polson, Dawn, 211–18
Polson, Vernon, 211–18
Portland Women's Forum, 142–43, 145
Prohibition, 57–58, 98
Protestantism, 49, 98, 212; liberalism, 104–5, 107–8, 201
Pryse, E. Morgan, 131–33, 153

Q
Quintoken, Charles, 130*fig.*, 205*fig.*

R
Racehorse, Lonnie, 170
Relander, Click, 21, 124, 127, 146, 164, 167–68
religion, 95–98, 189, 192. *See also* Indian Shaker Church; *names of religions*
resettlement, 22, 27, 65; cross-cultural relationships, 16, 19, 23, 27; displacement of Indigenous owners, 8, 17, 23, 29, 32–33, 38,

141, 227; land acts, 17, 28–29, 31–33, 35, 43. *See also* assimilation; Oregon Donation Land Act; settler colonialism; treaties

S

Sahaptin (language), 70, 163, 187
salmon fisheries: commercial industry, 56, 67, 175; Native, 7*fig.*, 71–72, 115, 125–26, 136, 179–80, 190; threat to, 6, 19, 85–86, 92, 115, 137–38, 194–95, 199. *See also* Celilo Falls; fishing
salmon ceremonies, 3–6, 5*fig.*, 10, 22, 117*fig.*, 156, 172, 195, 198; literary accounts of, 12, 177, 183–86
Saluskin, Alex, 126–27, 139, 144–45, 147–48, 156–59, 164, 169
"Save the Celilo Falls Committee," 21, 126
"Save the Columbia Gorge," 142–43
seasonal rounds, 29, 37, 67, 71, 78, 80, 83, 93, 118; restrictions on, 30, 40, 79, 85, 217
Seelatse, Eagle, 144
settler colonialism, 7–8, 16–17, 20, 31, 75, 82, 102, 123–24, 179, 210, 225; Native resistance to, 6, 10–11, 23, 28–30, 54, 70, 168, 184, 227
Sheer, David, 200–203, 207–8, 218
Slim Jim, James, 151–55, 152*fig.*, 258n59
Smith, John, 79
Society of American Indians, 15
songs, 70, 94–97, 192
Sookoit, Alice, 77–78
Sookoit, William, 77
sovereignty, 8, 16, 20, 137, 223, 226–27
Spooms, Jackson, 53–54
Stocket-ly, Chief, 10, 35

Struck, George, 86, 118
Struck, Gladys, 86, 118, 173

T

Teninos, 35, 70, 72–73
Termination, 20–21, 115, 138–39, 159, 205, 226, 232n28
TeWee, Edgar, 80–81, 93, 99
TeWee, Johnnie, 80–81, 93
The Dalles (city), 35–36, 46, 120
The Dalles Dam, 5, 206; campaign against, 19, 21, 124, 126–28, 139–50, 157–59, 169–70, 207, 219; effects of inundation, 6, 8, 19, 21, 124, 126, 134, 154, 187, 190–91, 195, 224, 226
Thompson, Davis, 135*fig.*, 183
Thompson, Flora Cushinway (*La moosh Cush-nee-yi*), vii, 7, 26, 117*fig.*, 121*fig.*, 130*fig.*, 135*fig.*, 174*fig.*, 196*fig.*, 205*fig.*, 210; adoption of granddaughter, 22–23, 188, 190, 195, 207–19; advocacy work, 16, 18–19, 22, 89–90, 92, 120–22, 128–31, 146, 163–64, 169, 194–95, 199–200, 224–25; children of, 80–81, 83, 93–97, 99–100, 188; conflict with Jimmie James, 127, 213–19; death, 195, 224; death of Tommy Thompson, 191–94; early life, 8–9, 15–18, 42–43, 50, 69–80; friendship with Martha, 12, 18, 90–91, 121–28, 129, 133–37, 155–56, 162–63, 173, 188–89, 193–95, 224; illnesses, 155, 188–89, 207; leadership roles, 10, 92, 120–21, 162, 185–86, 195, 198–99, 223; literary accounts of, 126, 133–37, 163, 173–74, 176–83, 222; longhouse rebuild, 195–98;

Thompson, Flora (*cont.*)
marriages, 9–10, 81–86, 91, 99–100, 116, 118, 119–20; oral histories, 199, 225; religious practices, 17, 94–98, 189, 218; salmon ceremonies, 3–6, 156, 172, 184–86; and settler colonialism, 28–31, 35, 42, 47, 50, 54–55, 79–80, 122–23, 163, 181–82, 223
Thompson, Henry, 135*fig.*, 184, 196–99, 219–21
Thompson, Richard, 183
Thompson, Chief Tommy, vii, 5, 35, 40, 47, 103*fig.*, 117*fig.*, 119*fig.*, 130*fig.*, 135*fig.*, 162, 174*fig.*, 195, 196*fig.*, 205*fig.*, 223, 225; advocacy, 6, 16, 85, 101, 127–33, 146, 162, 164, 169, 173; birthday celebration, 16263; friendship with Martha, 6, 12, 18, 8687, 90, 101, 115–16, 123, 155–56, 173, 224, 233n8; illness and death, 3–5, 10, 12, 155–56, 188–93, 201, 207; literary accounts of, 125–26, 133–34, 173, 176–78; marriage to Flora, 6, 9–10, 91, 118, 119–21; as salmon chief, 10, 85, 115–16, 120–21, 154, 156, 184–86, 254n68
Thurston, Samuel R., 32, 46
Totus, Watson, 144
treaties, 227; and access to resources, xi, 20–22, 39–40, 79, 115, 120, 126, 137, 158, 173, 194, 199–200; federal enforcement of, 40, 115, 137–38; federal violations of, 39–40, 85–86, 120, 126, 137–38, 142, 221, 269n19; reservation creation, 8–10, 33, 35–38, 86, 138, 165; signatory chiefs and tribes, 8, 10, 35; termination of, 20–21, 115, 138–39, 159, 205, 226

Turner, Wallace, 148, 151–52, 258n59
Tygh, 35, 70

V
Van Pelt, Jeff, 39
Vaughan, Thomas, 172

W
Walla Walla Treaty Council, 165
Warm Springs Indian Scouts, 41–42, 43*fig.*, 122, 171
Warm Springs Lumber Co., 153
Wasco County, 34, 60, 134, 198, 234n22
Wascos, 35, 70–71, 85
Washat, 94, 97, 192, 197
Weatherford, Leona, 142
Williams, Geraldine, 104
Winishut, Linton, 191–92
Winnier, William, 144
woman's lodges, 70, 74–76, 80
Women's National Indian Association (WNIA), 13–16, 43, 58, 81, 106, 136, 209
Woody, Elizabeth, 49, 225
Wright, A. O., 36–37, 70–71
Wyam, 3, 35, 123–24, 187, 222–23; DAR resolution, 170–71
Wynookie, Ida Thompson, 174, 188, 194*fig.*, 220–21

Y
Yakama Nation, 8–9, 98, 169, 170; opposition to The Dalles Dam, 127, 139, 144–51, 159, 161; treaty fishing rights of, 20, 35, 115, 120, 130, 157–58, 199
Yasui, Ray, 113

Z
Zonta International, 91, 109

EMIL AND KATHLEEN SICK SERIES IN
WESTERN HISTORY AND BIOGRAPHY

With support from the Center for the Study of the Pacific Northwest at
the University of Washington, the Sick Series in Western History and
Biography features scholarly books on the peoples and issues that have
defined and shaped the American West. Through intellectually challenging and engaging books of general interest, the series seeks to deepen
and expand our understanding of the American West as a region and its
role in the making of the United States and the modern world.

The Great Columbia Plain: A Historical Geography, 1805–1910,
by Donald W. Meinig

Mills and Markets: A History of the Pacific Coast Lumber Industry to 1900,
by Thomas R. Cox

*Radical Heritage: Labor, Socialism, and Reform in Washington and British
Columbia, 1885–1917,* by Carlos A. Schwantes

*The Battle for Butte: Mining and Politics on the Northern Frontier,
1864–1906,* by Michael P. Malone

*The Forging of a Black Community: Seattle's Central District from 1870
through the Civil Rights Era,* by Quintard Taylor

Warren G. Magnuson and the Shaping of Twentieth-Century America,
by Shelby Scates

The Atomic West, edited by Bruce Hevly and John M. Findlay

Power and Place in the North American West, edited by Richard White
and John M. Findlay

Henry M. Jackson: A Life in Politics, by Robert G. Kaufman

Parallel Destinies: Canadian-American Relations West of the Rockies, edited by John M. Findlay and Ken S. Coates

Nikkei in the Pacific Northwest: Japanese Americans and Japanese Canadians in the Twentieth Century, edited by Louis Fiset and Gail M. Nomura

Bringing Indians to the Book, by Albert Furtwangler

Death of Celilo Falls, by Katrine Barber

The Power of Promises: Perspectives on Indian Treaties of the Pacific Northwest, edited by Alexandra Harmon

Warship under Sail: The USS Decatur *in the Pacific West,* by Lorraine McConaghy

Shadow Tribe: The Making of Columbia River Indian Identity, by Andrew H. Fisher

A Home for Every Child: Relinquishment, Adoption, and the Washington Children's Home Society, 1896–1915, by Patricia Susan Hart

Atomic Frontier Days: Hanford and the American West, by John M. Findlay and Bruce Hevly

The Nature of Borders: Salmon, Boundaries, and Bandits on the Salish Sea, by Lissa K. Wadewitz

Encounters in Avalanche Country: A History of Survival in the Mountain West, 1820–1920, by Diana L. Di Stefano

The Rising Tide of Color: Race, State Violence, and Radical Movements across the Pacific, edited by Moon-Ho Jung

Trout Culture: How Fly Fishing Forever Changed the Rocky Mountain West, by Jen Corrinne Brown

Japanese Prostitutes in the North American West, 1887–1920, by Kazuhiro Oharazeki

In Defense of Wyam: Native-White Alliances and the Struggle for Celilo Village, by Katrine Barber

CPSIA information can be obtained
at www.ICGtesting.com
Printed in the USA
FSHW011736020519
57792FS

9 780295 743585